HOMEGROWN PANTRY

HOME GROWN PANTRY

A GARDENER'S GUIDE TO
Selecting the Best Varieties &
Planting the Perfect Amounts
for What You Want to Eat Year-Round

BARBARA PLEASANT

Storey Publishing

*The mission of Storey Publishing is to serve our customers by
publishing practical information that encourages
personal independence in harmony with the environment.*

Edited by Carleen Madigan and Sarah Guare
Art direction and book design by Jeff Stiefel
Text production by Erin Dawson
Indexed by Samantha Miller

Cover photography by © Hero Images/Getty Images, front (top); Jeff Stiefel, spine; © Kip Dawkins Photography, front
    (bottom left) and back (all); Mars Vilaubi, front (bottom right)
Interior photography by © Kip Dawkins Photography, except © Barbara Pleasant, 78, 103 (left); Mars Vilaubi, 6, 24 (right),
    42 (cauliflower), 43 (carrot, cucumber, radish), 48 (blackberry, blueberry), 49 (plum, rhubarb, strawberry), 52, 72, 74,
    80, 84, 85, 88, 98, 100, 108, 119 (top), 121, 135, 137, 146, 150 (right), 185, 187, 209, 258, 260, 276, 305; © Nicolevanf/
    Getty Images, 8 (top); Sarah Guare, 249
Map, page 135, by Ilona Sherratt

Storey Publishing
210 MASS MoCA Way
North Adams, MA 01247
storey.com

Printed in China by R.R. Donnelley
10 9 8 7 6 5 4 3 2 1

Library of Congress Cataloging-in-Publication Data
Names: Pleasant, Barbara, author.
Title: Homegrown pantry / by Barbara Pleasant.
Description: North Adams, MA : Storey Publishing, 2017. | Includes index.
Identifiers: LCCN 2016055527 (print) | LCCN 2016056917 (ebook) | ISBN
    9781612125787 (pbk. : alk. paper) | ISBN 9781612125794 (ebook)
Subjects: LCSH: Food crops. | Food—Preservation. | Vegetables. | Herbs. |
    Fruit.
Classification: LCC SB175 .P54 2017 (print) | LCC SB175 (ebook) | DDC
    635—dc23
LC record available at https://lccn.loc.gov/2016055527

To Gwen Steege,
for her ceaseless support

CONTENTS

WHY GROW
YOUR
Own Food?

The best food in the world starts in the garden and ends on your plate, perhaps after a comfortable stop in a well-stocked pantry or freezer. It never knows the back of a truck or the inside of a factory, and it holds no chemical or genetic secrets. The food you grow and preserve yourself is pure. Eating it feels comfortable and good.

This is why we garden our way through summer and can our way through fall, with the hum of the dehydrator in the background. Both a hobby and a lifestyle, provisioning yourself with homegrown, organic food brings tasty, tangible rewards that save you money, but it's the overall wholesomeness of the endeavor that makes food gardening so special. The package deal includes healthy exercise and mindfulness practice (weeding, cutting vegetables), for which you get a supply of fresh food that is renewed each year.

This book is about growing a garden that produces tasty, nutritious vegetables, herbs, and fruits, and then storing them for year-round use. This rewarding path leads to a fuller life, but it's a long and winding road from growing your first tomato to canning a batch of salsa. This is your guidebook for that journey.

THE DRIVE TO PROVIDE

My city mother fell in love with and married my country father, who grew a vegetable garden every summer because he liked it and thought that's the way life should be. With four kids to feed, Mom liked the money she saved with all the produce that came from the garden, but she didn't like the extra work involved in canning, at least most of the time. When the wild huckleberries in the woods ripened in early summer, she patiently picked the tiny berries and used them in muffins and pancakes, but she also made precious jars of huckleberry jam.

As her first assistant, I saw the time and care she took with that jam, and I knew it was not about saving money. She had devoted herself to those huckleberries by choice, and seeing that they were put to good use became a source of personal pride.

I should mention that my mother was Swedish, and that "Nothing wasted" was one of the mantras of my childhood, but this does not explain the compulsion to pick and preserve berries, which may be hardwired into our hunter-gatherer brains. As poetically stated by Wendell Berry, "Better than any argument is to rise at dawn and pick dew-wet red berries in a cup." In terms of things you can do to have a better life, picking berries simply works.

Growing and preserving at least some of your own food will also make you feel more secure in a wild and ever-changing world. News of war, sickness, and economic collapse loses some of its punch when you are sitting in the shade with a basket of snap beans in your lap or lingering in the kitchen to hear the last canning lids pop.

TWELVE COMMON TRAITS OF PANTRY GARDENERS

In 2010, Melissa A. Click from the University of Missouri and Ronit Ridberg from Tufts University published their examination of why people grow and preserve their own food. Their results showed complex motives, but food activism was a recurrent theme. After sorting through and analyzing more than 900 interviews with people who stock their pantries with homegrown food, the authors named their paper "Saving Food: Food Preservation as Alternative Food Activism." They wrote: "Food preservation emphasizes connection and relationships and thus has the potential to subvert the capitalistic logic of the global agro-food industry."

This came as a revelation to me and helped me become a better information sharer and listener. I had started lecturing on managing your homegrown food supply, and I will always remember a group waiting to hear what I had to say at the Mother Earth News Fair in Lawrence, Kansas. The room was full with people who were already growing and preserving some of their own food, and they wanted to do more of it. Many had children or grandchildren in tow. The energy was great, so we spent a lot of time talking about why we do what we do. What is it about growing and preserving your own food that makes it worth the time and trouble?

I was the only one there who had read Click and Ridberg's paper, but the Kansas group (and many others since then) validated and expanded the reasons why we commit to growing and preserving garden food, season after season. We pantry gardeners are a diverse, freethinking crowd, but here are 12 things many of us have in common.

1 You want to know what's in your food from seed to table. You perceive foods grown with systemic pesticides or genetic alterations as unacceptable, and you want to feel comfortable with what you eat.

2 You want to control how your food tastes in terms of sugar and salt, and you don't want synthetic preservatives or colors. Plain food is good food.

3 You want to feel confident rather than suspicious about the food you eat and serve to your children.

Several major medical schools have advised pregnant women and young children to eat organic food because of high levels of carcinogens and other toxins present in mainstream foods. This is not news to you.

4 You want your food to be consistent with your personal morals and beliefs. If you are a vegetarian, for example, growing and processing your own foods gives you a chance to eliminate animal-based ingredients.

5 You feel that growing and preserving your own food makes you a member in good standing of the global social movement toward clean, ethically grown food. Talking food sustainability is good, but acting on those beliefs makes you feel that you are part of something bigger.

6 You think of spending your money as a political act, especially when it comes to food. The belief in voting with your dollars is strong among gardeners who grow their own food, from the seed companies they patronize to the equipment and ingredients they buy for preserving food.

7 You feel empowered by knowing how to grow and preserve food to eat year-round. The transition from "I think maybe I can grow potatoes" to gaining the skills needed to grow, harvest, cure, and store a bumper crop brings a certain boldness of being.

8 You are willing to work hard for the reward of food security, and upon balance you think it's a good deal. Some days are easier than others, with persistence your only choice, but when the harvest is done you feel it was all worth it.

9 You regard growing and preserving your own food as an investment in your personal health, and that of your community and environment. By growing clean, nutritious food, using organic methods, you feel like you are doing your part.

10 You find that managing your own food supply connects you more deeply to nature and the earth. From the changing of the seasons to the hardness or softness of rain, you sense the world as a human and as a plant.

11 You feel a sense of family and social history when you grow and store your own food. Maybe it's making your grandmother's pickles, or your uncle's apple butter, but certain family recipes for preserved foods embrace us on deep levels, as sensory definitions of family.

12 You think a pantry filled with homegrown food is about the prettiest thing you've ever seen, and you like pretty things. To you, few things are more beautiful than abundance.

Sound familiar? Then it's time we got down to business.

HOW TO USE THIS BOOK

Homegrown Pantry is comprised of five chapters. Here in chapter 1, we will become grounded in our gardens and look at ways they can be managed to produce great food as efficiently as possible. While I hope beginning gardeners find this information easy to understand, it will make the most sense to people who have been gardening for a few years and have already gotten to know a number of different food crops firsthand. The more you grow, the more you know.

Chapter 2 provides step-by-step instructions for major food preservation methods, whether you are storing potatoes in old milk crates or making salt-fermented sauerkraut. This is where to look for simple canning instructions or for the many ways you can use a dehydrator to preserve summer produce for winter meals. Remember that practice makes perfect, and don't be discouraged by early mistakes. With gardening and food preservation, the next season brings new chances to succeed.

Chapters 3, 4, and 5 are encyclopedias of rewarding crops for the pantry garden, with details on how much to grow, how to grow it, and the best preservation options to consider when you have a bumper crop. These vegetables, fruits, and herbs were chosen based on their popularity, how well they are likely to grow using organic methods, and the ease with which they can be preserved. This is precisely the information I needed but did not have when I started food gardening in a serious way. Of special note are the Harvest Day Recipes, which are among the fastest and easiest ways to make use of a big harvest quickly.

YOUR CLIMATE, BY THE NUMBERS

There are several things about the place where you live that influence the crops and varieties you grow and how you preserve them. Becoming familiar with your climate zone, frost dates, latitude, elevation, and precipitation patterns will make you a better gardener and self-provisioner, too.

Average Frost Dates

As a vegetable gardener, the average dates of your last frost in spring and your first frost in fall provide reference points for when many vegetables should be planted. In general, these dates mark the beginning and end of the season for beans, tomatoes, and other warm-season vegetables that need warm soil temperatures and are easily injured by frost. Most cool-season vegetables are planted weeks before the last frost passes, and many of them stay in the garden until cold temperatures coupled with a short supply of sunshine stop their growth. Many Internet sites provide frost date calculators based on zip code, but you will get more detailed information from data collected by your state climatology service. Search "frost dates [*your state*]" to find the dates you need, and commit them to memory.

USDA Zones

In the United States, the Department of Agriculture has divided the country into numbered growing zones based on average minimum winter temperatures. Zone numbers from the US mainland range from Zone 3 in the far north to Zone 9 in Florida and southern California. The zone system aids communication among gardeners in general, but it becomes hugely relevant when you are selecting trees, berries, and perennials for your garden. Garden catalogs and plant tags use the zone system, making it easier to choose appropriate plants. If you are not sure which zone you are in, the mother map online (http://planthardiness.ars.usda.gov/PHZMWeb/) has a search function by zip code.

Latitude

Your latitude, or distance from the equator, determines day length patterns in your area. Locations close to the equator see less dramatic changes in day length than those that are farther away. For example, day lengths in New Orleans, near the 30th parallel, range from 10.1 hours on January 1 to 13.9 hours on July 1. Farther north, near the 40th parallel, which includes New York City and Salt Lake City, the shortest winter days last only 9.2 hours, but the longest summer days go to 14.8 hours.

Because they are solar beings, plants are much more attuned to these changes than are we humans. Especially when day lengths change quickly, in spring and fall, many plants respond by moving in or out of reproductive mode. The rapid lengthening of each spring day coaxes Asian greens and cilantro to bolt (produce flowers and seeds) at a young age, and most spinach varieties cannot hold themselves back from bolting once days get to be more than 13 hours long. In fall, when these triggers are absent, the plants have no interest in bolting and keep growing leaves. In the case of peppers, long August nights push the plants to load up with fruits.

Onions use multiple cues to form bulbs, including day length and temperature. This is why it is important to choose varieties that are right for your latitude, as discussed on pages 134–135.

Elevation

Higher elevations usually see more intense winds and cooler temperatures than lower elevations, with first and last frost dates that may differ from nearby areas at lower elevations by 2 weeks or more. In addition to an overall shorter growing season, altitude has a huge implication in food preservation because it changes the temperature at which water boils due to lowered atmospheric pressure. At sea level water boils at 212°F (100°C), but at 3,000 feet above sea level (the elevation at my house), the boiling point is only about 207°F (97°C). Because the food is cooking at a lower temperature, my canning jars must be processed longer to kill microorganisms.

Rainfall and Snowfall Patterns

In every place I have lived and gardened, there have been predictable patterns in when the weather will be wet and when dry conditions will prevail. Average monthly rainfall numbers for your location are easily accessed on the Internet, plus you can keep records of your own observations. A simple rain gauge and an outdoor thermometer will add much interest to watching the weather.

In an ideal season, most crops will receive regular rain during their juvenile growth phase and will be ready for drier conditions as they approach maturity. You can change planting dates and watering practices to keep them aligned with the natural precipitation patterns where you live.

CHOOSING WHAT TO GROW

When you are gardening to fill your pantry, consider these three questions when deciding what to grow:

1 Is this crop productive and easy to grow in my climate?

2 How much does my family like to eat it?

3 How much time and trouble is involved in storing this crop?

Choosing easy, productive crops is a simple matter of going with your garden's strengths. If the crop is in high demand in the kitchen and can be stored in cloth shopping bags in the basement, you have a winner. Potatoes, onions, garlic, pumpkins and winter squash, and sweet potatoes (where they grow well) should be priority crops because they often get positive answers to these three pivotal questions.

Crops that are easy to grow in one place may be huge challenges in another, and it just makes sense to repeat your successes. For example, if your carrots are seldom spectacular but your beans are robust, keep your carrot plantings small and grow as many beans as you can eat. Your soil's overall quality will improve over time when you use compost, organic fertilizers, and biodegradable mulches. This will change the script for crops that should grow well in your garden but fail to measure up.

Balancing Your Garden's
Food Groups

The concept of food groups is often used in diet planning, but it should be used in garden planning, too. Once they come into the kitchen, many vegetables cluster together in how they are eaten or preserved, which can lead to pantry overload or dinnertime boredom. Check out the kitchen food groups below, and strive for a happy balance within each set of similar choices.

Orange-fleshed vegetables. Carrots, pumpkins, sweet potatoes, and winter squash can be used in salads, soups, side dishes, breads, and desserts, but at some point your palate will tire of orange-fleshed vegetables and need some recovery time. This is a pity because sweet potatoes and winter squash are so easy to store. Do be realistic about how many orange-fleshed vegetables you enjoy eating, and adjust how much you grow.

Root crops. The growing popularity of fermentation has helped make better use of fall root crops — including radishes, rutabagas, and turnips — but you can still end up with a cold storage problem once you've eaten your fill of roasted root vegetables and hard freezes have begun. Among root crops, it's important to grow only as much as you can store in a refrigerated space.

Leafy greens. These wonderfully productive plants will surprise you, and many stems from chard, collards, and kale will be wasted if you plant more than you can use. The situation becomes more complicated if you also grow fall crops of turnip or mustard greens, so hard choices often must be made. I suggest changing things up from season to season, so that some years you skip growing a leafy green you like. Then, when you grow it again in a future season, you will be glad to have it.

When you find vegetables that excel in your garden, and grow as much of them as you are likely to eat, you will take a huge step closer to food self-sufficiency. Don't waste time and space growing more than you need or crops you really don't like to eat.

Work Your Shoulder Seasons

If your main growing season runs from May to October, your "shoulder seasons" are early spring and late fall. These are the times to grow salad greens and other veggies eaten fresh, and to enjoy early-bearing perennials like asparagus and rhubarb.

Strawberries, raspberries, blueberries, and other small fruits are easy to grow organically, but they are time consuming to pick. June-bearing strawberries and early raspberries help to open the harvest season early. They can be picked and stashed in the freezer before vegetable garden produce takes over your kitchen.

WORKING WITH TUNNELS

Not so long ago, a book of this type would include lengthy coverage of insect pests and what to do about them, and the crop entries in chapter 3 do note common pests to expect in your garden. But you will also read again and again my advice to keep at-risk plants covered with spun-bonded fabric row cover or lightweight tulle netting (also called wedding net) as a primary means of preventing pest problems.

Using row covers has caught on in a big way at organic farms everywhere, because row covers do more than protect plants from pests. They also tame strong winds, reduce temperature extremes, and moderate light in a way that pleases most plants. Plants growing under tunnels — hoops or frames covered with row cover — are protected from deer, dogs, and the heartbreak of hail, too.

You can expect amazing results with low tunnels, especially in transitional weather. Low tunnels have a proven track record of bringing on spring earlier for strawberries and spinach, and they are the best way to grow overwintering onions (see page 134). In cold climates, you can go with the increased insulation of plastic covers, but setting up a sheet plastic tunnel in a windy setting can be a futile exercise. When the edges are securely tucked in, a row cover tunnel will stand steady in strong wind.

Supports. Hoops or arches can be made from any smooth, non-snagging material like wire, pipe, or welded fencing. Most gardeners use hoops made from stiff, 9- or 10-gauge wire, or they make pipe hoops from inexpensive ½- to 1-inch-diameter poly pipe (the type used for underground water lines). Both types of hoops can simply be stuck in the ground, though pipe hoops are more likely to stay erect if they are slipped over sturdy rebar stakes or into sleeves made from rigid metal or PVC pipe. You can also attach them to the outside of framed beds with metal pipe strips. Even if you don't have raised beds, you can make wooden "running boards" for the long edges of your beds by outfitting them with tunnel-friendly holes or hardware.

Hoops should be of the right length to arch over your beds to a height of at least 16 inches. For 2-foot-wide beds, hoops should be at least 65 inches long. For 3-foot-wide beds, hoops cut 76 to 80 inches long are best. Hoops are

A low tunnel has three parts — the support hoops or arches, the cover, and the weights to keep the edges secure.

usually spaced 2 to 3 feet apart, so you may need a lot of them. The cheapest way to go is to buy a small spool of 9- or 10-gauge wire or poly pipe and cut the hoops yourself.

For winter use, arched wire fencing can withstand heavy loads of ice or snow without collapsing (as hoop-held tunnels are prone to do).

Covers. These are usually made from fabric row cover, which comes in different thicknesses and widths, or you can use a similar fabric from a fabric shop. Wedding net (tulle) works well because it does not retain heat, but it has tiny holes that insects cannot breach. When covers are not in use, store them in a dry place protected from sunlight to make them last longer.

Weights. The fabrics can be fastened to support hoops with clothespins and bunched together along the edges and held in place with weights. Use whatever is handy — bricks, pieces of firewood, lengths of scrap lumber, or sandbags filled with sand, soil, or gravel.

When used to exclude insects or other predators, feather-weight fabrics like tulle block only a little light and allow air to circulate freely.

Seasonal Calendar of
Food Preservation

Just as you keep track of planting dates in spring, it's an excellent idea to keep records of when your major crops are ripe and ready to be preserved. Make notes on a wall calendar of when you undertake big projects, and refer to it the next year so you can plan ahead to free up time for food preservation. The crunch time will vary with climate, but it will usually coincide with the ripening of your main crop of tomatoes. Here's a sample calendar of how preservation projects work through the seasons.

EARLY SPRING

Clean out freezer.

Sort and store empty canning jars and freezer containers.

LATE SPRING

Freeze or dry asparagus.

Freeze, dry, or can rhubarb.

EARLY SUMMER

Freeze or can strawberries and cherries.

Freeze peas.

Can beets.

Dry herbs and leafy greens.

MIDSUMMER

Cure and store garlic and onions.

Freeze or can blueberries, raspberries, and blackberries.

Make cucumber pickles.

Dry, freeze, or pickle summer squash.

Dry herbs and leafy greens.

LATE SUMMER

Cure and store potatoes.

Freeze or can peaches and plums.

Dry, can, or freeze tomatoes.

Freeze sweet corn.

Make and freeze herb pestos.

Can mixed vegetable relishes.

Dry beans and seed crops.

EARLY FALL

Cure and store sweet potatoes and winter squash.

Dry, can, or freeze apples, pears, and grapes.

Freeze or dry peppers.

Can mixed garden chutneys.

MID-FALL

Ferment cabbage and other vegetables.

Freeze or dry kale and collards.

Freeze spinach and chard.

LATE FALL

Process and freeze pumpkins and short-storing winter squash.

Make wine, jams, and jellies from frozen fruits.

MANAGING YOUR FOOD PRESERVATION GARDEN

Keeping up with everything happening in a diversified garden is a taxing load for most human brains, and it gets more complicated when you're handling food preservation, too. If food gardening had a gold medal event, it would be the marathon of planting, weeding, watering, staking, harvesting, washing, freezing, canning, and more that dominates our lives through the second half of summer.

Hundreds of small skills are involved, but here I want to share the big lessons you otherwise learn the hard way by making mistakes. The good news is that each new season provides opportunities to do better.

First Priority: Harvest What Is Ready

On any given day, you may have five things you want to get done in the garden, and you will end up doing only three of them because of lack of time. Refusing to admit this from the outset, you get busy planting, weeding, or whatever, and when the day is done, the world's finest lettuce is still sitting in your garden, waiting to be picked. Or maybe your pickling cucumbers are blowing up like water balloons, or birds are eating your blueberries for breakfast.

These things will not happen if you always make harvesting what is ready your top priority. To streamline the harvesting process, think in terms of strategic staging. Pick in the morning when you can, and stash your goodies in a shady spot or cooler to keep them cool.

Plan to Keep Planting

If you want to keep your garden productive all season long, you have to keep planting. Once a week, do a reality check in your head to see if anything is missing. A written or computer-based plan can help tremendously, or simply write your planned plantings on a wall calendar that you see every day. This will help keep good planting dates from slipping away, and you won't stop planting too soon. Until your fall garden is filled to capacity, your planting is not done.

When you have a big harvest day, make frozen water bottles from plastic drink bottles filled three-fourths full. Wrap the frozen bottles in small towels and place them among your harvested veggies or in an insulated cooler. This trick can save a lot of trips back and forth to the kitchen.

Provide Constancy of Care

Watering, weeding, and many other repetitive tasks fall under this guideline, so it's important to use methods that have some staying power. Drip or soaker hoses make it easy to water your crops while you attend to other things, and mulches are invaluable for keeping soil constantly moist.

Expect weeding to take up a good bit of time, even when you are armed with a dangerously sharp hoe — the most effective kind. Many evenings you will work until dark and look up to find yourself in the company of fireflies and sphinx moths. This is one of the best times to stop what you're doing, breathe deeply, and marvel at what you can achieve by combining sun, sweat, seeds, and soil.

Second-Season
Sowing

Spring fever energizes us to plant like crazy, but no such magic compels the planting of crops that mature in late summer and fall. Use the average date of your location's first hard freeze as a starting point, and count back 14 weeks (November 1 freeze date counts back to mid-July). Use this start date for this checklist for second-season sowing.

12 TO 14 WEEKS
BEFORE FIRST HARD FREEZE

Direct-sow a last planting of fast-maturing warm-season vegetables like snap beans, cucumbers, and summer squash. Also sow parsnips and rutabagas, and begin planting cilantro, lettuce, and radishes.

Start cabbage family seedlings indoors, and set out the seedlings as promptly as possible.

In climates with long autumns, add celery, bulb fennel, and parsley to your indoor planting list.

10 TO 12 WEEKS
BEFORE FIRST HARD FREEZE

Set out broccoli, Brussels sprouts, cabbage, cauliflower, kale, and kohlrabi seedlings, along with celery, bulb fennel, and parsley.

Direct-sow beets, carrots, collards, leeks, and scallions along with more lettuce and radishes. In some areas, fast-maturing peas and potatoes will make a precious fall crop when planted in late summer.

8 TO 10 WEEKS
BEFORE FIRST HARD FREEZE

Direct-sow arugula, Chinese cabbage, lettuce, mustard, pak choi and other oriental greens, spinach, and turnips. Sow more lettuce and radishes, including daikons.

6 TO 8 WEEKS
BEFORE FIRST HARD FREEZE

Make a final sowing of spinach along with mâche, which matches spinach for winter hardiness. Make a final sowing of leaf lettuce to grow beneath a protective tunnel or frame.

ON OR AROUND FIRST HARD FREEZE

Plant garlic, shallots, multiplying onion bulblets, and perennial nest onions.

Factor in Food Preservation Time

Experienced kitchen gardeners know that growing a great crop is only half of the story. As each crop comes in, you will still need to pick, cook, and/or store your fresh veggies in ways that preserve their flavor, nutrition, and other good eating qualities. Some crops will wait longer than others, but it's better to rearrange your work schedule than to allow tomatoes and peppers to go soft on the kitchen table.

Which method a preservation project uses determines how much time it will take. You can fill dehydrator trays with sliced tomatoes in 30 minutes, but you may spend 2 hours canning a batch of peaches because many more steps are involved. But canned foods are worth the time because they are easy to store and ready to eat.

Run only one active food preservation project at a time, and no more than two in one day. Otherwise, you will burn out long before the race has been run. Start each project in a clean kitchen, and put away your food preservation equipment as soon as you are finished using it. Canners, food processors, and cutting equipment will clutter up a kitchen fast.

It's also nice to have help. Peeling and paring veggies and fruits can be slow work alone. Many hands do make light work, and when you work with others, filling the dehydrator with apples or canning a batch of diced tomatoes is much more fun.

Food preservation is one area where you should never take shortcuts. You have gone to the trouble of planting, nurturing, and harvesting a crop, so you don't want to compromise quality when the crop hits the kitchen. The pressure of the harvest season pushes us to rush, but the hurrying needs to stop when a food preservation project gets under way. Whether you are blanching snap beans to stash in the freezer or canning your family's favorite bread-and-butter pickles, take the time to do things right. The reward is total confidence that your preserved foods are as nutritious and flavorful as they can possibly be.

COOKING FROM THE HOMEGROWN PANTRY

When you run out of something, you go to the store and buy more, right? This is a lifelong way of things for most of us, but cooking from the homegrown pantry requires an important new habit: shopping your own store first. When you start thinking of what you will cook in the next few days, begin by surveying what you have on hand that needs attention or sounds appetizing. This way you have a menu plan that partially originates in your garden, even in the middle of February.

As long as you have crops in cool storage, visit them at least once a week and fill a box with items you plan to cook. A butternut close at hand is more likely to get made into soup. If you find that you are not using up your cold-stored foods fast enough, you can cook and freeze or dry them, or share them with others. The same goes with freezer fare. If your main freezer is not in your kitchen, move selected frozen items to your kitchen freezer once a week to keep things moving.

Keep your dried herbs in a handy place so they are at the ready for cooking or making herb teas. When soup is on the menu, look to your dried veggies, which are at their best when slowly simmered in a tasty broth.

Enjoying
YOUR
Stored Foods

When you have grown and stored a number of crops from your garden, it's important to get into the habit of consuming them in logical order. Plan meals around veggies or fruits in need of attention, and take pride in your shrinking food supply. Below is the general consumption plan to follow, based on the shelf life of different stored foods. Of course you will skip around, but sticking to this overall plan helps minimize waste.

WITHIN 3 MONTHS

Use the veggies you have in cold storage, including pumpkins, apples, and pears, as well as onions, potatoes, and sweet potatoes. Some of these root crops will store longer, but they are at their best while they are fully dormant.

WITHIN 5 MONTHS

Finish off fermented foods and refrigerator pickles.

Cook and freeze any winter squash that have not yet been eaten.

When the onions are gone, start in on the shallots.

WITHIN 7 MONTHS

Empty freezer shelves of cherry tomatoes, peppers, summer squash, green beans, corn, greens, cabbage family crops, berries, and other fruits.

WITHIN 1 YEAR

Finish off shallots and garlic.

Consume all dried food, including tomatoes, peppers, summer squash, beans, pumpkin, kale, mushrooms, and herbs for cooking and tea.

Eat all pickled beets and cucumbers and vinegar-based relishes.

WITHIN 2 YEARS

Consume dried fruits and vegetables stored in the freezer.

Eat canned foods in sealed jars, such as tomato sauces (salsa and marinara), relishes and chutneys, fruits in light syrup, and jams and jellies.

BASIC
Food Preservation
METHODS

Knowing where your food comes from gives you confidence in its goodness, which is increased when you preserve your produce using safe, appropriate methods. Having a well-provisioned home is a tremendous convenience, because you must go no farther than your basement or freezer to gather much of what you need to make a meal. In early winter when your pantry, freezer, and basement are full, you may feel like you are living in a well-stocked organic grocery store.

Food preservation encompasses numerous skills that are easily learned through practice. As with other types of cooking, if you follow directions and pay close attention to details, you can expect great success with one food preservation project after another.

Do keep in mind that regardless of the methods used, only top-quality produce should be stored. Try to schedule food preservation projects when produce is in peak condition, which is usually right after it is picked. The crop profiles in chapters 3, 4, and 5 suggest the best short-term storage and long-term preservation options for each crop, which fall into these five categories: cold storage, freezing, drying, canning, and fermentation. In this chapter, each of these methods will be covered in detail.

FIVE BASIC FOOD STORAGE METHODS

1 **Cold storage, also called dormant storage.** If you provide them with cold conditions that make them think they are resting in cold soil, most root crops can be stored for months in a refrigerator, root cellar, or cold basement or outbuilding. Beets, carrots, turnips, and rutabagas will keep in the refrigerator for weeks or months. In a cool room or basement, potatoes, pumpkins, and winter squash will hold in a dormant state for several months; the dormancy periods for onions and garlic range from 3 to 10 months.

2 **Freezing.** When properly blanched and frozen, delicate veggies like asparagus, broccoli, or snap peas taste almost like the fresh versions. When you have no time to properly preserve any crop, you may be able to freeze the produce and take care of processing later. Frozen produce should be consumed within 6 months.

3 **Drying.** A food dehydrator is a huge time-saver for gardeners devoted to growing tomatoes and peppers, and it should be considered essential equipment if you have bearing fruit trees. Dried foods take up less space than canned or frozen ones, and drying is the best way to preserve herbs for cooking and teas. Under ideal conditions, dried foods last at least 1 year.

4 **Canning.** Storing foods in sealed jars is the most technical and time-consuming food preservation method, but with practice anyone can make excellent pickles, salsa, or delicious canned fruits. When you have huge batches of cucumbers for pickles or tomatoes for sauces, canning is usually the method of choice. Some fruits are at their best when canned.

5 **Fermentation.** When bacteria are allowed to digest the sugars in vegetables such as cabbage or radishes (controlled somewhat by a salty brine), the resulting fermented vegetables will store in the refrigerator for months. Wine is made by fermenting the sugars in fruits, with additional sugar added to raise the alcohol content.

COLD STORAGE OF HOMEGROWN PRODUCE

One of the reasons potatoes and onions are grown in gardens around the world is that they are so easy to store. The same goes for pumpkins, winter squash, and sweet potatoes. And if you think of your refrigerator as a device for cold storage, most root crops and some fruits make the list of good storage crops, too.

In a well-managed pantry garden, about half of the weight of your overall harvest should be from crops that do not need to be processed before they are stored. By making use of cold storage spots in your basement or garage, and perhaps adding a seasonal second refrigerator (or a temporary icebox made from a cooler), you can eat an abundance of these and other storage crops through the first half of winter.

Understanding Dormant Storage

The goal with most storage crops is to convince the root or seed capsule (for example, a pumpkin) that the plant is enjoying a natural period of rest under comfortable conditions. Lowering the temperature supports dormancy by reducing respiration; providing moisture and cold makes carrots and other crisp root vegetables sense they are still in the ground. Some staple storage crops, such as garlic, onions, and shallots, need dry conditions to support prolonged dormancy. Moisture can trigger them to start growing again.

Most storage crops benefit from a curing process before they go into storage, during which time you help them enter their dormant period in excellent shape. During the curing process, potatoes and sweet potatoes heal over small wounds to the skin, garlic and onions form a dry seal over the openings at their necks, and dry beans and grain corn let go of excess moisture that could otherwise cause them to rot.

Harvesting, curing, and storage requirements vary by crop, as reflected in the crop entries in chapter 3. If you harvest and cure your vegetables properly, they will last much longer in storage, but no fresh veggie lasts forever. Eat your cold-stored vegetables first, perhaps by combining them with goodies from the freezer. Move on to canned and dried foods when your supplies of "6 months or less" veggies run low.

Storing Carrots and Other Crisp Root Vegetables

Theoretically, carrots and other cold-hardy root vegetables that grow well below ground can be mulched over in fall and dug as needed in winter. This often works well with parsnips, but most gardeners risk losing much of an over-wintered carrot or beet crop to wireworms, voles, or other critters. Repeated freezing and thawing of the surface soil damages shallow-rooted root crops like turnips, rutabagas, and beets. It's always safer to harvest root crops, trim off the tops, clean them gently (no scrubbing), and secure them in cold storage.

Your refrigerator will provide perfect storage conditions for carrots, beets, radishes, and other root crops kept in plastic bags. But what if you run out of refrigerator space? Improvised, temporary cold storage should be tailored to your climate so that nature lends a helping hand.

- **Bury an old cooler halfway in a convenient spot,** and use it as a seasonal icebox for food you can't fit in your refrigerator. Place frozen water bottles in the cooler in warm weather, and secure the top with a bungee cord to prevent nighttime thievery from skunks or raccoons. You may need to pack roots in damp sawdust or sand to maintain high humidity. If your only concern is preventing vegetables from freezing, a cooler kept in the shade outside the kitchen door is handy for a few weeks in early winter. Simply cover it with a blanket on very cold nights.

- **Bins or buckets packed with damp sand or sawdust** will store roots crops nicely if you can find a place to put them with temperatures in the 32 to 40°F (0 to 4°C) range. Likely spots include an unheated garage or storage shed, or beneath your basement stairs. Check containers weekly and eat any roots that show signs of softening.

- **A seasonal second refrigerator** is worth considering if you have a lot of apples, pears, carrots, or beets to store; you live in a climate too warm for underground storage; or you want to store root vegetables to sell or trade later.

Crisp roots such as beets need high humidity to store well, so storing them packed in damp sand or sawdust is a good method to try. Sawdust is clean and lightweight, and the residue can be shaken out into the garden. Sand weighs more but is reusable — simply dry it in the sun and return it to a bucket or bin until you need it the next year.

Dry Storage for Potatoes and Onions

Potatoes, sweet potatoes, onions, garlic, and shallots like to spend their dormant period in dry conditions, with some leeway in temperature. A cool, dry basement where temperatures range from 50 to 60°F (10 to 15°C) is ideal, especially for potatoes, which need to be protected from light. I often store early-summer potatoes in bins and boxes under my bed, because it's the best cool, dry, dark place in my house in late summer.

Depending on the storage space available to you, you might use half-bushel baskets, small bins with loose-fitting lids (including low-profile under-the-bed bins), cardboard boxes, an old dresser with partially opened drawers, or plastic or wooden crates to store your dormant tubers and onion family crops. See page 167 for more resourceful ideas for storage spaces.

If you don't have a cool basement, look for other cool, dark places to store potatoes, such as an interior closet or under your bed.

Regardless of how perfect your dry root crops look when you move them to your basement or garage, do not forget to check them at least every 2 weeks. Sniff around for rotting problems, and watch for signs of new life. Each crop will decide when it's had enough rest and is ready to break dormancy, which is your sign to eat more onions, sweet potatoes, or whatever. This is a wonderful problem to have.

Storing Pumpkins and Winter Squash

When properly cured under warm conditions as described on pages 175 and 235, the rinds of pumpkins and winter squash harden, which in turn prevents moisture loss. But good squash can go bad suddenly even when kept in a cool, dry place. Check stored squash and pumpkins weekly for signs of mold, which is most likely to develop around the base of the stem. Promptly eat or preserve any that have developed minor blemishes, such as discoloration or soft spots.

Some types of storage squash store longer than others, so try to eat them in proper order.

Squash and pumpkins classified as *Cucurbita pepo* have thin rinds, so they usually keep for only 2 to 3 months. Examples include acorn squash, delicata or sweet potato squash, spaghetti squash, and many pumpkins. Eat these semi-perishable winter squash in the fall. Process pumpkins into frozen purée in late fall, while they are still in good condition.

Buttercup and kabocha squash (*C. maxima*) will keep for 4 months under good conditions, but after 2 months the fruits should be watched closely for signs of softening or mold. Many squash pie devotees bake up all questionable buttercups in early winter and stash the mashed squash in the freezer. This is a wise move, because it's easy to make a pie or batch of muffins if you have squash purée waiting in your freezer.

The smooth, hard rinds of butternut squash (*C. moschata*) help them store for 6 months or more, so eat your butternuts last. Many gardeners grow more butternuts than other types of winter squash because they are so easy to store.

FREEZING YOUR HOMEGROWN BOUNTY

In the homegrown pantry, a freezer is like a kitchen assistant. When you're faced with a food preservation challenge, your freezer can probably provide a fast and easy solution. Some vegetables and fruits are at their best when frozen, and many others can be frozen in a pinch. For example, the bulk of my stored tomatoes are dried or canned, but by fall I have also saved up several gallons of whole tomatoes in the freezer — all from days that brought perfectly ripened tomatoes and no time to deal with them.

The shadow side of using your freezer for catch-all food preservation is that it is very easy to lose track of what you have. Some people keep lists of their freezer contents, but you can do pretty well by simply dividing your freezer space into logical sections or dedicated shelves for veggies, fruits, meats, dried foods, and juices and stocks. Also make a habit of cleaning out your freezer every spring, when it should be close to empty. Dried foods and seeds can be stored for more than a year in the freezer, but other foods should be consumed after 6 months or so.

In some cases, it is beneficial to temporarily store excess vegetables and fruits in the freezer and process them for long-term storage later. Whole, frozen tomatoes can be thawed and transformed into sauce, and prefrozen cherries dry better than fresh ones. Frozen berries can be made into jams or preserves as easily as fresh ones, and freezing and thawing breaks down cell walls, which works wonders preparing apples or pears for fermenting into wine.

Containers for Freezing

Many people who grow and preserve their own food are motivated in part by purity. It is therefore with reluctance that we use food-safe plastics for freezing food. Paper-thin and capable of expanding slightly along with its crystallizing contents, plastic freezer bags (or freezer-grade vacuum-sealer bags) do what good freezer containers should do — provide airtight conditions in a puncture-resistant package. Foods frozen in bags are stackable if you freeze them flat on a plate or cookie sheet.

Choose containers with screw-on lids when freezing liquids like cherry juice. Pop-on lids tend to pop off as liquids freeze and expand.

Rigid plastic food containers make good freezer containers, too, though snap-on plastic lids tend to warp and crack with time. If you are buying new round plastic food containers primarily for use in the freezer (for example, plastic "freezer jars" for frozen fruit juice), pay extra if you must for screw-on lids.

A few summers ago, a visiting friend was aghast when I poured blackberry juice into a clean canning jar and screwed on a used lid before stashing it in the freezer. Jan said I had broken two rules — freezing in canning jars and reusing lids — but some rules can be carefully broken. You can freeze in clean canning jars as long as you leave plenty of headspace, because liquids expand as they freeze. I leave 1½ inches in pints, or 2 inches in quarts.

Lids should never be reused for canning, because they cannot be trusted to form a sound seal. But when freezing in canning jars, you don't want a seal, and the expansion of the freezing contents will push on a seal anyway. I screw on lids loosely at first, and tighten them after the jars have frozen solid. Canning jars take up a lot of freezer space, so I mostly use them for fruit and veggie juices, which are messy to handle in bags. I also use canning jars to freeze dried fruits and vegetables, which last 2 years in the freezer but only 1 on a cabinet shelf.

Expelling Air to Prevent Freezer Burn

Unless you are freezing liquids (which require space for expansion), it is important to remove as much air as possible from within the freezer container. Freezer burn — the formation of ice crystals that refreeze around the edges of the food and compromise its taste and texture — is reduced when the food fits tightly in the bag, with very little air. With Ziplock freezer bags, air is squeezed out by hand, or you can use a drinking straw to suck out extra air before sealing the bag. Or use the pressure of water to push air from bags. Submerge the bags almost to the seal in water, then zip.

Electric vacuum sealers suck out air as they seal the bags. A vacuum sealer and bags are an extra expense, but devotees say they are worth it because they make frozen and dried foods last longer.

Freezing Vegetables and Herbs

Freezing vegetables is fast and easy, and many kitchen vegetables from asparagus to zucchini can be frozen. Part of the beauty of freezing vegetables is that you can do it in small batches, to use odds and ends from your garden, or in big batches when you are buried in green beans.

Unlike with canning, you don't have to pay attention to acidity or salt when freezing vegetables. Instead, you can mix and match veggies based on pleasing colors and flavors — for instance, using carrots for color, bulb fennel for texture, and green-leafed herbs for extra flavor in mixed packages of frozen goodies. You can also include blanched mild onions in your frozen combos (a good use for bolted onions that won't store well), but don't include garlic, black pepper, or other "seed spices," which can undergo unwanted flavor changes when frozen.

Use only veggies in excellent condition that have been thoroughly cleaned. Except for peppers, tomatoes, and a few other food crops, veggies should be cooked before they are frozen. This is usually done by blanching the vegetables in steam or boiling water as described below, but you also can use your oven or grill to prepare foods for freezing. Blanching or cooking stops enzyme activity that causes vegetables to lose texture and nutrients; frozen veggies with no flavor and a cardboard texture were not cooked long enough to destroy these enzymes.

As an alternative to blanching, you can roast or grill vegetables before freezing them, which often adds flavor. Peppers and squash in particular benefit from grilling or broiling. You also have the option of freezing complete dishes, ready to thaw, cook, and serve, such as slow-cooked green beans or creamed corn. Instead of freezing pumpkin or squash purée, some people go ahead and make pies, and freeze the tightly wrapped, ready-to-bake pies.

HOW TO FREEZE VEGETABLES

1 Set up a two-piece steamer or pot of boiling water for blanching on the stove. Also set out a large baking dish to use for cooling the blanched vegetables. Bring the water to a slow boil.

2 Thoroughly clean and pare the vegetables into pieces of uniform size.

3 Place about 3 cups of the prepared veggies in the steamer basket or boiling water, put on the lid, and set your timer for a minimum of 3 minutes. Check for a color change, which indicates the pieces are almost cooked through. Err on the side of doneness. It is better to go 1 minute too long than to underblanch the vegetables.

not cooked   cooked

4 Put a dozen or so ice cubes in the baking dish, and transfer the hot, blanched vegetables to the ice bath as soon as you remove them from the steamer or pot. Blanched veggies keep their color best if they are immediately cooled in ice.

5 When the vegetables are cool enough to handle, pack them into freezer-safe containers and freeze immediately. Or arrange the pieces on cookie sheets in the freezer, and place them in freezer-safe containers after they freeze hard.

Veggie Freezing Tips

- When freezing green beans, include a few pods of a purple-podded variety, and use them as blanching indicators. The purple color will change to green when the beans are perfectly blanched.

- Use a silicone muffin pan (shown at left) for freezing pestos or other vegetable or herb purées, or any veggies you often use in small amounts. After the food is frozen hard, transfer to freezer-safe containers.

- Blanch perfect leaves from cabbage or collards and freeze them flat for later use as stuffed cabbage leaves. Blanch and freeze hollowed-out summer squash or sweet peppers for stuffing, too.

- Freeze vegetables and companion herbs together — for example, snap beans with basil or creamed sweet corn with parsley or cilantro. Add the herbs during the last minute of steam blanching, so they barely wilt.

- Add color to your frozen vegetables by including carrot, golden beet, radicchio, or other colorful edibles.

Freezing Fruits and Berries

If you have fruit trees or berry bushes, your freezer will play an essential role in making sure you have top-quality homegrown fruit to eat year-round. Blueberries, raspberries, and strawberries can be frozen as they are harvested, and you can transform them into preserves, jam, juice, or wine when you have time. Freezing is also a convenient way to store apples, cherries, and other tree fruits that will be used in baking. Home winemakers often freeze fresh fruit before fermenting it, because the freezing and thawing process encourages any fruit to release its juices.

Freezing Fruit with and without Sugar

Most of us would like to eat less sugar, and there is no sound reason to add sugar to bags of frozen berries or any fruits that will eventually be blended into smoothies or processed into preserves or wine. No sugar is needed when individual berries or cut pieces of fruit are frozen on cookie sheets and then moved to long-term storage containers. However, sugar has a tenderizing effect on fruit, which is especially beneficial with soft-fleshed fruits like strawberries and peaches. When you plan to use any frozen fruit as a dessert topping, tossing the fruit with sugar (½ cup sugar for each pint of fruit) or covering it with a sugar syrup (half sugar, half water) before freezing will enhance the fruit's color and texture, and upon thawing you will have a delicious fruit syrup, too.

Preventing Discoloration in Fruit

When exposed to air, many cut fruits oxidize, which causes them to darken. Unwanted color changes can easily be prevented by placing cut apples, pears, or peaches into cold acidified water, then draining the water before freezing the fruit. Simply place a large bowl of cold water next to your cutting board, and add to it any of the following acidifying agents.

- **Vitamin C or ascorbic acid** is highly effective and does not change the flavor of the fruit. Dissolve one 1,500 mg tablet in 1 quart of water.

- **Citric acid** is widely available as a powder, and while it does prevent discoloration, it also introduces a noticeable acidic flavor to some fruits.

- **Lemon juice** contains both ascorbic acid and citric acid and makes a handy acid bath when 3 tablespoons are mixed into a quart of water. The slight lemon flavor is pleasing in some fruits, such as pears.

DRYING VEGETABLES, HERBS, AND FRUITS

The most convenient foods in a homegrown pantry are those that are stored dried. Dried foods take up little space and can keep for a year or more, and they are terrifically easy to use in the kitchen. From herbs to add to marinades to casserole-ready squash or potatoes, dried foods are the quick go-to ingredients you will depend upon when fresh and frozen food runs low. You will reach for other dried foods almost every time you cook.

Often you will need only a little of something, like a few rings of jalapeño pepper, or maybe some kale to add color and flavor to a winter soup. In these situations, dried foods are perfect because they are ready in amounts large and small — enough tomatoes for a pot of chili, or a pinch of crushed parsley for a cold salad.

The essence of drying is the removal of water from the food, which in turn makes the food too dry for microorganisms to ruin. A food dehydrator is the best way to remove moisture. You may have success with a solar food dryer if you live in a climate with low humidity, but most of us require an electric food dehydrator to dependably dry the foods we grow. Compared to canning and freezing, drying food with a dehydrator is less time consuming and requires less energy.

Once foods have been dried, they can be rehydrated with a 20-minute soak in hot water, or you can add them directly to liquid dishes like soups or casseroles. Apples and many other dried fruits are tender enough to make enjoyable eating out of hand, but most dried vegetables are best used in casseroles or soups. Prepare to be happily surprised when those dried chips of zucchini plump up in a bubbling, savory sauce. Like magic, they go back to being summer squash.

First we will look at the equipment and basic steps involved in drying food, and then I'll go into more details for drying vegetables, herbs, and fruits.

Basic Equipment for Drying

The first dehydrators I ever saw were lightweight cloths spread over clipped boxwoods, where my country neighbors were drying apples, just as they had done for decades. At night they gathered up the corners of the cloths and brought the apples indoors to protect them from night dampness and dew. The apples were finished in a few days, and then placed in a 150°F (65°C) oven for 30 minutes to spook out any hiding creatures. If you have the weather for it, this is the most natural way there is to dry food.

Unfortunately this natural method is so slow that the food becomes exposed to contaminants over an extended period of time — unless you live in a very dry climate.

Food dehydrators are simple appliances that consist of a container equipped with a heating element and fan. The fan is in the back of square dehydrators (left), which helps large batches dry evenly. Modestly priced round dehydrators (right) have their fan in the top, and they are great for smaller jobs.

In arid climates, a simple solar food dehydrator is easy to make from cardboard boxes and aluminum foil. Designs vary, but usually the base of a solar dehydrator is a foil-lined box that amplifies solar heat, which is channeled upward over trays of drying food.

If you don't want your preserved food to be subject to the whims of the weather, an electric food dehydrator is all you need. An oven will not do, because the minimum temperature on most ovens is 150°F/65°C (too hot for herbs and fruits), and there is no practical way to circulate air continuously through a warm oven. Dehydrators come in a range of sizes, and you can make your own choice based on consumer reviews. Choose a model with trays that are easy to remove and clean, because tomatoes in particular can be messy.

Preparing Food for Drying

One of the great things about drying tomatoes and many other garden goodies is that they can be dried raw. Tomatoes that are dried as slices even benefit from having their skins left on, so prepping them is a simple matter of washing and slicing. Herbs being dried for cooking or tea are dried while still attached to their stems, and many thin-walled hot peppers can be dried whole.

Many foods do require special preparation if they are to dry into a product you will look forward to eating. Kale tastes better if it is lightly rubbed with oil and salt before drying, and most fruits need to be dipped in an acidic solution (see page 23) to keep them from turning brown. The charts on pages 28–29 note pretreatment procedures that benefit different fruits and vegetables, and it is well worth the extra time to do things right. After all, you are preparing the convenience foods you will be using until they run out or next year's crop comes in, whichever comes first.

The question of whether or not to blanch foods before drying them comes up again and again in food dehydrating circles. Some foods such as potatoes and other root crops should always be cooked through before they are dried, but with many other foods, like apples and peppers, whether or not to blanch is up to you. Most dried vegetables (and many fruits) are too coarse or chewy to

eat as enjoyable snacks, but if you blanch and season the pieces before drying them, they will become more tender. Squash, apples, and pumpkins that are blanched and tossed with spices before they are dried have an appealing melt-in-your-mouth quality that may be worth the extra trouble, at least for a few batches.

It is difficult to prescribe specific drying times for different foods, because they vary not only in how long the dehydration process requires but also how long it takes for moisture levels to equalize within the plant tissues. For this reason I recommend starting with 2 to 4 hours and then pulsing drying times. Once the initial moisture has been removed from foods, I like to slow down the drying process by turning on the dehydrator for short periods of an hour or two the next day. By the time the food is ready to be stored, it is evenly dried and in need of little or no conditioning time.

Conditioning and Storing Your Dried Foods

Some pieces will dry faster than others, so you need to allow time for the moisture content to equalize among the pieces of dried food. This is done by "conditioning" the dried food, usually by placing it in an airtight container for a couple of days, and then checking its moisture content again. If the food feels a little too moist, a quick run through the dehydrator or a brief bask in a warm oven should set things right. Always condition your dried foods for a day or two before packing them away for long-term storage.

Dried foods must be stored in airtight containers. Vacuum-sealed bags are ideal, but you can also use freezer bags or clean, dry canning jars. Each time a container is opened, air will enter that may change the moisture level in the dried food, so it is best to store dried foods in small containers.

Dried foods must be protected from light and warm temperatures above 60°F (16°C). A low, dark cabinet is ideal, or you can use your freezer. Foods that have been properly dried will keep at cool room temperatures for 6 months to a year, but in the freezer they will keep for twice that long.

Four Degrees
OF
Dryness

Foods vary in the degree to which they should be dried. The following terms are often used to describe degrees of doneness in dehydrated foods.

Half-dried. Food is dried until surface moisture is gone, but it is still soft and moist inside. Raisins, cherry or paste tomato halves, or seasoned squash slices can be dried only halfway and then stored in the freezer.

Leathery. You can feel no wet or sticky places with your fingers, and the food is easy to fold and twist. Most fruits with a high sugar content, such as apples or ripe plums, are best dried to the leathery stage.

Hard. Most vegetables should be dried until they are as hard as cardboard, because less moisture is better for long-term storage.

Crisp. Herbs, leafy greens, and hot peppers should be dried until they are crisp. Molds quickly develop in herbs that have not been sufficiently dried.

Drying Vegetables

Except for mushrooms, for which drying is always the best preservation method, drying is one of several ways vegetables can be preserved. Many crops that are typically frozen also can be dried, and diversification is comforting when it comes to your homegrown food supply. You also can team up your food dehydrator and freezer by making half-dried vegetables, which are stored frozen. Half-dried tomatoes are a prime example. Thick-fleshed paste tomatoes are cut into halves, sprinkled with sea salt, and dehydrated until they collapse. When frozen in this half-dried state, tomatoes become compact, non-drippy ingredients for pasta, pizza, or even salads.

Making Vegetable Powders

Once vegetables have been dried, you can take small batches out of storage, dry them again until they are quite crisp, and use a dedicated coffee grinder or mini food processor to turn them into a powder. Small amounts of tomato, spinach, or beet powder can be used to add color and flavor to homemade pasta dough, and vegetable powders are handy for adding flavor to soups and stews. Dried garlic can be made into garlic powder or garlic salt, and you can stock your spice cabinet with your own paprika (from dried chili peppers) and cumin (from dried seed of the cumin plant). For the strongest flavor punch, freshly pulverized vegetable powders are best.

Freeze half-dried tomatoes seasoned with summer herbs in portions suitable for use in pasta, sandwiches, or pizza.

Drying Seeds for Storage

Beans, peas, and other crops that are consumed as seeds, such as dill and coriander, are easy to dry indoors at normal room temperatures. Slow drying allows organs within the seeds to enter dormancy in a mature state, so allow a couple of weeks for dry beans and peas to harden. Most dry beans are so pretty that a bowl of them on the kitchen table is as attractive as a bouquet of flowers. You can't help but stir through them with your fingers at least once a day.

With small seeds such as dill, fennel, celery, or others you want to harvest for eating or replanting, cut the seed heads into a paper bag and bring them indoors to dry. After a couple of weeks, crunch through the dried seed heads with your hands. Seeds, being heavy, will accumulate at the bottom of the bag for easy collection and cleaning.

Best Vegetables
FOR
Drying

For the vegetables pictured below, drying is a preferred preservation method. Numerous vegetables not included here — for example, asparagus and broccoli — are also candidates for drying if you do not have freezer space for them. You also may want to dry small amounts of cabbage, carrots, or other soup veggies, simply in the interest of convenience.

KALE

Pretreatment: Preseason with oil, salt, and various spices such as curry or chili powder.

Tips: Kale chips can be nibbled as a snack or crumbled into cooked dishes or green smoothies.

LEEKS

Pretreatment: None required. You can blanch sliced leeks in hot water for 10 seconds to float out bits of grit.

Tips: The best onions for drying, sliced leeks dry fast and store a long time.

MELON (MUSKMELON)

Pretreatment: An acidic dip in pineapple or orange juice helps preserve color.

Tips: Drying until almost leathery concentrates flavor. Try freezing half-dried melon in bite-size pieces.

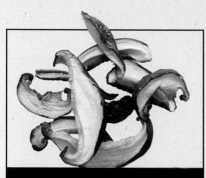

MUSHROOMS

Pretreatment: None required. Clean mushrooms thoroughly before slicing and drying them.

Tips: Shiitakes and many other mushrooms dry quickly and store a long time.

PEPPERS

Pretreatment: None required. Smoking peppers before drying them further enhances flavor.

Tips: Drying concentrates flavor, turning a vegetable into a spice. Paprika and chili powder are made from pulverized dried peppers.

POTATOES

Pretreatment: Blanch or bake until done, then dehydrate immediately. Dry until hard.

Tips: Dry your cull potatoes for use in scalloped potatoes, as hash browns, or in soups and casseroles.

PUMPKIN

Pretreatment: None required. Pare away the rind and soft tissues near the seed cavity. Dry ½-inch-thick slices or pieces.

Tips: Sliced pumpkin dries into hard chips, which readily rehydrate in soups and stews. Cook until soft to make pumpkin purée.

SUMMER SQUASH

Pretreatment: None required. Blanching or pre-seasoning is optional.

Tips: Drying saves room in the freezer and makes it easy to add small amounts of squash to pasta, pizza, or soups.

TOMATOES

Pretreatment: None required. Clean and cut into uniform pieces.

Tips: Dry cherry tomato halves into "raisins." Use dried tomato slices in soups and stews.

Drying Herbs

From zesty kitchen herbs like rosemary and sage to mints and other tea herbs, you can save bundles of money by growing and drying your own herbs. See chapter 5 for descriptions and growing instructions for 15 easy-to-grow herbs. When your favorite herbs produce more leaves or flowers than you can use, dry as many as you can for off-season use in cooking and teas.

Drying Leafy Herbs

The leaves and stems of herbs contain much less moisture compared to vegetables, so they are quick to dry in a dehydrator. Harvest leafy herbs for drying when they are in pristine condition. A day or two before you plan to harvest, use a fine spray from your hose to wash down the plants. The best time to harvest herbs for drying is late morning, just after the dew has dried.

1 Use scissors or pruning shears to gather herbs, and keep them in large pieces to make handling easier.

2 Clean the herbs under clean running water, shake off the excess water (or use a salad spinner), and arrange on dehydrator trays. Dry at a low heat setting for 2 hours, then turn over the herbs and dry for another hour.

3 Allow the herbs to sit overnight, and finish drying the next day. Dry herbs until they are crisp.

A dehydrator does a good job of helping dry herbs retain their colors and flavors, but you also can dry many herbs by hanging them in small bunches in a dark, well-ventilated room. Be careful, because light will bleach out the colors of many herbs, and high humidity can cause them to become moldy. In addition, tiny insects easily survive in air-dried bunches but not in herbs dried in the dehydrator or even a slightly warm oven.

Clip out large stems before storing your dried herbs, but try to keep the leaves in large pieces as you pack them into airtight containers (I use glass canning jars). Herbs will retain more of their aromatics if leaves are unbroken until just before they are added to a dish or steeped into a tea.

Store dried herbs in a cool, dark place. Light and high temperatures will ruin the color and flavor of dried herbs.

Drying Blossoms for Tea or Medicine

Blossoms take longer to dry compared to leaves, and pulsed dehydration sessions of an hour or so, over a couple of days, do the best job of evenly drying the dense interiors of big blossoms. Tiny chamomile flowers almost dry themselves, but whole blossoms of herbs harvested as flowers will take time. In Zone 6 and warmer, you can grow hardy hibiscus organically and gather and dry the green seed capsules just after the petals fall.

Drying Fruits

The next best thing to having fresh fruit to eat is having dried fruit you grew yourself. Apples, pears, plums, and other tree fruits are prime candidates for drying, and you can dry seedless grapes into raisins. Drying berries is possible but can be very slow. Freezing and juicing are better methods for preserving your homegrown berries.

When properly dried and stored, dried fruits can last for up to 2 years, which matches the bearing cycles of many backyard trees. Especially if you are able to store dried apples or pears in your freezer, you won't mind as much when your trees don't make a crop, and because drying is so easy, you will waste less in years when you're buried in fruit.

Drying concentrates sugars, so dried fruits are much sweeter than the fresh version. High sugar amounts also give dried fruits slight elasticity, and most are at their best when dried just to the leathery stage. It's easy to dry fruits. Just follow these three steps:

HOW TO DRY FRUITS

1 To prevent discoloration, dip all fruits in an acidic solution (see page 23) before they are arranged on trays.

2 Place the prepared pieces in the dehydrator and dry at medium temperature for 3 to 4 hours, or until the fruit no longer feels wet to the touch. Allow to rest for a few hours to equalize moisture.

3 Finish drying until the pieces are leathery.

Many of the dried fruits sold in stores have been preserved by candying, a time-consuming process in which foods are slowly impregnated with sugar before they are dried. This sugar-based preservation method is interesting to try, but it doesn't result in nutritious food. Besides, most fruits taste so sweet after they are dried that they can pass for candy without any added sugar.

Making Fruit Leathers

Any type of concentrated fruit "butter," such as apple, plum (shown here), or even pumpkin butter, can be dried in sheets that can be rolled up like leather. Check the owner's manual of your dehydrator for directions on drying fruit leathers in your dehydrator, which usually involves spreading the fruit purée over nonsticky silicone sheets and drying it. You also can use small plates. If the leather sticks to the plate after it has dried, an hour in the freezer will make it pop free. Because fruit leathers retain some moisture, it is best to store them in the freezer.

Best Fruits
FOR
Drying

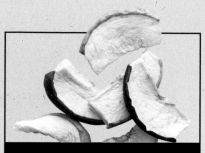

APPLES

Pretreatment: Acidic dip; organic apples do not require peeling.

Tips: Toss the prepared apples with small amounts of brown sugar and cinnamon to make spiced dried apples.

CHERRIES

Pretreatment: Pit the cherries and cut in half. Dry immediately or freeze covered with a little sugar. Thaw and drain before drying.

Tips: Freezing and thawing breaks down cells and speeds drying. Save and drink the juice.

GRAPES

Pretreatment: Pour boiling water over seedless grapes to soften and break skins before drying them.

Tips: Raisins made from red grapes are a taste treat. Before drying, some people pre-freeze grapes, as with cherries.

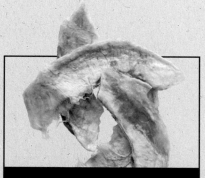

PEACHES AND NECTARINES

Pretreatment: Peel if the fruit is not organic. Use an acidic dip to prevent discoloration of slices.

Tips: Slices dry much faster than halves. Preserve by canning and freezing, too.

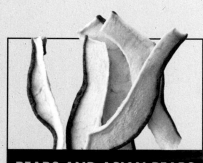

PEARS AND ASIAN PEARS

Pretreatment: Allow pears to ripen fully before drying. Use an acidic dip to prevent discoloration.

Tips: Cut dried pears into small pieces with scissors for use as raisin substitute.

PLUMS

Pretreatment: Halve, then cut into slices. Use an acidic dip to prevent discoloration.

Tips: Slices dry much faster than halves. Plum slices rehydrate quickly and work well in mixed salads.

CANNING YOUR HOMEGROWN HARVEST

The wonderful thing about canning is that once it's done, you have food that will store for a year or even two as long as it is protected from temperature extremes and light. Pickles and relishes are good projects for beginning canners, or you might get started with simple jams or preserves. Tomatoes and tomato-based sauces like salsa are among gardeners' most popular canning projects, and tree fruits will keep the canning equipment busy well into fall.

Some crops are better candidates for canning than others. The canning process cooks the food inside the jars, so delicate vegetables that cook quickly may turn to mush when canned. This is why freezing and drying are often better ways to preserve many of the food crops you grow, as noted in the crop entries in chapter 3. But for fruit juices or jam, relishes and pickles, and delicious tomato-based sauces, canning is often the best way to go.

What Canning Does

As foods are processed inside heat-resistant glass canning jars, heat inside the jars causes the contents to expand, and some steam is forced out. This is why you leave some headspace between the food and the lids and don't tighten down the screw bands before the jars are processed. After processing, as the jars cool, a vacuum forms that pulls the lids downward, forcing the rubber compound on the lids to make an airtight seal.

In addition to the steam action that seals the jar, in most cases the canning process uses heat to kill microorganisms that would otherwise cause the food to spoil. The heat of processing also neutralizes enzymes in the food, which preserves vitamins and other nutrients. The type of canner needed and the processing time vary between recipes because factors such as density and acidity can affect how long it takes for the food inside jars to heat evenly to the temperature needed for safe preservation. Acidic foods processed in a water-bath or steam canner usually need to be heated to 212°F (100°C), while low-acid vegetables processed in a pressure canner need to be heated to 240°F (115°C). Any product that contains meat requires processing at 250°F (120°C), which can only be achieved at 15 pounds pressure in a pressure canner.

Types of Canners

The type of canner you use depends in large part on what you are canning. High-acid foods can be safely canned in a water-bath or steam canner, but low-acid foods require pressure canning, which exposes them to the higher temperatures needed to kill microorganisms in a low-acid environment. See The Role of Acidity on page 34 for more discussion of how the acidity of foods affects the composition of good canning recipes.

Water-Bath Canner

A water-bath canner is a large pot with a basket that fits inside for suspending jars above the bottom, so that simmering or boiling water can circulate around all sides of the jars. During processing, the jars must be submerged over their tops with boiling water. Be very careful when handling big pots of boiling water!

If you are new to using a water-bath canner, start with small half-pint or pint jars until you see firsthand how things work. Do not be alarmed if bubbles float from the hot jars when you put them in the simmering water. The bubbles are from air trapped in the bands and from steam pushing out through the seals.

Steam Canner

A steam canner is a three-part pot with a water reservoir, an inner rack for holding jars, and a tall cover that allows trapped steam to flow around the jars. A steam canner requires a little more than a quart of water to process seven pint jars of high-acid foods, compared to about 2 gallons of boiling water in a water-bath canner. A steam

You can use a waterbath canner (left) or steam canner (right) to process jams, pickles, and acidified vegetables and sauces.

canner saves significant time and energy, doesn't heat up the kitchen, and requires less heavy lifting compared to a water-bath canner.

For more than a decade, information on the safety of steam canning has remained incomplete. But researchers from several universities have recently concluded that steam canners can be as safe and effective as water-bath canners when used to preserve acidified or naturally acidic foods. The same safety guidelines used for water-bath canning apply to using a steam canner.

Pressure Canner

A pressure canner is so airtight that it can pressurize steam, thus raising the temperature inside canning jars to 240°F (115°C) — the temperature needed to safely process low-acid vegetables like sweet corn and potatoes. Like steam canners, pressure canners use little water. Even at high temperature under pressure, low-acid foods take a long time to process, so it is best to use pints rather than quarts. For example, pints of sweet corn must be processed at 10 pounds of pressure for 55 minutes, but quarts need 85 minutes.

Pressure canners vary slightly in how they operate. Become familiar with the instructions that came with your canner, and follow them closely to ensure good results.

Altitude and Processing Times

Water boils at lower temperatures at high altitudes, so home canners at altitudes above 1,000 feet must compensate by processing food longer to kill bacteria inside the jars. As a general guideline, add 5 minutes of processing time if you are at 1,000 to 3,000 feet elevation, add 10 minutes at 3,000 to 6,000 feet, and 15 minutes at 6,000 to 8,000 feet.

Steam also expands more at high altitudes, so headspace should be slightly increased for all types of canning, but never by more than ½ inch.

The Role of Acidity

Processing foods at high temperature theoretically sterilizes them, but what if bacteria survive the heat treatment? This is where pH becomes important, because an acidic pH of 4.6 or lower makes it extremely difficult for microorganisms to grow. Published canning recipes that are in keeping with USDA guidelines (including the recipes in this book) depend on the interaction between processing times and pH to achieve food safety.

Most fruits are naturally acidic, but you can never be sure. It is always better to be safe than sorry, so even when canning acidic foods like applesauce or tomatoes, a small amount of lemon juice, vinegar, or citric acid is often added to make sure the pH is solidly below 4.6. For example, the natural pH range for tomatoes is 4.0 to 4.6. By adding a little lemon juice or vinegar to each jar of your homemade tomato sauce, you make sure your home-canned tomato sauce is not a borderline case.

Pickling recipes often combine low-acid foods like cucumbers or summer squash with a high-acid, vinegar-based brine. You can make small changes to flavoring ingredients used in pickles such as garlic or dill, but do not change the brine.

Tomato-based sauces like salsa or marinara sauce require the addition of significant acidifiers because they include low-acid vegetables like onions and peppers. Never omit or reduce the vinegar or lemon juice in these recipes.

Making Jams, Jellies, and Preserves

One of the best ways to preserve fruits and berries — either fresh or frozen — is to can them as jellies, jams, and preserves. The differences between the three hinge on how much fruit is in the finished product. Jams and preserves are mostly fruit in a jelled sugar syrup, while jellies are made from clear juice. All are easy to make and can be processed in a water-bath or steam canner. Many old recipes will direct you to let hot jars seal on their own, without processing, but processing jams and jellies greatly reduces the likelihood that you will see nasty molds forming on the top of your jam.

Some fruits like green apples and blackberries are rich in pectins — the compounds that help jams and jellies to thicken. Working with the natural pectins in fruits involves substantial guesswork, so most people use commercial jelling products to make sure their preserves and jams turn out right. If you want to reduce the sugar in your fruit preserves, you can choose between regular pectins intended to be used with one-third less sugar and low-methoxyl pectins that gel when they are mixed with calcium. Be sure to follow the directions that come with your pectin product, and don't forget the lemon juice if it is part of the recipe. The acids in lemon juice are sometimes important for jams and jellies to thicken the way they should.

Canning Jar Basics

Canning jars and lids lined with rubber seals have become the standardized containers for home canning. With good care, glass canning jars can be reused dozens of times, or until they develop a crack or chip. And although canning jars are made of heat-resistant glass, they will break apart if you place a very hot liquid into a cold jar. This will never happen if you hold your clean canning jars in a warm oven while you finish preparing the food.

Most home canners have a collection of jars in various sizes that include pretty half-pints for jams, chutneys, or relishes; pints for often-used recipes; and quarts for foods consumed in large quantities, such as fruit juices. Pint-size jars hold about 2 cups of food, which is a convenient size for general cooking needs, so you will probably need more pints than other sizes.

Your last choice is between regular and wide-mouthed jars. Why not try both? Wide-mouthed jars are easier to fill when you are trying to get a tight pack of pickled beans or beets, but jars with regular-size mouths have a smaller seal area, and the lids cost a little less.

Always use new lids, because previously used ones may not form a sound seal due to grooves in the rubber ring. You can reuse lids when using your canning jars to store foods in the freezer or on cabinet shelves. Discard lids that become dented or rusted.

Before you get started, clean the fruits or veggies you plan to preserve, and then clean the kitchen. Assemble all the things you will need for the project:

- Large ovenproof baking dish, for holding hot jars
- Clean jars, rings, and new lids (prepare one extra)
- Measuring cup
- Large stainless steel pot
- Knife or mandoline
- Large stainless steel cooking spoon and ladle
- Canning funnel
- Table knife
- Clean, damp paper towels
- Jar-lifting tongs
- Water-bath, steam, or pressure canner (follow recipe directions)
- Timer

I. Thoroughly clean and rinse the baking dish and the jars. Place the jars in the baking dish and place them in a warm (150°F/65°C) oven. Wash the rings and lids, and set aside.

2. Prepare the food to be canned according to the recipe directions, and measure all ingredients. Whenever possible, the food should be very hot when it goes into the jars.

3. Place the canner on the stove to heat.

4. Remove the pan of jars from the oven, and place the pot of prepared food next to the hot pan. As you fill the jars to within ½ inch of the rim, use the canning funnel to keep the rims clean.

STEP 4

5. Use the table knife to go around the inside walls of each jar to release any trapped air bubbles. Add or subtract food or liquid to correct the filling level to ½ inch from the rim.

STEP 5

6. Carefully wipe the rim of each jar with a damp paper towel to remove any food residue that will interfere with the sealing of the jars. Also wipe the lids with a clean cloth. Place the lids on the jars and screw the rings in place, tightening them "finger tight." You should be able to loosen the ring without holding the jar with your other hand.

7. Use the jar-lifting tongs to place the hot jars in the canner, taking care to keep them upright. Place the lid on the canner, and spend 3 or 4 minutes slowly bringing up the temperature of the water or steam. When the water in a water-bath canner returns to a slow boil, or a plume of steam is produced by a steam canner, set the timer for the appropriate processing time.

8. Keep a close watch on the stove to keep the temperature in the canner as steady as possible. Turn off the heat when the timer goes off.

9. Follow the instructions provided with your canner for removing the jars. Carefully lift jars from a water-bath canner and place them on a heatproof surface to cool. If you are using a steam canner, wait until the water stops boiling and you no longer see steam coming out of the vent hole. Lift the top at an angle with the top tilted toward you, so trapped steam is released a safe distance from your face. Lift jars with a jar lifter and place on a heatproof surface to cool.

10. Listen for popping sounds as the jars seal. Allow to cool completely before removing the rings. Write the date and contents on the lid, or place pretty labels on jars you are likely to give as gifts. Store in a cool, dry place.

STEP 7

STEP 10

When Jars Don't Seal

Some home canners never have a failed seal, but I am not one of them. Even when I do everything right, about 1 out of 30 jars develops a problem. How can you tell? Lids that don't seal as they cool from the canner are obvious, but once the jars are in storage I start sniffing for trouble. Gases leak from jars that are not sealed, so if you can smell pickling brine, fruit, or other aromas that should not be escaping, check each lid of the suspicious batch.

- Look at the unopened jar for signs or unusual discoloration or mold, especially near the top edge of the food.

- Open the jar, and listen for the seal to break. If it barely gives a gasp, there could be trouble.

- Immediately smell the food. One sniff, and you should recognize the fragrance of summer tomatoes, applesauce, or fall pears. There should be no mold inside the jar.

Compost the contents of suspicious jars, and check the jar for problems. On several occasions I have found bumps, lumps, or chips in the top edges of the glass jars that sabotaged the seals. I use the defective jars for other things, or I recycle them.

But try not to worry. Most jars will seal just fine. Each time a batch of jars is set aside to cool, you can listen to lids popping as a reward. When you take the time to listen, each pop brings a spurt of joy, announcing that the canning project is a success.

THE MAGIC OF FOOD FERMENTATION

Fermentation is one of the oldest, safest, yet most mysterious forms of food preservation. For thousands of years, people around the world have used fermentation to turn cabbage into sauerkraut, cucumbers into pickles, milk into cheese, and fruit juice into wine. Home fermentation was fading as a lost art when health-minded foodies rediscovered the benefits of fermented foods for the digestive system. Bioactive fermented foods are good for you, and fresh ferments made at home are best of all. The packaging and processing required to make fermented foods stable enough to sell in stores reduces the density of probiotic elements in the food.

Fermenting Vegetables

The type of fermentation used with vegetables is called salt fermentation, because high salt levels in the liquid (brine) limit the growth of unwanted microorganisms. At the same time, controlled salt allows certain strains of bacteria, primarily those called lactobacilli, to flourish. Using sugars in the raw food for energy, the lactobacilli produce lactic acids, which further protect the food from spoilage while imparting a tangy flavor. Once a fermented food has soured (gone tangy), it can be repacked into clean jars and stored in the refrigerator or a cold root cellar or basement for at least 4 to 5 months, assuming there is any left. This is doubtful, because fermented veggies are so delicious and nutritious that you might hide jars in the back of the fridge, but you won't forget they are there when you want a fat-free, vitamin-rich, probiotic snack.

Use only fresh, flawless produce that has been thoroughly cleaned. Use clean hands, knives, and chopping surfaces when preparing produce for fermentation. While canning is about precise ingredients and procedures, fermentation is much more intuitive and revolves around nurturing microscopic life-forms rather than killing them.

Basic Fermentation Equipment

Glazed fermentation crocks are great for making big batches of salt-brined pickles, but for everyday fermenting, any upright container with a mouth wide enough to reach inside with your hand will do. I like glass for easy cleaning, and I've found that a 2-quart canning jar is almost perfect for fermenting vegetables. Most foods shrink as they ferment, so you simply downsize to a smaller jar.

Fermentation produces gases that must escape, but you also need a barrier to keep out insects, dust, and airborne microorganisms. There are many ways to modify canning jar lids so they do exactly this; the simplest version involves drilling a hole in a plastic screw-on canning jar lid and fitting it with an airlock of the type used by home winemakers. Or forget the lid and use a clean cloth or coffee filter, held in place with a rubber band, to cover the top of the fermentation jar.

When fermenting foods in large crocks, use weights to keep the food submerged, because fermenting foods that are exposed to air may develop unwanted molds. If you have a crock but no weights, use a large plate held in place with a clean quart jar filled with water. When fermenting foods in a wide-mouthed jar, a sandwich bag filled about two-thirds full of water makes an ideal weight for keeping the food submerged while allowing gas bubbles to escape around the edges of the bag. One of the reasons I recommend using a water-filled plastic bag as a weight is that it minimizes release of unpleasant odors, probably by reducing how much oxygen is available to the bacteria. Open fermentation, in which the container is covered with a cloth or coffee filter, gives rise to much punchier aromas.

Do You Need an Activator?

Many fermentation recipes include a small amount of whey (a lactobacillus soup produced during the cheese-making process) as an activator to kick-start the fermentation process, but it is not necessary and may alter the finished product. Whey will indeed get a fermentation project off to a rollicking start, but the microbes at work will be very different from those that occur naturally on vegetables. These naturally occurring microbes will carry on the fermentation process quite nicely, the way they have been doing for thousands of years.

One of the ways I've improved my fermentation projects is by copying the ingredients on products I found wonderfully delicious. In this way, I discovered that adding a small amount of chopped apple or pear to a batch of garlicky fall kraut or kimchi (about 2 tablespoons per quart) improves the flavor and quality of the food and provides a fleeting dose of sugar, which helps kick off the fermentation process.

You also can use brine from a recently finished fermentation project to inoculate the brine in a new one, but again, you are altering the natural process. Fermentation involves a succession of different microbes that do different things to the vegetables they are working on. Putting late-stage microbes into an early-stage ferment can result in uneven fermentation, in which small pieces are done days before sturdier ones.

Making Sense out of Salt

It can be difficult to use the right amount of salt in veggie fermentation projects, because some salt is rubbed into the vegetables and then more is added in the brine. You will need to learn to taste your way through the first few days of vegetable fermentation projects.

Start with the general measure of 1 tablespoon salt rubbed into the vegetables and 1 tablespoon salt added to the brine (both measurements per well-filled quart). By the second day of fermentation, after the vegetables have released some of their juices, they should taste slightly saltier than you would want to eat them, and the brine should taste about as salty as seawater.

If the brine tastes too salty on the third or fourth day, when the salt from the vegetables and the brine have merged together and the vegetables have shrunk, it's fine to pour out half of the brine and replace it with fresh water. Taste again after 12 hours or so, and further dilute if it is not in the edible range. With practice your taste buds will quickly tell you when the salt level is in a favorable range for fermentation. To teach your tongue the right salt level, dissolve a tablespoon of salt in 2 cups of water, and taste the solution at room temperature.

Ferment in Season

Make fermented vegetables in cool weather. The fermentation process itself generates a few degrees of heat, so room temperatures above 75°F (24°C) can push the temperature of a fermentation project above 80°F (27°C). Veggies that ferment under warm conditions tend to go soft and slimy; under cooler temps they stay crisp.

Fall is generally the best season for fermenting, though you can ferment in summer as long as you have a cool place in which to do it. If you have enough cool weather to get a project started but then a heat wave moves in, you can finish fermenting jars inside of a cooler, chilling the space with frozen water bottles that are replaced daily.

Work with Clean Hands

After you have done the dishes and cleaned up the kitchen is a great time to work your fermentation projects because your hands are at their cleanest of the day. Clean hands are the best tools for mixing and pushing down fermenting foods.

1. To start a fermentation project, chop or slice vegetables into bite-size pieces, and place them in a large bowl or baking pan. Cabbage and radishes make a good first ferment. Sprinkle the chopped vegetables with salt, and crunch the salt into the veggies with your hands for at least 5 minutes. Feel free to add spices for color and flavor, including chili powder, ginger, turmeric, and caraway or fennel seeds.

2. Place the veggies in a wide-mouthed glass jar, and press down with your fingers. Leave at least 2 inches between the salted veggies and the top of the jar.

3. Mix 1 tablespoon salt with 1 pint water, and pour over the vegetables until they are barely covered. Fill a plastic sandwich bag with cool water, and stuff it into the top of the jar. The water-filled bag serves as a weight and an airlock. Place a cloth over the top of the jar. Place the jar in a cool location, somewhere it won't be disturbed (do not refrigerate).

STEP 3

STEP 2

4. The next day, stir a bit with a clean spoon, and add a small amount of water if needed to completely cover the fermenting vegetables with liquid. Then press down the veggies with clean hands, and replace the water-filled sandwich bag. Repeat this procedure daily, and don't worry about funky smells, especially when fermenting cabbage or radishes. Days 3 to 6 tend to be quite aromatic, though the water-bag method goes a long way toward minimizing fermentation odors.

5. After 5 days at cool room temperature, start tasting the fermenting vegetables to see how you like them. The flavor of the food often begins to change after 3 days, but you need to wait for a second flavor change, to tangy-sour with a slight buzz, before calling the project complete. This may take 3 weeks in a cool basement or only 5 to 7 days in a typical kitchen.

6. Refrigerate fermented foods as soon as they are done. If the brine is very cloudy, pour it off and replace it with a fresh salt brine.

FINISHED FERMENT

Best Vegetables
FOR
Fermenting

It is possible to ferment almost any vegetable, but these veggies work so well in fermentation projects that you will want to try them at least once.

CABBAGE

How to use: Chop or coarsely grate any cabbage; use as a base ingredient in mixed ferments.

Tips: Garlic and dill provide more levels of flavor in fermented "salads." Radishes are a natural fermentation partner.

CAULIFLOWER

How to use: Cut into bite-size florets and ferment with cabbage, carrots, and other fall vegetables.

Tips: Store in the refrigerator, in a fresh brine solution, and serve with pickled peppers and other homegrown condiments.

KOHLRABI

How to use: Slices or chunks provide texture in mixed ferments.

Tips: Kohlrabi combines beautifully with carrots.

CARROTS

How to use: Thin slices ferment faster than thick ones, and pieces should be uniform in size.

Tips: Mixtures of different colored carrots are lovely to see and eat. Add grated carrots to mixed ferments to boost color.

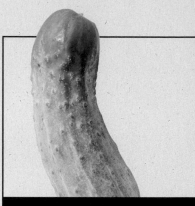

CUCUMBERS

How to use: Use only whole pickling cucumbers. Keep cukes submerged with weights.

Tips: A grape leaf placed in the bottom of the jar enhances crispness. Pack in fresh salt brine before storing fermented sour pickles in the refrigerator.

PEPPERS

How to use: Ferment jalapeño slices; purée and ferment hot peppers for making into sauces.

Tips: As fermentation advances, many seeds will drop to the bottom, where they are easily removed.

RADISHES

How to use: Essential for adding crunch, color, and peppy flavor to mixed ferments.

Tips: Super-productive daikon and Chinese radishes work great and can be combined with cabbage to make kimchi.

SNAP BEANS

How to use: Choose perfect beans trimmed to fit vertically in pint jars, regular mouth preferred. Use basil or dill as herbal accents.

Tips: Close the jars for a few hours each day and turn them upside down. The rest of the time, leave the jars vented so gases can escape. Include yellow wax beans for color.

TURNIPS

How to use: Fermentation mellows the flavor of turnips, which provide toothsome texture in mixed ferments.

Tips: Small salad turnips do not need to be peeled before fermenting. All turnips combine well with cabbage.

Making Wine from Fruits

The pleasure of wine is doubled when you make it yourself for a few cents a bottle, using your own fruits, and without unnecessary additives. Home wine making is an excellent way to preserve any type of excess fruit, from apples to strawberries, and you also can make wine from herbs such as sage and parsley. I have even heard of tomato wine! With a little imagination, whatever fruit you have too much of can be made into some kind of wine.

Some fruit wines are easier to make than others. Grapes are the simplest fruit to ferment because grapes give off their juice willingly, tend to ferment quickly, and the waste, called lees, readily separates from the wine. Dark-colored berries like blackberries and black raspberries make great wine, too, whether you use them alone or combine them with other fruits like apples or pears. In home wine making, you always have the choice between fermenting fruits by themselves or in combinations chosen to enhance flavor, color, and aroma. For example, I can make a batch from all apples to yield a light white wine, or add a pound of frozen blackberries to the fermenting apples to make a berry pink rosé with blackberry aroma. Or I can make the two batches separately and blend them later on, when the wine is within a few weeks of being ready to bottle.

Fruits and fruit juices for wine making can be held in the freezer, and freezing and thawing has a tenderizing effect on apples, pears, and other low-juice fruits. Another option is to can fruits or fruit juices in a water-bath or steam canner for later use in wine.

The Role of Sugar

The alcohol content of wine or cider is determined by how much sugar is available for yeast to convert to alcohol. For the finished wine to be stable in the bottle, it should have an alcohol level between 8 and 12 percent. Winemakers use a simple instrument called a hydrometer to test the sugar content (as reflected in specific gravity) of a newly composed batch of wine, but that measurement becomes approximate when you top off with water or add additional sugar-laden juice. Old-time winemakers routinely added additional juice or sugar to raise the alcohol content of their country wines, which were valued more for their headiness than their flavor.

The recipe on pages 46–47, which uses 2 pounds of sugar per gallon of wine, will generally yield a wine with an alcohol level around 10 percent. Very sweet fruits like wine grapes do not need this much sugar, but apples or pears may need a little more. Some winemakers prefer corn sugar for wine making, but any type of sugar — including honey — can be used to make wine.

Making Wine without Additives

If you were to buy a wine-making kit, it would come with these or similar additives, which shorten the time you must wait to bottle the wine. Over the years, wine-making kits have changed to include fewer sulfites but more clarifying agents. A natural winemaker lets time take care of yeasts and clarity, but the choice is yours.

- **Bentonite** is a fine volcanic clay that pulls particles from the wine, helping them accumulate at the bottom of the fermenter. This clarifying agent is used mostly with white wines.

- **Kieselsol and/or chitosan** are gel-like clarifying agents, made from sea creatures, which are used to remove haze from wines.

- **Pectic enzyme** may come with a fruit wine kit, and even natural home winemakers use this enzyme, usually in liquid form, to help fruits break down and release their sugars.

- **Potassium metabisulfite** is a sufite used to sanitize equipment, and in the past it was used to stabilize wine. It is sold as a powder or as campden tablets.

- **Potassium sorbate** is the sulfite used to stabilize wine, which means killing yeasts so they cannot process remaining sugars. Sweet wines depend on the use of this sulfite, but dry wines can be allowed to become still on their own.

Blackberries and other fruits that are too tart and seedy to eat fresh make wonderful wine.

Recipes for fruit wines, sometimes called country wines, vary only slightly from one another, and you have tremendous leeway in the fruits and fruit juices you use. The measurements here are for a 1-gallon batch. You will need:

- 4–6 pounds fresh fruit, cut into small pieces

- 2 pounds sugar

- 3 quarts water, boiled

- Juice of 1 lemon

- 6 drops liquid pectic enzyme

- 1 can frozen white grape juice concentrate (optional)

- 1 packet wine yeast (champagne or Montrachet strains)

1. Place the fruit in a fermentation bag inside a sanitized primary fermenter. Combine the sugar with 2 quarts of the hot water and pour over the fruit. Add the lemon juice, pectic enzyme, and grape juice concentrate (if using), and additional boiled, cooled water to bring the water level up to 1½ gallons. When the temperature cools to 72°F (22°C), test the specific gravity or taste the liquid. It should taste quite sweet, as sweet as light syrup. Sprinkle on the yeast and cover the primary fermenter after providing a way for gases to escape, such as using an airlock or covering the container securely with several folds of cheesecloth or a clean towel.

2. At least once a day for 5 to 6 days, use clean hands to knead the fruit in the fermentation bag and turn it, so a different side floats to the top. The liquid will become cloudy and slightly fizzy; with some fruits, large bubbles form on the top. Taste the liquid just before washing it from your hands. The sugar level should drop noticeably by the fifth day.

3. After about a week, when the fruit in the fermentation bag has become a gooey mess, lift it from the container and let the juice drip back into the wine (shown below). Spend a few minutes with this, but do not squeeze the bag. Compost the fermented fruit, and let the wine rest for a couple of days.

4. Without jiggling the wine, siphon the clear part into a clean glass bottle that can be fitted with an airlock. Allow about 4 inches of space between the top of the liquid and the bottom of the airlock. If needed, top off the wine with boiled, cooled water to bring the liquid to this level. Install the airlock.

5. Place the wine in a dark place where temperatures range between 60 and 70°F (16 and 21°C). Cover the bottle with a cloth sleeve to protect the wine from light, which can change its color. Old T-shirts make convenient wine covers for big bottles.

6. After about a month, siphon the wine again (this is called racking; shown below) into a clean bottle. Move the wine to a cool place, and check it monthly to make sure the airlock is clean and functioning properly. Rack again after 3 months.

7. If you do not use sulfites to kill any live yeasts remaining in the wine, you must wait for the wine to become "dry," or without sugars, to consider bottling it. This takes about 6 months. During the last month, the wine should be moved to normal room temperatures, just in case higher temps stimulate activity by surviving yeast.

8. Wine is finished and ready to bottle when no air can be seen moving through the airlock for several days, and no bubbles are present around the top edge of the wine (see below). When in doubt, wait. Wine that is bottled before it becomes still will pop its cork, which creates a nasty mess.

9. Allow the bottled wine to age for at least a year before tasting it. Wine that tastes too rough to swallow at bottling time often matures into amazing wine, but you must give it time. Two years is not too long to wait for naturally made wine from your organically grown fruits.

Best Fruits

FOR

Home Wine Making

APPLES

Make a light white wine, a good base wine for blending; best when aged at least 2 years.

BLACKBERRIES

Make a bold red wine, best when aged 2 years; or combine blackberries with apples or pears.

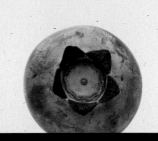

BLUEBERRIES

Make a light rosé that is ready to drink young at only a year.

CHERRIES

Delicious jewel-tone cherry wine is great for holidays and special occasions, best when aged 2 years.

GRAPES

Fast, clean fermentation makes grapes the top fruit for wine making. Can be blended with other fruit wines.

PEACHES

Messy to make, but peach wine delivers great aroma in a full-bodied white wine.

PEARS

Pear wine can taste flat on its own, but is much improved with addition of raspberries.

PLUMS

Plum wine made from chopped fruits has excellent character and color; matures young and is ready to drink after 1 year.

RASPBERRIES

Use raspberries on their own, or combine with other fruits to improve the color and aroma of wines.

RHUBARB

Rhubarb wine is easy to make, but the wait is long for fully developed wine, up to 4 years.

STRAWBERRIES

A sweetheart of a wine, strawberry wine has a long fermentation period, so don't rush to bottle it. Best when aged for at least 1 year.

VEGETABLES

FOR THE

Homegrown Pantry

Every crop you plant requires an ongoing investment of time and energy, so it pays to be choosy. You want to grow plenty of the crops your family especially likes, but consider your garden's abilities as well. Crops that are easy to grow organically are usually a good fit to the site and soil. If a nearby organic farmer does well with a certain crop, you can probably grow it, too.

When the crop hits the kitchen, it gets judged under new rules. How difficult is it to store? A pie pumpkin that will sit patiently on your porch for a month suddenly sounds great, and it's hard to beat the fulfillment brought by a nice basket of cured potatoes resting in the basement.

Storage crops should be the backbone of your homegrown pantry, but you will grow dozens of other plants for eating fresh and putting by. You will get to know 28 great vegetables in the following pages, which are sorted alphabetically by crop. Herbs are covered separately in chapter 5.

Deciding which food plants to include here was difficult, and I wish I had endless pages to cover great homestead crops that grow in limited climates and soils. One of the exciting things about food gardening is that you can spend a lifetime exploring the possibilities and deciding for yourself what your priority crops should be.

Dig in.

In hospitable climates, a well-maintained asparagus bed will start bearing 1 year after planting, reach maximum productivity within 5 years, and stay productive for 10 to 15 years.

ASPARAGUS

(Asparagus officinalis)

HOW MUCH
15 plants per person

- -

STELLAR VARIETIES
'Guelph Millennium' for cold climates, 'Apollo' for warmer ones, and 'Jersey Giant' in Zones 4 to 6

- -

BEST WAYS TO PRESERVE
Freeze, pickle, or dry

Cold hardy and long lived, asparagus is the first big vegetable of the year to come into the kitchen. It is perfectly fine to eat every last spear fresh, which only makes sense. By late spring your store of put-by foods will be running low, making your asparagus crop even more welcome. Should you have extra, asparagus can be frozen, pickled, or even dried. When used to make a warm and creamy soup, dried asparagus easily passes for the real thing.

A hardy perennial adapted in Zones 3 to 7, asparagus grows best in well-drained soil with a near-neutral pH, in climates that get cold enough in winter to kill back the fronds. Asparagus can be grown in warmer climates, albeit not happily. In hospitable climates, a well-maintained asparagus bed will start bearing 1 year after planting, reach maximum productivity within 5 years, and stay productive for 10 to 15 years, or more.

Best Asparagus
FOR THE
Homegrown Pantry

Because asparagus stays productive for so long, it is important to plant the best variety available for your area, especially if you live in a very cold or hot climate.

In cold climates where winter takes its time leaving, 'Guelph Millennium' and other varieties that emerge late often escape damage from spring freezes.

In warmer climates, early, heat-tolerant varieties like 'Apollo' and 'UC 157' produce well before the weather turns hot.

In Zones 4 to 6, gardeners have a wider choice of varieties, including 'Jersey Giant', 'Jersey Knight', and other hybrids bred in New Jersey for improved disease resistance and better productivity.

Many hybrid asparagus varieties are able to produce seven or more spears per mature plant because they are mostly male plants that do not expend energy producing seeds. Seed-producing female plants produce fewer spears, and those spears are also thinner, which some gardeners like. If you keep a patch of mixed-gender plants, you will harvest spears in a range of sizes. Female plants develop red seed capsules in late summer, so they are easy to identify should you decide to dig them out to make room for more productive male plants.

Female asparagus plants produce berries that are eaten by birds, and they sometimes give rise to volunteer seedlings. They usually produce thin spears compared to male plants.

HOW TO
Grow Asparagus

When: Plant asparagus crowns (dormant roots of 1-year-old plants) in spring, at about the same time you would plant potatoes, but don't rush to plant them in cold soil.

- -

Where: Choose a site with fertile soil that is clear of perennial weeds and grasses. A single row of plants set 18 inches apart will fill in to form a 24-inch-wide bed, or you can grow a double row in a 36-inch-wide bed. Wider plantings are difficult to manage. Locate asparagus along the back or side of your garden, because 5-foot-tall asparagus fronds will shade nearby plants.

- -

Planting: A few improved varieties (including purple ones) can be grown from seed. Start seeds indoors in spring and set out the seedlings when they are 12 to 14 weeks old, just after your last spring frost has passed. Consider carefully, because starting with crowns eliminates a full year of tedious weeding.

Asparagus craves phosphorus, which is usually abundant in compost made from kitchen waste or in composted manure. Work a 2-inch layer of rich, weed-free compost into the soil before planting. Shape a planting trench 4 inches deep and 10 inches wide, and arrange the crowns in the bottom, about 15 inches apart. Refill the trench without stepping on the bed. Lightly mulch with grass clippings, weathered leaves, or another organic material to suppress weeds.

Maintenance: Regular hand weeding is required to control weeds during the first two seasons after asparagus is planted. Pull out weeds early and often, and mulch to suppress weeds and maintain moisture.

In early winter, after several hard freezes have damaged the fronds, cut them at the soil line and compost them to interrupt the life cycles of insects and diseases. Then fertilize the bed with a 1-inch layer of weed-free compost or composted manure, topped by 3 inches of straw, rotted sawdust, or another weed-free mulch. In spring, clean spears will push up through the mulch. Fertilize your asparagus again in early summer, when you stop cutting spears. You can top-dress with a balanced organic fertilizer or scatter another inch of rich, weed-free compost over the decomposing mulch.

HOW MUCH TO PLANT?

For eating fresh and having extra to freeze, pickle, or dry, plant about 15 plants per person, which translates to 6 pounds per asparagus eater. A bed of 25 plants will produce about 10 pounds of asparagus per year.

Asparagus Pests and Diseases

Two species of asparagus beetles damage asparagus spears and fronds throughout North America: the common asparagus beetle (black, white, and red) and the twelve-spotted asparagus beetle (red-orange with black dots). Both are about ⅓ inch long.

Prevention. Asparagus beetles overwinter in plant debris, so removing fronds in winter will reduce their numbers. Lady beetles and several small wasps are major asparagus beetle predators.

Treatment. Hand-pick adults early in the morning, when it's too cool for them to fly. Asparagus beetle eggs look like stubby brown hairs on new spears; they can be wiped off with a damp cloth. Once they are feeding on fronds, asparagus beetle larvae (soft gray-black sluglike creatures) are unable to crawl back up the plants when swept off with a broom. Spinosad-based pesticides will stop feeding by asparagus beetles at all life stages.

HARVESTING AND STORING
Asparagus

When: The exact dates of your spring picking season can vary by 2 weeks or more due to variations in soil temperature from year to year. As a rule, asparagus spears will develop when soil temperatures reach 50°F (10°C). The first spears are often lost to hard freezes if left unharvested, but covering beds with row cover tunnels during the first weeks of the harvest season can help limit cold damage.

Long-lived asparagus plants need time to grow large root systems, so it is best to let them keep all of their stems for at least a year. As long as a new planting grew vigorously its first season (and your growing season is not extremely short), you can harvest spears for 2 weeks when your planting is 1 year old. The next season, harvest all spears that appear for the first 4 weeks of active growth. In the third season, you can harvest asparagus for 6 weeks; by year 4 the plants will be strong enough to tolerate a full 8-week harvest season.

How: Snap off spears that are longer than 4 inches at the soil line as soon as they appear in spring. In cool weather, you can let the spears grow longer. Promptly refrigerate harvested asparagus, and eat or preserve within a few days.

Asparagus
FOOD PRESERVATION OPTIONS

When you tire of eating fresh asparagus but the spears keep coming, you can freeze some, make a batch of pickled asparagus in a vinegar brine, or dry bite-size pieces into threads in your dehydrator.

Freezing. Choose your prettiest spears for freezing, even if it means working in small batches. Follow the steps for blanching and freezing vegetables on pages 21–22. Try to keep as much length as you can when trimming spears, because if you later want to grill or sear your thawed asparagus, you will be happy to have large pieces. Always blanch asparagus before freezing it, because blanching actually increases the nutritional value of this veggie by altering enzymes.

Canning. A low-acid food, asparagus requires processing in a pressure canner for 30 minutes, which causes it to become overcooked. However, you can make pickled asparagus in a vinegar brine (recipe on page 59) to showcase this vegetable's beauty in cold salads and sandwiches.

Drying. One-inch-long pieces of asparagus that have been blanched and cooled will dry into tiny threads of asparagus, which do an amazing job of regaining their shape when cooked in simmering water or stock. If you plan to use your stored asparagus mostly in soups or casseroles, drying is a great method to try.

> **If you plan to use your stored asparagus mostly in soups or casseroles, drying is a great method to try.**

Pickled Asparagus

You can increase the sugar in this recipe if you want the asparagus spears to taste more like bread-and-butter pickles.

Makes 4–5 half-pint jars

20	asparagus spears, more or less
3	tablespoons salt, plus 1 teaspoon
5	small garlic cloves
2	cups vinegar
¼	cup sugar
1	teaspoon mustard seeds
⅛	teaspoon ground turmeric

1 Cut the asparagus into uniform pieces that will fit inside the jars, leaving ½ inch of headspace.

2 Place the asparagus in a large bowl and sprinkle with 3 tablespoons of the salt. Cover with cold water and allow to sit for 3 hours.

3 Drain in a colander, and rinse off the excess salt. Tightly pack the asparagus into warm jars, and place 1 garlic clove in each jar.

4 Bring the vinegar, sugar, mustard seeds, turmeric, and the remaining 1 teaspoon salt to a simmer, and pour over the asparagus. Process in a water-bath or steam canner (page 33) for 10 minutes.

'Rocdor' bush snap bean

'Tiger Eye' and 'Cranberry' dry beans

'Royal Burgandy' bush snap bean

'Northeaster' pole bean

'Christmas' lima bean

'Contender' bush snap bean

BEANS

(*Phaseolus* species)

HOW MUCH
15 row feet per person for bush beans, plus 5 row feet per person for pole types

- -

STELLAR VARIETIES
'Provider' bush snap beans, 'Northeaster' pole snap beans, and 'Calypso' dry beans

- -

BEST WAYS TO PRESERVE
Freeze, pickle, pressure can, or dry

A bona fide native American vegetable, beans are easy to grow no matter where you live. All beans grow best in warm weather, whether you are growing them for crisp snap beans or for dry beans to cook in winter. Most gardeners use their limited time and space to grow snap beans for freezing, pickling, and canning and grow one or two strains of dry beans as treasured culinary crops.

Historically, snap beans were preserved by drying. Hung on strings near the fire, the beans dried into "leather breeches," which were a practical and essential winter food before electricity became widely available. After being soaked in a pot of water overnight, the beans were simmered on the woodstove for several hours, resulting in a delicious dish to eat with cornbread or biscuits as the main mid-day meal.

Today we are more likely to freeze, pickle, or can green beans — and perhaps dry some for snacks, too. Base your gardening and preservation plans on how you like your beans. Frozen snap beans are convenient for casseroles or tossing into pasta salad, and pickled green beans (see the recipe on page 69) accented with fresh herbs do a marvelous job of capturing the taste of summer in a jar. You will need a pressure canner to can low-acid green beans, or you can go back to the old way and dry them.

Best Beans

Homegrown Pantry

Delicate little filet beans (also called "haricots verts") are great for fresh eating, but varieties with larger, more substantial pods hold up better when frozen or canned. Among gardeners who preserve what they grow, the types and varieties named below have legions of dedicated fans. Most are available in retail store seed racks.

Bush snap beans are so uniform and predictable that they are easy to love. And because bush beans mature quickly, in 50 to 60 days, plantings can be scheduled so they escape damage from pests or inhospitable weather. 'Provider' and 'Contender' set the standard for green-podded varieties, which mix beautifully with yellow or purple-podded snap beans when frozen or pickled. The pods of 'Royal Burgundy' and other purple-podded varieties turn green when cooked, but 'Rocdor' and other yellow varieties keep their color through processing.

Pole snap beans usually have a high leaf-to-pod ratio, so the pods tend to be large and numerous compared to bush beans. 'Blue Lake' produces straight, 5-inch-long pods and performs best in mild summer climates. 'Kentucky Wonder' does better in heat, though all pole beans are prone to shedding blossoms during heat waves. The large, flat pods of 'Northeaster' (also known as 'Kwintus') quickly fill a picking basket and hold up well when canned.

Dry beans deserve a place in the garden because they are such a high-protein vegetable, easy to grow, and a cinch to store. Every gardener should try a few varieties in search of strains they find productive and tasty, so that nutritious dry beans become part of your garden's repertoire. You might start with bush-type 'Calypso' beans, also called Yin-Yang beans or Orca beans because of their black-and-white splotches. Or grow pole-type dry beans like 'Hidatsa Shield' as "cornfield beans" by planting them among widely spaced corn or sunflowers when the support crop is knee-high. This is perhaps the easiest way to grow dry beans without giving up prime-time garden space.

HOW MANY TO PLANT?

As a season-long goal, try to grow 15 row feet of bush beans per person for fresh eating and preserving, and another 5 row feet per person of pole beans. With good care and regular harvesting, you would get a pound per row foot from the bush beans, and slightly more from the pole varieties. As a hedge against pests and bad weather, the bush beans can be grown in two plantings made a few weeks apart.

Dry beans are not super-productive plants, but they are too beautiful and nutritious not to grow. Expect about 1½ pounds of dry beans from a 12-foot double row of bush-type dry beans, or 2 to 3 pounds from a pole type.

'Northeaster' pole beans

More Bountiful Beans for
Hot Climates

Gardeners in warm climates can grow regular snap beans in spring and fall, but high temperatures in summer can cause blossoms to fail, resulting in few beans. Lima beans, tepary beans, and yard-long beans don't have this problem and thrive in weather too hot for other beans.

Lima beans (*Phaseolus lunatus*) thrive in warm, humid weather and often resist pests that bother regular beans. At their best in warm, muggy weather, pole-type varieties including 'Christmas' (also known as 'Large Speckled Calico') and white-seeded 'King of the Garden' can produce huge yields when given a secure trellis. Bushy 'Jackson Wonder' can be grown for freezing or drying, though dried limas are much easier to shell compared to the tender green ones needed for freezing.

Tepary beans (*P. acutifolius*) are native to the Southwest and Mexico, where they have been part of the traditional diet for thousands of years. Planted during the summer rainy season, tepary beans have smaller leaves than regular beans and also adapt well to the alkaline soils found in many arid climates. Tolerant of heat and drought, tepary beans like 'Blue Speckled' or 'Tohono O'odham White' are excellent low-care beans for hot summer areas.

Yard-long or asparagus beans (*Vigna unguiculata* ssp. *sesquipedalis*) are grown for their long, slender pods, which are harvested when they are 12 to 18 inches long. Depending on variety, pods may be green, burgundy, or streaked. Yardlong beans need a trellis at least 8 feet high, but plantings of these super-productive peas can be kept small — only a dozen plants will keep the pods coming all summer. After they are cut into bite-size pieces, yardlong beans can be blanched and frozen just like other snap beans. Unlike regular purple-podded snap beans, which turn green when cooked, 'Red Noodle' and other dark-podded yardlong beans keep their color.

HOW TO
Grow Beans

When: Start planting beans in late spring, after the last frost has passed. Seeds germinate best when soil temperatures range between 60 and 70°F (16 and 21°C).

Most people plant bush snap beans two or three times, with sowings 3 weeks apart. Where summers are hot, make a late-summer sowing about 10 weeks before your first fall frost is expected.

Choose planting dates for dry beans that will lead to the crop maturing during the driest part of summer, or in early fall.

- -

Where: Beans need a sunny, well-drained site, but they adapt to most types of soil as long as conditions are warm. Beans are a good crop for beginners because the large seeds grow into big, fast-maturing plants. The plants have no tolerance for frost and will not grow under cold conditions.

- -

Planting: Like other legumes, beans form partnerships with soil-dwelling bacteria that enable them to capture and utilize nitrogen from the air. If you grew beans in your garden the previous year, scatter a few spadefuls of soil from last year's bean patch into the new planting site to inoculate it with beneficial rhizobia. Also provide a bit of a balanced organic fertilizer when preparing planting space for beans, because it takes a while for the nitrogen-fixing machine to get going.

Do not soak beans in water before planting them, as is done with many other seeds. With beans, only a few hours under oxygen-deprived conditions can injure the growing embryo. Plant beans dry. The most space-efficient spacing for beans is to plant them in double rows, with 12 to 14 inches between the rows. Thin seedlings to only about 6 inches apart, because beans like close company.

Tripod Trellis

Provide a sturdy trellis for pole beans at planting time. A tripod design in which poles come together at the top becomes more stable when it is loaded with vines. Long bean trellises can be made from a series of tripods, attached at the top with a horizontal pole. Trellises should be 5 to 8 feet tall, depending on how long the vines will grow.

Short pole beans, known as half-runners, run to only 5 feet compared to the 8- to 12-foot vines common in other pole beans. Even for long-vined varieties, a 6- to 8-foot-tall trellis will do, because the vines will double back upon themselves when they reach the top of the trellis. Wire mesh fences also make great trellises for pole beans.

- -

Bean Pests and Diseases

Sometimes beans enjoy a carefree season with few problems, but in some years trouble seems to lurk around every corner.

Brick-colored Mexican bean beetles sporting black spots often lay clusters of yellow eggs on bean leaves, which hatch into yellow larvae that rasp tissues from leaves. Hand-pick this pest in all life stages, and try spraying neem to control light infestations. Late plantings of bush beans sometimes escape damage.

Brightly colored Japanese beetles and deer both love to munch bean foliage. Hand-pick the beetles, or use lightweight row covers to hide your beans from both pests.

Night-feeding cutworms often sabotage beans grown in sites that recently supported grasses, cutting down seedlings at the soil line. Save survivors by sticking toothpicks into the soil beside the main stems (cutworms cannot girdle wood, only tender stems). Diatomaceous earth sprinkled over the soil's surface can help reduce losses.

Several fungal and bacterial diseases cause dark spots and patches to form on bean leaves; most are aggravated by wet conditions. To keep from spreading diseases among plants, avoid working in your bean patch when the foliage is wet.

HARVESTING AND STORING
Beans

When: Harvest snap beans when the pods reach full size but are still tender. Harvest at least twice a week. Most bush beans will produce a second or third flush of beans after the first one is picked, and pole beans will produce continuously for more than a month. Don't worry if you miss a few. The mature beans of all snap bean varieties are edible and usually make good soup beans.

Gather some of your soup beans at the mature green stage, when the pods begin to feel loose and leathery, and use them in succotash and other summer dishes. Let the rest finish as dry beans. Allow dry beans to stay on the plants until the pods turn tan and the beans inside show good color and a hard, glossy surface.

How: Bean plants can be brittle, so use two hands when harvesting pods. Immediately rinse snap beans in cool water to clean them, then pat them dry between clean kitchen towels. Store in plastic bags in the refrigerator until you are ready to cook or preserve them, but not for more than a few days.

If damp weather sets in just when your soup beans should be drying, pull up the plants and hang them upside down in a dry place. Place picked pods in paper bags or open trays kept in a dry, well-ventilated place, preferably indoors. Most dry beans are easiest to shell after the pods have dried to a crisp, or are at least leathery. After shelling your beans, allow them to dry at room temperature for at least 2 more weeks before storing them in airtight containers. If you think insects might be present in your stored beans, keep them in the freezer.

Superior snap bean varieties like 'Northeaster' have crisp, fleshy pods that do not become stringy until the beans inside begin to gain size.

The pods of dry beans like 'Black Turtle' and 'Calypso' become tough at a young age, and waste no time producing mature edible seeds.

Save Bean Seeds for Replanting

Beans are self-fertile and open-pollinated, so they are one of the easiest crops from which to save seeds for replanting. To save dry beans for replanting, simply select the largest, most perfect seeds from your stored beans. With snap beans, it is usually best to not pick beans from plants grown for seed production purposes. That way, the plants will channel all of their energy into big seeds that will grow into big seedlings. Be patient, because snap bean varieties that have been bred to stay tender for a long time are often very slow to develop mature seeds. It can take 6 weeks for pods to mature from green to tan. Under good conditions, bean seeds will store for at least 3 years.

Bean
FOOD PRESERVATION OPTIONS

You can preserve snap beans several ways, including freezing, pickling, pressure canning, and drying. As you choose preservation projects, think about how you will use your beans in the kitchen. Either canned or frozen beans can be used to make green bean casseroles, but the frozen version is better for pasta salads or stir-fries. Pickled green beans are wonderful to have on hand during the spring and fall salad seasons, and they add crunch to sandwiches, too. Canned and dried beans have very long shelf lives, with canned beans in particular worth the small trouble needed to make them.

> Either canned or frozen beans can be used to make green bean casseroles, but the frozen version is better for pasta salads or stir-fries.

To freeze beans, follow the procedures for blanching, chilling, and freezing given on pages 21–22.

Dry snap beans rehydrate slowly, so they are best used in slow-cooking soups.

Freeze some of your blanched and chilled snap beans on cookie sheets and transfer them to a large freezer bag when frozen hard so you will have loose beans for adding in small amounts to various dishes. Also combine blanched snap beans with other veggies and herbs to make frozen mixtures that vary from week to week. As the summer progresses, many gardeners cook up savory pots of "shelly beans" made from young pods mixed with shelled beans from older ones, seasoned with plenty of fresh herbs. Because they are completely cooked and seasoned, I label these as "ready-to-eat" beans in the freezer.

Drying Snap Beans

When time and dehydrator space permit, dry a few trays of your best snap beans after blanching them first. For dried snap beans destined for use in winter soups, cut the beans into uniform 1-inch pieces. You also can dry seasoned green beans for snacking. After beans are blanched and chilled, pat them dry before tossing with a seasoning oil mixture. Dry the seasoned green beans until leathery, and then store in the freezer.

Canning Snap Beans

Beans are a low-acid vegetable, so unless they are in an acidic pickling brine, a pressure canner is needed to can them safely. Processing time is short, only 20 to 25 minutes at 10 to 15 pounds pressure (depending on altitude); increase time when snap beans or cooked dry beans are combined with other vegetables in soup mixes.

Pickled green beans are new to some gardening cooks, but not for long! When preserved in a vinegar brine, green beans stay crisp for months while picking up flavors from herbs, garlic, or other seasoning spices. When basil is used as the seasoning herb, they are called basil beans.

Pickled Green Beans

Makes about 7 pints

7 dill sprigs or basil leaves

7 small garlic cloves

5 pounds green or yellow beans, cut into uniform lengths

4 cups vinegar

4 cups water

½ cup sea salt or pickling salt

2 tablespoons sugar

1   Place 1 dill sprig or basil leaf and 1 garlic clove in the bottom of hot, clean jars. Place the beans in the jars and arrange so they stand upright, packing them as tightly as possible.

2   Bring the vinegar, water, salt, and sugar to a simmer and pour the liquid over the beans, leaving ½ inch of headspace. Screw on the lids and process in a water-bath or steam canner for 10 minutes.

Little round beets are
great for canning whole,
but varieties with a
cylindrical shape cook
and peel quickly, and
yield more uniform slices.

BEETS

(Beta vulgaris)

HOW MUCH
5 row feet per person for fresh eating, plus 20 row feet for storing and preserving

- -

STELLAR VARIETIES
'Ruby Queen' or 'Cylindra' for canning; all beets store well in the refrigerator

- -

BEST WAYS TO PRESERVE
Place in cold storage, pickle, ferment, or can

Few veggies you can grow in a garden offer as many storage options as do beets. The trimmed roots will store in the refrigerator for months, or they can be pickled or canned. In most climates you can grow a second crop of beets in the fall, which have the advantage of maturing when the soil is chilling down. Cool soil brings out the sweetness in beets and contributes to their ability to store under refrigeration well into winter.

If you like beets, you will want to go into winter with a nice store of pickled beets (which can be processed in a water-bath or steam canner) or pressure-canned beets, which require no added sugar. I like to get my beet canning done with a spring-to-summer crop, because beets grow fast as days become longer and warmer in spring. Fall-grown beets are slowpokes and need at least 10 weeks of growing time before cold weather stops their growth. The most challenging part of growing a good fall crop of beets is getting the planting up and growing in hot summer weather, a task for which shade covers are invaluable.

Best Beets

FOR THE
Homegrown Pantry

Beet varieties vary in shape, color, and uniformity. All types of beets can be used in pickles and relishes, but the varieties named below are often preferred for canning crops.

- **Round red beets** include many popular varieties, but some are better for canning than others. Try 'Ruby Queen' if you want to can small, whole beets, but opt for larger 'Detroit Dark Red' if you plan to slice or dice beets before pickling or canning them. Under good conditions, 'Early Wonder' and 'Lutz Green Leaf' will keep getting bigger until they become worthy of cold storage in the fall.

- **Cylindrical red beets** are shaped like blunt 6-inch-long carrots, and this shape makes them fast to cook, peel, and slice into uniform pieces. The upright plants of the 'Cylindra' or 'Taunus' varieties are easy to grow, and the roots push up out of the ground when they are ready.

HOW MANY TO PLANT?

Most gardeners have fresh beets in the refrigerator and on the table from midsummer to late fall, so the canned beet supply needs to last only about 6 months. For your spring planting, plan on 5 row feet per person for eating fresh, and another 20 row feet to make 12 to 14 pints of pickled or canned beets.

How many fall beets you grow is limited mostly by your available cold storage. Fall-grown beets can be big, so only 15 row feet would give you 5 pounds for fresh eating and 10 pounds for storage into early winter.

What about Yellow Beets?

Yellow beets were a Burpee seed company novelty in the 1940s, but germination rates of yellow or "golden" beets have remained low until recently, with the introduction of more vigorous sprouters like 'Touchstone Gold'. Mild, sweet, and never messy because they do not bleed, yellow beets make gorgeous pickles.

In addition to yellow beets, white and bicolored beets look pretty on the plate, but they are less productive and uniform compared to red beets. This is fine if you want a rainbow of beets for fresh eating and refrigerated storage, but not if you are trying to stock your pantry with pickled beets.

HOW TO
Grow Beets

When: In spring, plant beets about 2 weeks before your average last frost date. Beets can be sown earlier if the planting is covered with a row cover tunnel. In fall, plant beets 10 weeks before your average first frost date.

- -

Where: Full sun and rich, finely cultivated soil are needed to grow beautiful beets. When growing a canning crop, use every opportunity to enhance the uniformity of the planting. Some gardeners say beets can be started in containers and transplanted, but my experience with transplanted beets has been disappointing. Direct-seeded beets simply grow better.

Beets need a range of nutrients, so be sure to mix in a standard dose of a balanced organic fertilizer and a generous helping of compost as you prepare the bed. Beets need a soil pH between 6.0 and 7.0; a light application of wood ashes can be helpful in more acidic soils.

- -

Planting: You can improve the germination of beet seeds by soaking the seeds in water for 4 to 6 hours before planting them. Plant the primed seeds ½ inch deep and 1 to 2 inches apart in rows spaced at least 10 inches apart. To provide perfect germination conditions, cover the seeded bed with a piece of cloth or other shade cover, which prevents soil crusting and compaction. A row cover tunnel provides similar benefits.

- -

Maintenance: Beet seed capsules often contain two or more seeds, so thinning is essential to growing plump roots. Use your fingertips or a small pair of scissors to snip out extra seedlings to turn twins into singles. When beet seedlings are 2 inches tall, thin them to 3 inches apart. Fall beets being grown for winter storage need more space and can be thinned to 6 inches apart.

Beets are set back by drought, so provide water as needed to keep the soil lightly moist at all times. Hand-weed early and often, but stop weeding when the plants are within 3 weeks of maturity lest you disturb the beets' roots, which can cause them to lose interest in plumping up. If your beets start pushing up during a period of very hot, sunny weather, use a light mulch of grass clippings or erect a shade cover over the bed to keep the shoulders from becoming green and tough.

Beet Pests and Diseases

Flea beetles and leaf miners. Beets have few insect enemies beyond flea beetles, which make tiny holes in leaves but would rather eat arugula. Leaf miners leave behind meandering tunnels in beet leaves. Neither pest is likely to cause significant damage, but row covers can be used preventively in areas where pest pressure is high — for example, near commercial sugar beet fields.

Boron deficiency. Dark corky spots in and on beets are a symptom of boron deficiency, easily prevented by amending the soil with compost or mixing in a dusting of household borax when preparing the bed for planting. Note that beets are inefficient users of boron, so deficiency symptoms in beets do not mean your soil is bereft of boron.

Fungal diseases. Under very rainy conditions, beet leaves can become blighted with several fungal diseases. Frequently the plants will regain their health if the damaged leaves are cut away and composted.

Animal pests. Rabbits will eat beet greens, while voles may attack beets from below, often chewing off the taproot. Mature plants that suddenly wilt may have been fed upon by voles. Fine mesh hardware cloth fencing, buried vertically around the bed, is the only sure way to protect beets where vole populations are high. Unfortunately, deer love beet greens, too, so plan ahead to protect your crop.

HARVESTING AND STORING
Beets

When: Begin pulling round beets when they measure 2 inches across. In fall, harvest beets after the first frost but before the first hard freeze.

- -

How: Gently swish the roots in cool water to remove excess soil, but do not scrub them. Cut off all but 1 inch of the beet tops, but leave the taproot intact to prevent bleeding. Set aside the youngest, most tender beet greens for fresh eating. Pat the roots dry with clean towels and place in plastic bags in the refrigerator until you are ready to use them.

If you live in a cold climate and have a root cellar or other place where near-freezing temperatures can be maintained, fall beets can be packed in buckets with damp sand or sawdust for winter storage. See page 17 for more ways to cold-store beets. Be sure to check stored beets weekly for signs of trouble.

Beets push up out of the soil as they mature, which takes the guesswork out of when to harvest.

Vary your knife work when making pickled beets and beet relishes. One batch might be uniform slices and another matchsticks, with relishes made from finely diced or grated beets.

Beet
FOOD PRESERVATION OPTIONS

Cold storage in bins or boxes or an extra refrigerator is the easiest way to store a robust crop of fall beets, but summer beets are best pickled or pressure canned fresh from the garden. Beets are a low-acid food, but using a vinegar-based pickling brine makes it possible to process pickled beets in a water-bath or steam canner. Pressure canning beets is not difficult, assuming you are familiar with your canning equipment.

Tip: Simply scrubbing and simmering for half an hour makes beets easy to peel.

Canning Pickled Beets

Naturally firm and colorful, pickled beets will create beginner's luck for any new home canner. For the base brine, use 4 cups vinegar, 2 cups water, and 2 cups sugar (no salt is necessary). As long as you stick with

this high-acid brine for low-acid beets, the flavorings you choose can go in several directions:

- Most traditional recipes include finely sliced onions, cinnamon sticks, and whole cloves, with everything simmered together for a few minutes before the jars are filled.

- Orange peel, thin slices of fresh ginger, and mustard seeds give pickled beets a flavor profile that pairs beautifully with Asian foods.

- Relishes in which the beets are finely chopped and combined with cabbage are easy to make and look great on the plate or on a sandwich. No water is added to equal parts vinegar and sugar when making a brine for beet-based relishes.

Follow the standard home canning directions given on pages 36–37 when making pickled beets. The general guideline for canning pickled beets is to process pints in either a water-bath or steam canner for 30 minutes. This is a long processing time for a pickled vegetable, but beets are so dense that they rarely suffer from prolonged heating.

Pressure Canning Beets

A straightforward veggie to handle in the pressure canner, cooked beets cut into bite-size pieces are often lightly salted with ½ teaspoon salt per pint. The general guideline for canning beets is to process pints for 30 to 35 minutes at 10 to 15 pounds pressure, depending on altitude.

Using Beets in Fermentation Projects

Like most other root crops, raw beets tend to stay woody when fermented on their own or used in mixed ferments. For this reason, beets are usually cooked before being added to the fermentation crock. Red beets will turn everything else in the crock red, too.

Fermented Beet Kvass

This recipe produces a tangy, salty-sweet fermented drink that continues to improve after it is moved to the refrigerator. Sweeten your kvass with a touch of honey just before drinking it.

Makes 2 cups

3 cups scrubbed, unpeeled beets, cut into ½-inch cubes

1 cup chopped cabbage

2 garlic cloves, crushed

2 teaspoons sea salt

1 tablespoon honey, or more to taste

1 Place the beets, cabbage, and garlic in a clean quart jar and sprinkle with the salt. Cover with warm water, leaving 1 inch of headspace. Cover with a coffee filter, held in place with a screw ring.

2 Keep in a warm room for 5 to 7 days, or until you can taste fizziness in a sample sip. Check daily, and use a spoon to remove any mold that forms on the top.

3 After 5 to 7 days, strain the liquid into a clean jar, stir in honey, and add enough water to make 2 cups (1 pint). Your beet kvass is ready to drink. Dilute with water if it is too salty, and add more honey if you want more sweetness. Kept refrigerated, kvass will continue to improve for a few weeks, or until it is gone.

BROCCOLI

(*Brassica oleracea*)

HOW MUCH
3 plants per person for fresh eating, 9 plants per person for freezing

STELLAR VARIETIES
Large-headed 'Diplomat' and sprouting 'DeCicco'

BEST WAY TO PRESERVE
Freeze

Broccoli is a crop that needs to be attentively courted before it will become your sweetheart. Garden broccoli has more precise cultural requirements compared to other vegetables, and most gardeners spend several seasons learning how to grow it. On every level — timing, soil fertility, spacing, and pest management — broccoli's rather exact needs must be met. But once you learn broccoli's secrets for success in your garden, you can look forward to bountiful yields of this popular and nutritious vegetable.

Garden-fresh broccoli is remarkably tender, so it is always in high demand at the table. In the garden, however, large-framed broccoli plants need lots of space, so try not to get carried away on a broccoli binge. A cool-weather crop best grown in spring or fall, broccoli tastes sweetest when it matures in autumn, after nights turn chilly. Freezing is the best way to preserve broccoli.

Best Broccoli

FOR THE

Homegrown Pantry

Fresh eating quality is all that counts when choosing broccoli varieties. The two best-tasting types are large-headed hybrids like those you see in grocery stores, and sprouting varieties that produce numerous small heads over several weeks.

Large-headed varieties produce familiar domed heads composed of numerous clustered florets, or beads. Many varieties produce smaller side shoots after the primary head is harvested, especially when grown in spring. Hybrid varieties like 'Diplomat' mature in a uniform way, so you can harvest and freeze all of the crop in one day.

Sprouting and gailon varieties grow into bushier plants that produce numerous small heads. Italian strains like 'DeCicco' (*Brassica oleracea* var. *italica*) have long been popular among gardeners, and they have recently been joined by Asian "gailon" types, classified as *B. oleracea* var. *alboglabra*. These sprouting broccolis produce continuously for more than a month, and they are ideal for mixing with other vegetables in frozen packets or for bringing raw crunch to any salad. Pick just before the flowers open for best quality. Sprouting and gailon varieties are different from broccoli raab (*B. rapa* var. *ruvo*), a mustard cousin with much sharper flavor.

A broccoli head is made up of many tender green "beads," which are immature flower buds. After the main head is cut, many varieties produce smaller secondary heads a few weeks later.

HOW TO
Grow Broccoli

When: For your spring crop, start seeds indoors 6 weeks before your last spring frost, and set out hardened-off seedlings when they are about 4 weeks old. Striving for very early crops can backfire, because seedlings exposed to cold often produce tiny heads (a syndrome called "buttoning"). In spring, wait until the weather warms to set out your broccoli. You can also seed broccoli directly into a nursery bed and transplant the seedlings to your garden. Experiment with planting dates, which are key to growing great broccoli. Be careful when purchasing seedlings. They are often overgrown, so they already have one strike against them. Broccoli does not like any type of stress.

For your fall crop, start seeds indoors 12 to 14 weeks before your first fall frost, and grow the seedlings in filtered shade until they are about 4 weeks old. This is usually the height of summer, so it helps to cover the little plants with a row cover or tulle tunnel to filter strong sun and protect them from grasshoppers and other insects. Have the tunnel ready the day you transplant your broccoli.

Where: Broccoli is a heavy feeder, and the plants take up nutrients most easily when the soil pH ranges between 6.0 and 7.0. Choose a sunny site with fertile, well-drained soil.

Planting: Loosen the planting bed and mix in 1 inch of mature compost. Unless your soil is already very fertile, also mix in a high-nitrogen organic fertilizer such as alfalfa meal or composted poultry manure, or you can use a balanced organic fertilizer. Water the fertilized bed thoroughly before setting out seedlings. Allow 18 to 20 inches between plants for most varieties. Dwarf varieties can be planted 12 inches apart.

Maintenance: In spring, protect young seedlings from cold winds with cloches, or you can grow them beneath a row cover tunnel. Wait until the soil warms to mulch broccoli. Just before heads form, drench plants with an organic mix-with-water fertilizer, or scratch a dusting of any high-nitrogen organic fertilizer into the soil around the plants.

Broccoli Pests and Diseases

The same pests that bother cabbage are often seen on broccoli, which make it a favorite host plant for velvety green cabbageworms, green cabbage loopers (which loop their bodies, inchworm-style), and blackish armyworms. All are easily controlled with a biological pesticide that has *Bacillus thuringiensis* as its active ingredient. In summer, brightly marked harlequin bugs and grasshoppers can devastate young plants. The best way to prevent summer pest problems is to grow plants beneath floating row covers.

Plants that suddenly collapse may have been hit by cabbage root maggots — rice-size fly larvae that feed on broccoli roots. Where this pest is common, plant seedlings deeply and press the soil firmly around the stems. A loose collar of cloth wrapped around the base of the stem will further discourage egg laying by adults.

Almost-ripe broccoli heads will continue to grow when shielded from strong sun. Tie or pin the top leaves together to create an instant sun shade.

HARVESTING AND STORING
Broccoli

When: As soon as you see tiny heads forming in summer broccoli, use clothespins or string to bind the topmost three leaves together into a sunshade (shown at left), which will help the heads ripen more uniformly. Avoid overhead watering to keep the growing head as dry as possible. Check the plants daily for the size of the heads and the condition of the beads, which are actually immature flower buds. Harvest when the beads around the edges of the head show slight loosening, but most of the rest of the beads are still tight.

Light frosts improve the flavor of broccoli that matures in the fall, and the best broccoli of the year comes between the first frost and the first freeze.

- -

How: Use a sharp knife to cut off the heads at an angle, which will limit how much water pools inside the cut stem. Chill harvested broccoli immediately by placing the heads in the refrigerator or in a cooler kept cold with frozen water bottles. Clean the heads under cool running water. If you see tiny cabbageworms in the heads, soak large pieces in warm salt water for 10 minutes to float them out. Enzymes in broccoli cause the tissues to toughen after the heads are cut, so blanch and freeze bumper crops right away to preserve broccoli's tenderness.

If you continue to water and weed healthy broccoli plants, many varieties (or sometimes individual plants) will develop secondary branches that produce lovely little heads for fresh use or for mixing with other summer vegetables in frozen packages. Sprouting broccoli is a cut-and-come-again crop that will produce new buds each time it is cut.

HOW MUCH TO PLANT?

For eating fresh, allow three plants per person, but triple that amount if you want to freeze a year's supply comprising 4 to 5 pounds per person. In most climates, you can divide broccoli into spring and fall plantings.

Broccoli
FOOD PRESERVATION OPTIONS

For the best home-preserved broccoli, steam blanch bite-size pieces and freeze them in vacuum-sealed bags. Also include broccoli in bags of mixed summer vegetables and herbs you put by in your freezer.

Broccoli florets that have first been blanched to preserve their color — about 4 minutes in steam — can be made into refrigerator pickles using the same recipe used for cucumbers (see page 112). You also can dry blanched broccoli florets, but expect the green to become tinged with brown as the pieces dry to crisp.

BRUSSELS SPROUTS
(*Brassica oleracea* var. *gemmifera*)

HOW MUCH
4 plants per person for eating fresh, plus more for freezing

STELLAR VARIETIES
'Diablo', 'Dimitri', and 'Nautic'

BEST WAY TO PRESERVE
Freeze

If asparagus and rhubarb are the season openers in the homegrown pantry, Brussels sprouts are the crop that brings the gardening year to a satisfying end. Growing Brussels sprouts is not without its challenges. In many parts of North America, the best planting dates are early to mid summer, when the weather is inhospitable to seedlings and most of your garden space is fully occupied. But if you nail down good planting dates and nurture the stately plants through hot weather, you will have garden-fresh organic Brussels sprouts for more than a month as fall turns to winter.

Do not expect an overload, because Brussels sprouts' productivity is on the stingy side. This is a crop to grow for its late harvest period and culinary appeal, which is off the charts when dinner includes tender, freshly picked Brussels sprouts. Should you have extra, freezing is the best way to preserve them.

Best Brussels Sprouts

FOR THE

Homegrown Pantry

Varieties are few for this cool-season cabbage cousin, and I suggest choosing a hybrid that is recommended by a regional seed company or your state Cooperative Extension Service. Seeds of high-quality hybrids such as 'Diablo', 'Dimitri', and 'Nautic' are worth their high cost because they deliver vigorous growth under less-than-perfect conditions.

> Seeds of high-quality hybrids are worth their high cost because they deliver vigorous growth under less-than-perfect conditions.

HOW TO

Grow Brussels Sprouts

When: Unlike cabbage and broccoli, Brussels sprouts are seldom successful from plants set out in spring. Hot weather that arrives just as the plants start developing sprouts ruins the crop by causing the sprouts to become loose, leafy, and bitter. It is much better to wait until late spring or early summer to start Brussels sprouts seeds. Recommended seeding-starting dates from Cooperative Extension Service literature include March 30 in Zone 4, May 15 in Zone 5, June 5 in Zone 6, and July 1 in Zones 7 and 8.

Where: Most veggies like light, cushy soil, but Brussels sprouts need the opposite — heavy clay with a few rocks in it. Brussels sprouts grow into stiff, top-heavy plants with skinny bases that are easily damaged by rocking in the wind. Light, sandy soils cannot adequately anchor Brussels sprouts plants, even when they are propped up with stakes and have soil mounded up around the base. A slightly acidic to near-neutral pH is ideal.

Planting: Enrich the planting site with a generous helping of a balanced organic fertilizer because Brussels sprouts are heavy feeders. They also need more boron than other crops. A little household borax mixed into the watering can every few weeks is a good therapy in soils that may have little boron to offer.

Harden off the seedlings before setting them out in well-prepared soil, and cover them with lightweight row cover or tulle tunnels to exclude insect pests. When the plants are 12 inches tall, top-dress them with a high-nitrogen organic fertilizer such as composted manure.

Pruning the Plants

It is normal for Brussels sprouts plants to shed their oldest leaves in late summer. Gather these up and compost them to reduce slug habitat and risk of diseases. About a month before your first fall frost, you also can pinch out the growing tips from each plant, which helps them channel energy into the sprouts. As the plants grow, stake them to keep them from falling over. Upright Brussels sprouts plants produce better than crooked ones.

Brussels Sprouts Pests and Diseases

The same pests that bother cabbage are often seen on Brussels sprouts in summer. If cabbage white butterflies get beneath the row covers in summer, treat plants with a *Bacillus thuringiensis* pesticide to bring them under control.

Colonies of cabbage aphids can appear on your Brussels sprouts well into autumn, when most insect pests have disappeared. A black sooty mold, which grows on aphid honeydew, is often present as well. Remove badly infested sprouts and leaves, and spray plants with a strong spray of water to dislodge some of the aphids. Then apply insecticidal soap, and repeat the treatment after 1 week.

HOW MANY TO PLANT?

Grow as many plants as you have room for, starting with four plants per person (about 2 pounds Brussels sprouts). Go up to five plants per person if you have space. Brussels sprouts production is slow but steady. Starting in late fall, Brussels sprouts will produce 4 to 5 sprouts per plant, per week, for about 6 weeks.

HARVESTING AND PRESERVING
Brussels Sprouts

When: Frost improves the flavor and texture of Brussels sprouts, which are at their best after a light freeze or two.

- -

How: Twist off the sprouts, a few at a time, as soon as they are at least ½ inch in diameter; the first sprouts are often much smaller than those produced later in the season. As you harvest sprouts from the bottom of the plants, break off the lowest leaves to give the next sprouts more room to grow. Refrigerate harvested sprouts immediately.

Food Preservation: Stored in plastic bags, Brussels sprouts will keep in the refrigerator for 2 weeks, though the outer leaves will turn yellow. Blanch and freeze any extras after trimming them and cutting them in half. If you have a cold basement, you can pull plants from the garden in late fall, clip off the leaves, and stick the roots in buckets of damp sand for short-term cool storage. At temperatures just above freezing, Brussels sprouts stored this way will keep for more than a month.

The best way to harvest Brussels sprouts is to pop them off by hand, using a pushing-twisting motion.

A hard red cabbage with roots buried in moist garden soil waits in the basement for its turn in the kitchen.

CABBAGE

(*Brassica oleracea* var. *capitata*)

HOW MUCH
3 to 4 small heads per person for spring crop, 5 to 10 heads per person for fall

STELLAR VARIETIES
'Gonzales' spring cabbage and 'Late Flat Dutch' fall cabbage

BEST WAYS TO PRESERVE
Ferment, freeze, pickle, or dry

A vigorous crop by nature, cabbage is easy to grow once you find the right planting dates and learn to manage pests preventively. A cool-season crop, cabbage can be grown in both spring and fall, with much of the fall crop put by as kraut and frozen wrappers for cabbage rolls. In either season, growing cabbage is an excellent investment of time and space. Commercially grown cabbage is bombarded with pesticides from cradle to grave, and organically grown cabbage can get expensive since it is sold by the pound. The solution is to grow your own, which opens the door to trying distinctive varieties that vary in size, density, leaf type, and color.

Cabbage keeps surprisingly well in cold storage, especially hard heads that mature in the fall. Leafier savoy cabbage can be fermented, frozen, or dried for long-term storage, or you can make savory relishes put by in jars. Don't forget to blanch and freeze perfect outer leaves so you will have them for making cabbage rolls in winter.

Best Cabbage
FOR THE
Homegrown Pantry

In most climates, you can grow two crops of cabbage: a spring crop that matures just before the weather turns hot in early summer, and a summer-planted crop that matures in fall, a couple of weeks after your first fall frost.

For spring cabbage, choose fast-maturing hybrids that produce smallish heads if you are pushed for space. The 'Gonzales' and 'Pixie' varieties quickly produce lovely softball-size heads, but any variety rated at less than 75 days to maturity will do. Among open-pollinated varieties, semi-conical 'Early Jersey Wakefield' is a good choice for spring.

For the fall crop, choose slower-growing storage types, which produce dense, heavy heads in 85 to 100 days, depending on variety. In many areas, it is important to choose varieties that resist soilborne fusarium yellows. Rarely seen in stores, squat flat-headed varieties like 'Late Flat Dutch' or 'Mammoth Red Rock' can be great fun to grow. Dense storage cabbages will hold in the garden until fall turns to winter.

> A cool-season crop, cabbage can be grown in both spring and fall, with much of the fall crop put by as kraut and frozen wrappers for cabbage rolls.

THE RED CABBAGE ADVANTAGE. Rabbits and deer are fond of cabbage, though red-leafed varieties are of less interest than green cabbage. In addition, cabbageworms and other common pests are generally less numerous and easier to spot on red-leafed cabbage.

HOW MUCH TO PLANT?

Estimating how much spring cabbage to grow is easy, because most of it will be eaten fresh. Simply grow three to four small heads for each person in your household.

For the larger fall crop, growing 5 to 10 plants per person should fill your needs, with the number of plants dependent on the size and weight of the mature heads. An average market cabbage weighs 3 pounds, but if you are growing a variety that produces very large heads, you will need fewer of them.

HOW TO
Grow Cabbage

When: Start seeds for spring cabbage indoors, at normal room temperatures, 8 to 10 weeks before your last spring frost. Provide bright fluorescent light and begin hardening off seedlings when they have three true leaves. Transplant to the garden when your cabbage seedlings are about 6 weeks old, and use cloches to protect them from cold winds and critters. For your fall crop, count back 12 to 14 weeks from your first fall frost to find your best seeding date. For example, if your first fall frost date is October 15, fall cabbage seeds should be started by mid-July.

- -

Where: Cabbage is as a heavy-feeding crop, in part because the roots do not stretch very far into the soil, and so they must find the nutrients they need in the square foot of soil beneath the plants. Cabbage takes up nutrients most efficiently in soil with a slightly acidic pH between 6.0 and 6.5. Full sun is required to grow good cabbage.

- -

Planting: If you buy cabbage seedlings in six-packs, immediately transplant them to 4-inch-diameter pots if it is not yet time to set them out in the garden. Interruptions in growth due to cramped roots are never good for cabbage.

Space cabbage plants 24 inches apart, or 18 inches apart for mini cabbages. Very large varieties grown in cool climates need 36 inches between plants. Weed regularly for the first few weeks your cabbage is in the garden.

- -

Maintenance: When watering is required, use soaker hoses or carefully hand-water the plants' root zones, because sprinklers or overhead watering can cause excess moisture to accumulate in the growing cabbage heads, leading to musty mildews you can taste. Use your own judgment when deciding when and how to mulch your cabbage. Large cabbage leaves shade the soil between plants the same way a mulch would, so mulching is not necessary in moist climates and may encourage slugs, especially in the spring crop.

Cabbage seedlings set out in summer face a different set of challenges, and they benefit from a mulch of grass clippings or chopped leaves — any biodegradable material that will keep the soil cool and moist through the hottest part of summer. Fall cabbage (which is set out in summer, while it's still hot) also should be protected from pests with a row cover or tulle tent from the day the seedlings are set out in the garden.

When heads begin to form, drench the root zones with a high-nitrogen liquid fertilizer, or scratch a light application of a balanced organic fertilizer into the soil around the plants. Harvest cabbage early in the morning, while the heads are cool.

Cabbage Pests and Diseases

Most cabbage diseases are regional in nature and can be prevented by growing resistant varieties recommended by your state Cooperative Extension Service. Insects are another matter, because the lengthy list of cabbage pests requires preventive management. The good news is that cabbage loves life under row covers, which give you a very high level of protection from insect pests.

Note that as cabbage plants approach maturity, they naturally shed two or three of their oldest leaves. Removing the basal leaves as soon as they start to turn yellow or appear ragged may have the additional benefit of making conditions less favorable to slugs, snails, caterpillars, earwigs, and other creatures attracted to the cool, moist shelter provided by a stately cabbage plant.

In seasonal order, these are the pests to watch for on cabbage:

- **Cutworms** sever seedlings at the soil line, usually at night. You can prevent cutworm damage by making rigid collars from plastic cups or food containers, which are pushed into the ground around newly planted seedlings.

- **Slugs** chew irregular holes in cabbage leaves. A few slugs among the lowest cabbage leaves are not a problem, but slug traps and hand-picking are often needed in slug-friendly climates.

- **Cabbageworms** are green leaf-eating caterpillars, the larvae of cabbage white butterflies. The butterflies cannot lay their eggs on plants protected with lightweight row cover or tulle. Two organic pesticides, Bt and spinosad, provide excellent control when applied every 10 to 14 days. Using these sprays preventively is very worthwhile in the fall, when other small moth larvae, including dark little armyworms, may infest growing cabbage.

- **Earwigs** sometimes seek shelter in the base of cabbage plants during periods of rainy weather. Trap them with rolls of damp newspaper placed beneath plants.

- **Harlequin bugs** appear in summer, so spring cabbage often escapes damage. Summer-planted cabbage requires protection with row covers or tulle tunnels, which will keep grasshoppers from eating young cabbage seedlings, too.

- **Cabbage aphids** appear in fall, often in large numbers. They are more likely to colonize kale or Brussels sprouts before attempting to gain a foothold in cabbage. Repeat applications of insecticidal soap are needed to get cabbage aphids under control.

HARVESTING AND STORING
Cabbage

Cabbage can be harvested anytime after the heads become firm and well formed. When spring cabbage is cut early and high, with a generous stub of basal stem left in the ground, the plants often will produce a cluster of loose mini heads that make wonderful cooked greens. Spring cabbage heads are often leafy and lightweight compared to those that mature more slowly in cool fall weather.

The core of a cabbage head will continue to grow after the head has reached prime condition for harvesting. When plants holding slightly overripe heads are exposed to drenching rain, the core's sudden growth spurt can cause the heads to split. Lesson: It is better to harvest perfect cabbage heads when they are ready, and store them in the refrigerator, than to let them stand too long in the garden.

Cool weather slows down the growth rate of cabbage, making the heads less likely to split, and cool temperatures also trigger the production of sugars in the leaves. Ideally, fall cabbage should reach mature size just after your first frost occurs and be perfect for harvesting for another month. Light to moderate frosts are good for cabbage, so don't be in a rush to harvest fall cabbage until hard freezes become frequent. A brief overnight freeze will not injure a good head of cabbage, but cabbages that are allowed to freeze hard are never the same.

> **When spring cabbage is cut early and high, with a generous stub of basal stem left in the ground, the plants often will produce a cluster of loose mini heads that make wonderful cooked greens.**

Cabbage
FOOD PRESERVATION OPTIONS

Whole, trimmed cabbage heads packed into plastic bags will keep in the refrigerator for several weeks. They also can be kept in a cold root cellar or in an insulated cooler kept outdoors. Some gardeners with cold, roomy basements (but little refrigerator space) pull up plants with roots attached, trim off most of the outer leaves, and "plant" them in buckets of slightly moist soil to extend their storage time. On or off the roots, it is better to process cabbage for long-term storage while it's fresh and perfect than to hold heads in cold storage any longer than necessary.

Your long-term cabbage food preservation options include fermentation, freezing, pickling, and drying. You can choose your preservation projects based on how much cabbage you have that needs to be made pantry ready.

Fermenting Cabbage

It's easy to preserve cabbage as salt-fermented kraut, as spicy kimchi, or in mixed vegetable ferments as long as you have fresh, organically grown cabbage; have cool conditions for fermentation; and follow good sanitation procedures. Cabbage comes from the garden laden with the bacteria needed for fermentation to occur, so you do not need a starter culture when working with mixtures that are at least half cabbage. Once the fermentation process is complete, which takes only 7 days or so, fermented cabbage will store in the fridge for about 6 months, or until it is gone.

Step-by-step directions for fermenting cabbage and other vegetables are given in the fermentation section on pages 40–41. The Savory Salt-Fermented Sauerkraut recipe on page 93 is a good project for beginning fermenters. Because cool conditions are needed to ferment cabbage, the best time to do it is in the fall, but much depends on climate. I often make a small, one-head batch of fermented cabbage from my spring crop so we will have sauerkraut in the fridge as a summer

condiment, but the rest of our summer cabbage is eaten fresh or added to relishes. Most of my larger fall crop goes into various fermentation projects that keep us in fermented foods until the New Year, and sometimes beyond.

Crispy Chinese Cabbages

If your favorite form of fermented cabbage is Korean-style kimchi, you will want to grow both Chinese cabbage (also called napa cabbage, *Brassica rapa* var. *pekinensis*) and pak choi or bok choy (spoon cabbage, *B. rapa* var. *chinensis*) in your fall garden. The fast-growing plants are ready to start eating in only 6 weeks, and unlike spring crops, Chinese cabbage and pak choi grown in the fall seldom bolt and are barely bothered by flea beetles. Both plants make excellent additions to fall fermentation projects that include radishes, carrots, and other crisp vegetables. In the garden, handle Chinese cabbage or pak choi the same way you would grow a fall crop of Swiss chard (see page 213).

Canned Cabbage Relishes

Shredded cabbage is a primary ingredient in several popular relishes, including piccalilli, which is called chowchow in the South. An acidic brine made from vinegar and brown sugar preserves the cabbage and companion vegetables (onions, tomatoes, and peppers), so piccalilli can be canned in a water-bath or steam canner.

You can process cabbage in a pressure canner, but the results will be mushy compared to cabbage that is blanched and then frozen or dried.

Freezing and Drying Cabbage

Two of the most convenient ways to stretch your cabbage supply into the off-season is to freeze small batches or to dry larger ones. In either case, it is important to blanch the cabbage quite thoroughly, preferably in steam, before packing it away in freezer containers or arranging the blanched pieces on dehydrator trays.

You also can freeze whole, blanched outer leaves for making stuffed cabbage rolls in winter. Simply select perfect leaves slightly larger than an outstretched hand, wash well, and cut a 2-inch slit in the primary leaf vein to help the leaf lie flat. Blanch in steam for 4 minutes or so, until the color changes, and cool. You can freeze the blanched leaves flat, or roll two or three leaves into loose rolls and freeze them like giant cigars. Thaw completely before using to make your favorite cabbage roll recipe.

I first tried drying cabbage in hopes it would make a tasty snack, but it turned out that dried cabbage is better for cooking than as a popcorn substitute. When coarsely chopped and blanched before drying until leathery (for freezer storage) or crisp (for cool, dry storage in vacuum-sealed containers), dried cabbage does an amazing job of regaining its succulence when added to slow-cooked dishes. Especially in spring when the cupboard is looking bare, it's great to have some humble dried cabbage to add flavor and fiber to a nourishing soup.

TOP: Coarsely shredded cabbage can be blanched and dried, then added to slow-cooked dishes.

BOTTOM: Slitting the stems of blanched leaves makes them easy to freeze for later use making cabbage rolls.

Savory Salt-Fermented Sauerkraut

Many gardening cooks make sauerkraut as their first fermentation project. To ensure a fast start, this recipe includes a small amount of diced apple, which provides the beneficial bacteria with a bit of natural sugar. Dill or fennel seeds enhance the flavor of this delicious kraut.

Makes about 1 quart

2	small or 1 large head cabbage (5–6 pounds), grated or chopped
10–15	radishes, chopped
1	medium onion, diced
2	tablespoons sea salt
½	medium apple, peeled and diced
1	teaspoon dill seeds or fennel seeds
1	quart water

1 Combine the cabbage, radishes, onion, and salt in a large pan. Massage the salt into the vegetables with clean hands for 5 minutes or more. Mix in the apple, and press the mixture into a clean 2-quart canning jar or fermentation crock.

2 Pour in the water. It will not cover the vegetables, but wait a day to add more water if necessary, because the salt will pull juices from the veggies. Cover with a top equipped with an airlock, or use a screw band to secure a cover made from a coffee filter or piece of lightweight cloth.

3 Check the kraut daily to make sure the food is covered with salt brine; if needed, use a water-filled sandwich bag as a weight (see page 39). At cool room temperatures, the sauerkraut will ferment in less than 1 week, and it can be stored in the refrigerator for months.

'Yellowstone'

'Dragon'

'Red Cored
Chantenay'

Grow colorful red and yellow carrots
in spring for fresh eating, then switch
to heavier orange Chantenay types for
harvesting in fall and storing into winter.

CARROTS
(*Daucus carota* var. *sativus*)

HOW MUCH
20 row feet per person

- -

STELLAR VARIETIES
'Early Nantes', Chantenay, Danvers, and 'Purple Haze'

- -

BEST WAYS TO PRESERVE
Refrigerate, place in cold storage, freeze, or pickle

Carrots that are freshly pulled from moist ground have a vibrant flavor that is unique and habit forming, but carrot flavor is a combination of nature and nurture. You will always grow your sweetest carrots in the fall, when the soil is getting cooler, but sweetness isn't everything. To eat carrots year-round, grow fast-maturing varieties in spring, and make summer sowings for a season-stretching fall crop.

Several preservation methods befit carrots, but except for carrots grated into relishes for color and texture, or carrot slices added to packets of mixed frozen vegetables, you should regard carrots as an almost year-round fresh-from-the-fridge crop. Summer carrots will store in the refrigerator until they are gone, and fall carrots can be dug as needed until the ground freezes. After that, they can be refrigerated or kept in cool storage for 3 months or more.

Best Carrots

FOR THE

Homegrown Pantry

Most open-pollinated carrot varieties are identified as belonging to one of the four variety groups below, but with hybrids there is substantial crossover between types. You need not worry about the distinction — just keep trying varieties until you find a few that like your garden as much as you like them.

When considering color, red carrots provide novel nutrients and beautiful color, but red carrots taste best when cooked. Orange carrots are generally the sweetest. It can be great fun to grow mixtures of carrot varieties in different colors, which make cooking more interesting.

- **Nantes** types are good all-season carrots, but especially fine in spring because they grow fast and keep their sweet flavor in warm soil. Roots are usually 5 to 6 inches long, with a crisp, juicy texture. Nantes types like 'Early Nantes', 'Nelson', and 'Mokum' make great fresh eating carrots and store for weeks in the refrigerator.

- **Chantenay** carrots develop stocky, conical roots that become sweeter as the soil cools in the fall, so

they are a choice carrot to harvest in late fall for fresh eating in winter. Some varieties are remarkably cold hardy. Chantenay carrots are rarely seen in stores, which is all the more reason to grow them. I like to grow them as my last carrot planting of spring, and I let them stay in the garden until the soil cools in the fall. Handled this way, Chantenays grow up to 3 inches across, so that only a couple of them will feed a family.

- **Danvers** carrots probably descended from Chantenays, but they are straighter and therefore easier to clean and cut for processing. These thick carrots excel in cool climates, where the roots can take their time sizing up without being stressed by extreme heat.

- **Imperator** carrots are luxuriously long with silky skins, as you might expect of crosses between Nantes and Chantenay types. Most varieties in this group need deep, sandy soil to be at their best. But even a not-quite-perfect yellow 'Yellowstone' or orange-and-purple 'Purple Haze' is a very impressive carrot.

Chantenay (shown here) and Danvers are best for cold storage.

In the kitchen, raw carrots are invaluable for providing crunchy texture in salads, slaws, and legions of other dishes, so your first concern should be growing plenty of fresh carrots. For me, this means making two plantings in spring and two more in late summer for fall harvest. I could grow more, but other orange vegetables including pumpkins, sweet potatoes, and butternut squash are easier to grow and store compared to carrots, and you can only eat so many cooked orange vegetables. I concentrate on growing lots of fresh and refrigerated carrots for eating raw, plus extra for adding color and texture to pickles, frozen vegetable mixtures, and fall fermentation projects.

For all of these needs, about 20 total row feet per person per year is a good estimate, which should yield 15 to 20 pounds of carrots. Carrot size is a big variable, because a fully mature Chantenay carrot will be three times bigger and heavier than a Nantes type. Flavor matters, too. Sometimes a sowing of carrots will turn out so pretty and delicious that you wonder why you didn't plant more.

HOW TO
Grow Carrots

When: Begin sowing spring carrots about 2 weeks before your last frost date, and make a second sowing 2 weeks later. In cool climates, you can continue planting every 3 weeks until midsummer — keep records to find your best planting dates. Sow fall and winter carrots 10 to 12 weeks before your first fall frost. Carrots are a good choice to plant after spring peas, or following a summer crop of buckwheat.

- -

Where: The best carrots are grown in sandy loam soil or in raised beds enriched with plenty of organic matter. My soil is enriched clay, and I am prone to spend a ridiculous amount of time digging through the bed to mix in compost and pick out rocks. I also mix in a balanced organic fertilizer, because carrots need an array of nutrients, but using composted manures can cause them to become forked and misshapen. It's important to do everything you can to support fast growth, because carrots grow slowly by nature.

- -

Planting: Carrots need constant weeding for 6 weeks or so, or until they claim their space. You can reduce weed competition from day 1 by sowing carrot seeds in shallow furrows and then covering the seeds with weed-free potting soil. Or try seed tapes, which eliminate tedious thinning and give you straight rows that are easy to weed. In spring, you can grow radishes between rows of carrots to suppress weeds and make good use of space. When planting carrots in summer, lay boards between seeded rows to retain moisture and smother weeds.

Keep the soil constantly moist for a week after planting carrot seeds, which are slower to germinate compared to other vegetables. To reduce surface evaporation during the germination period, cover newly seeded soil with a double thickness of row cover or an old sheet, loosely arranged over the seeded bed. With summer-sown carrots, I get the best germination by planting them along a soaker hose.

- -

Maintenance: Carrots must be thinned to at least 2 inches apart, or 4 inches for big Chantenay varieties. You can do this during routine weeding, which is also mandatory with carrots. Feathery, upright carrot leaves allow room for all kinds of weedy invaders, but a patch that is kept weeded will eventually close its canopy to shade out weeds.

- -

Carrot Pests and Diseases

Carrots do sometimes suffer from insect pests, including carrot rust flies and carrot weevils, but the worst problems come from animal pests, including rabbits and deer. Damage from insects and animals can be prevented with row covers held aloft with hoops. Or use fine-mesh wire cages to exclude hungry critters from your carrot planting.

Misshapen carrots can be caused by roots running into obstacles or being bitten off by creatures, by excessive fertilization, or by disfiguring diseases. In warm climates, root knot nematodes cause galls to form on roots. Where nematodes are common, grow carrots after a cover crop of French marigolds, which starves them out. In cooler climates, a naturally occurring soil bacterium, *Agrobacterium tumefasciens*, can cause carrots to be hairy and misshapen. To avoid this problem, grow carrots in compost-enriched soil far from grapes and nut or fruit trees, which often host this parasitic bacterium.

For best flavor, wait until carrots push up out of the ground to harvest them.

Carrots

When: Do not be in a rush to harvest carrots, which always taste best when fully mature. As carrots mature, the foliage often turns a darker shade of green, and the roots begin to push up out of the soil. Hill up soil or mulch over the shoulders of maturing carrots to keep them from turning green.

Pull or dig your summer crop when roots reach mature size, start pushing up out of the soil, and show rich color and full flavor. Taste improves as carrots mature, but do not leave mature carrots in warm soil any longer than necessary lest they be damaged by critters. Before pulling carrots, use a digging fork to loosen the soil just outside the row.

Summer-sown carrots that mature in cool fall soil can be left in the ground longer, but they should be dug before the ground freezes to preserve their quality. You can experiment with overwintering young carrots sown in late summer, but harsh winter weather or hungry animals may do them in.

- -

How: Rinse harvested carrots with cool water, or swish them in a bucket of cold water to remove clods of soil. Use a sharp knife to cut off the carrot tops, which will prevent moisture loss. Pat the carrots dry with clean towels and store in plastic bags in the refrigerator or a cold root cellar. Wait until just before using your carrots to give them a good scrub.

- -

Food preservation: Carrots will store for months in the refrigerator or in very cold storage in a root cellar or unheated basement. As long as temperatures are kept constantly cool, ideally around 40°F (4°C), carrots packed in damp sand or sawdust will keep for 3 months or more.

Use your refrigerated or cold-stored carrots as needed to add color to pickles and frozen vegetable mixtures, but mostly enjoy eating them raw. Should a planting have issues from root-tunneling insects that render the roots unworthy of long-term refrigeration, cut the good parts into sticks or slices, blanch until barely done, and either freeze or dry the pieces.

Trimmed carrots packed in damp, weathered sawdust will store for weeks at cool temperatures around 40°F (4°C).

CORN

(Zea mays)

HOW MUCH
50 row feet per person

STELLAR VARIETIES
'Luscious', 'Ambrosia', and 'Bodacious'

BEST WAYS TO PRESERVE
Freeze, can, or dry

One of the top taste treats of summer, sweet corn belongs in every garden large enough to grow it. A block of two parallel rows at least 15 feet long is needed, because the best pollination occurs when the pollen (released by tassels at the tops of the plants) drifts to the silks that emerge from the tips of the ears. In small plantings of fewer than 30 plants, you must hand-pollinate corn by sprinkling pinches of pollen onto the silks. Growing sweet corn requires warm soil (above 65°F/18°C), so early summer is prime planting time.

Plant corn in blocks rather than rows so that all of the silks will be showered with pollen, which results in more uniform, well-filled ears.

Best Corn

Homegrown Pantry

Corn genetics can be quite confusing, but one type of sweet corn has what is called the "sugary enhanced" gene, often abbreviated as *se* in seed catalogs. Various *se* varieties are consistent winners in field trials and in gardens, and you can find varieties with yellow, white, or bicolored kernels. Unlike older types of sweet corn, varieties with the sugary enhanced gene stay sweet for more than 1 week (giving you more time to harvest and process the crop) and feature tender texture combined with rich corn flavor.

All *se* sweet corn varieties are hybrids, but many are available as certified organic seeds. When choosing varieties to grow as freezer crops, you will get top productivity from midseason varieties, which mature about 75 to 85 days after planting. Midseason sweet corn varieties develop larger ears than early varieties, so harvesting and processing goes a little faster. Excellent varieties include 'Luscious' and 'Ambrosia' (bicolors) and 'Bodacious' (yellow).

> **Midseason sweet corn varieties develop larger ears than early varieties, so harvesting and processing goes a little faster.**

HOW MUCH TO PLANT?

The simple answer is "as much as you can grow," but that might not leave much room in your garden for anything else. If you have plenty of space and want to preserve a year's supply, plant about 50 row feet (about 60 ears of sweet corn) for each household member.

HOW TO
Grow Corn

When: In late spring or early summer, sow seeds in warm, fertile, and well-worked soil that contains plenty of nitrogen.

- -

Planting: Corn requires more nitrogen than other vegetable crops, so plan ahead for this need. To stock the soil with nitrogen, thoroughly mix in a 1-inch layer of fresh grass clippings; composted chicken manure or other well-rotted manure; and alfalfa meal, soybean meal, or another high-nitrogen organic fertilizer (follow label directions). Sweet corn seed must germinate rapidly or it will rot. For best germination, soak seeds in clean water overnight before sowing in warm soil. Many gardeners sow their early sweet corn when apple trees are in full bloom.

Sow seeds 1 inch deep and 4 inches apart, in blocks of two or more rows spaced about 24 inches apart. Two weeks after planting, thin plants to at least 12 inches apart.

- -

Watering: For the first 6 weeks, sweet corn needs only an average supply of water, but things change when the plants reach their reproductive stage. Starting when the tassels emerge and continuing until the crop is ripe, sweet corn needs at least 1 inch of water per week, or 1½ inches per week in very hot weather. Soaker hoses or drip irrigation lines are the easiest and most efficient ways to water sweet corn.

Maintenance: Use a sharp hoe to keep weeds under control. When the plants are knee-high, top-dress the planting with a balanced organic fertilizer scratched into the soil's surface. Fertilize again when the tassels emerge, using a high-nitrogen organic fertilizer in granular or liquid form.

If plants are blown over by gusty summer thunderstorms, give them a few sunny days to right themselves. It won't hurt nearly mature plants to grow crooked, but you may need to prop up young plants that don't get back up by themselves. To prevent this problem, called "lodging," hill up soil over the base of the plants as you hoe out weeds.

Hand Pollination

When the tassels emerge from the top of a sweet corn plant, the pollination process has begun. Pollen grains shed by the tassels fall on sticky strands of silk, and if all goes well, lines of perfect corn kernels are born. Excellent pollination produces ears that are filled with wall-to-wall kernels; poor pollination leads to ears with lots of missing kernels. To ensure big, well-filled ears in a garden planting of sweet corn, hand-pollinate your sweet corn by clipping off pieces of pollen-bearing tassel and tapping them over the silks to release small clouds of pollen. This maneuver is especially useful with plants on the ends of the rows, which may not receive as much pollen as those in the middle of a planting. Hand-pollinate in the late morning, when corn pollen is in prime condition. If you hand-pollinate your corn daily for 3 or 4 days, you can be sure of getting plenty of large, well-filled ears.

In small plantings, you can hand-pollinate corn by tapping pollen-filled tassels over silks where they emerge from the tips of the ears.

HARVESTING AND STORING
Corn

When: Once an ear feels hard and full when you squeeze it, and the silks at the end have dried to a dark brown or black color, pull back the shuck near the tip and examine the kernels. The kernels on ripe ears are plump and tightly packed together, with a glossy sheen. Taste and texture change as ears ripen, too. Ears that are not quite ready taste sweet but lack good corn flavor, while overripe ears have tough, wrinkled kernels that taste starchy.

- -

How: Refrigerate the ears immediately or put them in a cooler kept chilled with frozen water bottles. Process within 24 hours.

Corn Pests and Diseases

Raccoons and birds. Raccoons closely monitor sweet corn's progress and stage nighttime raids just as it reaches perfection. To protect nearly ripe ears, tape the ears to the stalk with packing tape. In areas with severe raccoon pressure, you will need at least two strands of electric fencing to protect your corn, installed 4 and 8 inches from the ground. To keep birds from ruining the tips of almost-ripe ears of corn, cover them with paper bags held in place with clothespins or rubber bands.

Corn smut. A fungal disease called corn smut causes kernels to become large and distorted, so they look like monstrous blobs. Although ugly, smutty kernels taste like mushrooms when cooked and are considered a delicacy in some parts of the world. Still, it's a good idea to remove smutty ears from your garden to limit the spread of fungal spores.

The kernels on ripe ears of sweet corn have a glossy sheen and a rounded shape, and the corn tastes good when sampled raw.

Corn

Freezing makes it possible to enjoy sweet corn that tastes summer-fresh at any time of year. Sweet corn also can be canned in a pressure canner, but long processing times (almost an hour for pints) can create a product that seems overcooked compared to the frozen version. In addition to freezing, you can dry a batch of kernels to include in soups or slow-cooked meals. For some families, summer would not be complete without a batch of colorful corn relish hot from the canner.

Freezing Sweet Corn

Choose freezing methods for your sweet corn based in part on how much freezer space is available. Corn off the cob takes up less than one-fifth of the space required for whole ears, which can quickly fill up a shelf. After hearing good reports from gardeners who freeze their corn in the shucks I had to try it, but it's a shortcut I will never take again. The thawed corn had a mealy texture and flat flavor. Lesson learned! When you want to freeze whole ears, take the time to shuck, clean, and blanch them first. Thaw ears for at least 1 hour, then handle them as if they were fresh-picked ears.

Freeze most of your corn off the cob. Cutting the kernels from raw ears naturally creates creamed corn when milky juice and kernels cook together. If you cook the ears before cutting off the kernels, they will resemble whole-kernel corn sold in cans. The choice comes down to personal preference, but I find that the creamier style is a fast and easy way to get corn into the freezer, and it always gives great results. Use a sharp serrated knife to cut the kernels from raw ears, and then use a spoon to scrape the remaining milky juice off the cobs. Bring the mixture to a simmer, then allow to cool and freeze.

> Cutting the kernels from raw ears naturally creates creamed corn when milky juice and kernels cook together.

A Bundt pan becomes food processing equipment when you use it to hold ears of corn as you cut off the kernels.

Canning Sweet Corn

Corn is a very low-acid vegetable, with a pH range of 6.0 to 6.8. A pressure canner is therefore necessary to can sweet corn on its own. The base processing time for pints is 55 minutes; processing in quarts takes so long that the corn becomes overcooked.

A strong pickling brine (made of 2 cups vinegar, ⅔ cup sugar, and 1 tablespoon salt), with no water added, will lower the pH of sweet corn to acceptable levels for processing in a water-bath or steam canner. A small batch of sweet corn relish is a great way to use odds and ends of ripe red peppers, and small jars are a rare treat when added to springtime salads. Adding a small amount of turmeric to the pickling brine helps to lift the color in corn relishes.

Drying Sweet Corn

If you are drying some of your corn — a smart strategy in the event of freezer failure — you should pre-cook ears to obtain whole-kernel corn. Corn used as animal feed is dried on the cob, but not sweet corn. With sweet corn it is best to boil or steam ears until just done, and then cut off the whole kernels and dry them. The small kernels can scorch because they hold so much sugar, so keep the temperature moderate. Store your dried corn in the freezer or in vacuum-sealed bags in a cool, dry place. Dehydrated sweet corn is wonderful in soups and stews that cook for more than 1 hour.

Sunday Dinner Creamed Corn

When you have 20 or so ears of corn to get into the freezer, this recipe is a great time-saver. The corn steams in a little butter and its own milk, and kernels around the edges roast to brown. The delicious results are ready to eat when thawed and heated.

Makes 4 to 5 pints

20 ears sweet corn

1 teaspoon salt

3 tablespoons butter, cut into small pieces

1 Use a sharp serrated knife to cut the kernels from the raw ears. Then use a spoon to press out the juice and remaining bits of corn.

2 Place the corn in a very large ovenproof pan and sprinkle with the salt. Dot with the butter, and cover loosely with aluminum foil.

3 Bake at 350°F (180°C) for about 40 minutes, until the corn is hot and bubbly and your house smells like roasting corn. Cool, pack into freezer-safe containers, and freeze.

'County Fair'
pickling

'Marketmore'
slicing

CUCUMBERS

(Cucumis sativus)

HOW MUCH
8 plants

- -

STELLAR VARIETIES
'Little Leaf', 'County Fair', and 'Marketmore'

- -

BEST WAY TO PRESERVE
Pickle

The cool crunch of fresh cucumbers has made them summer staples for more than 3,000 years, and cucumbers were probably the first vegetable to be preserved using salt fermentation to turn them into pickles. Pickling is still the best way to preserve cucumbers, and methods range from simple refrigerator pickles to salt-brined beauties accented with garlic. If you are a first-time canner, there is little to go wrong with bread-and-butter pickles, which are preserved in a spiced brine made from vinegar and sugar.

Productive and fast to mature, cucumbers are easy to grow in fertile, organically enriched soil with a near-neutral pH. Training the vines up a fence or trellis increases the plants' productivity and makes the cucumbers easier to pick. Cucumbers and dill for pickling can be grown together in early summer, the best season to grow cucumbers.

You can make sliced or chopped pickles and condiments using productive slicing cucumbers, but small-fruited pickling varieties are best for fermenting or canning whole.

Best Cucumbers
FOR THE
Homegrown Pantry

The size and shape of cucumbers vary with variety, and the best ones for pickling are small pickling cucumbers. These specialized varieties have a low peeling-to-flesh ratio, so they hold up better to canning, and they are the only cucumbers you can use to make salt-fermented pickles. Pickling cucumbers produce all at once, over a 2-week period, and must be picked daily. They are fine for eating fresh, too.

That said, you can make most types of pickles (aside from salt fermented) from American cucumber varieties, which are the dark green, oblong cukes seen in supermarkets. These varieties have been bred for uniformity, productivity, and high levels of disease resistance. As long as they are picked young, American cucumbers make good pickles when sliced, cut into chunks, or finely diced.

Use thin-skinned greenhouse cucumbers only for making refrigerator pickles (see page 112). Thin-skinned greenhouse cukes are meant for eating fresh.

HOW MANY TO PLANT?

Cucumbers are very productive plants, so you won't need many to produce enough cucumbers for several pickling projects — no more than 8 to 10 plants of a disease-resistant pickling variety like 'County Fair' or 'Little Leaf' or a productive all-purpose cucumber like 'Marketmore'. When kept picked, each plant can produce more than a dozen fruits over the 3-week harvest period, so it is easy to grow too many cucumbers. It is the nature of canned cucumber pickles to start going soft after a year, so there is no point in making more pickles than you are likely to eat in 9 months. You may also be pickling other vegetables like asparagus, beets, or green beans — another factor to keep in mind when estimating how many cucumbers to grow for making into pickles.

Even when provided with a trellis, cucumber vines need plenty of sunny space to ramble.

HOW TO
Grow Cucumbers

When: Sow seeds directly into prepared rows or hills 1 to 2 weeks after your last spring frost has passed, and make a second planting a month later. Or start seeds indoors under bright fluorescent lights 2 weeks before your last spring frost date, and set out the seedlings when they are 3 to 4 weeks old, during a period of warm weather.

- -

Where: Choose a sunny site with fertile, well-drained soil. Cucumbers can be grown in rows or in hills spaced 6 feet apart, and you can double yields per square foot by training cucumber vines up a low trellis.

Planting: Mix a 2-inch layer of rich compost into the planting site, along with a light application of a balanced organic fertilizer. Plant seeds ½ inch deep and 6 inches apart. When the seedlings have three leaves, thin them to 12 inches apart, which is also the proper spacing for transplanted seedlings.

Use a trellis to increase the leaf-to-fruit ratio of your cucumbers, which will increase yields of flawless, flavorful fruits. Any trellis that offers several tiers of horizontal support will work, from string trellises to wire tomato cages. Trellising small-fruited pickling cucumbers also makes them easier to pick.

Cucumber Pests and Diseases

To protect plants from all types of pests while providing warm growing conditions, grow cucumbers under row cover tunnels until they begin blooming heavily and need to be visited by pollinating insects.

Bacterial wilt. A common disease of garden cucumbers, bacterial wilt is spread from plant to plant by cucumber beetles. Initially a single stem wilts, followed by another, and within a week infected plants are barely alive. If bacterial wilt is common in your area, grow resistant varieties like 'County Fair' or 'Little Leaf' pickling cucumbers, or protect plants with row covers until they start blooming.

Cucumber beetles. Two species of yellow-and-black, ¼-inch-long beetles often visit cucumber plants. Striped cucumber beetles have black stripes down their backs, while spotted cucumber beetles are yellow with black spots. Both species can be monitored and/or controlled using yellow sticky-cup traps, which are yellow cups stapled to wood stakes that are covered with a sticky substance like Tangle-Trap. Nearby plantings of borage may help suppress cucumber beetle populations by attracting big bumblebees to the area.

Powdery mildew. This fungal disease often infects old cucumber plants, though many varieties offer some genetic resistance. Powdery mildew turns cucumber leaves dull gray, and the plants stop growing. Pull up and compost badly infected plants.

When preparing cukes for fermentation, scrub gently on the blossom end, which old-timers believe is the "activator" spot that contains important starter bacteria for effective fermentation.

HARVESTING AND STORING
Cucumbers

When: Cucumber plants self-regulate how many fruits they will carry at a time. Even if you see dozens of female blossoms being worked by bees, only a few of them will develop into cucumbers. To maximize production, promptly harvest fruits as soon as they reach picking size. Pick daily, because cucumbers can get big fast after warm rains.

How: Lightly scrub, pat dry, and refrigerate harvested cucumbers right away. When preparing cukes for fermentation, scrub gently on the blossom end, which old-timers believe is the "activator" spot that contains important starter bacteria for effective fermentation. When you have saved up enough cucumbers, make a batch of pickles.

Cucumber
FOOD PRESERVATION OPTIONS

Cucumbers and pickles are such closely related subjects that some gardeners talk of growing pickles. But then, cucumbers are better at picking up secondary flavors than other vegetables, and truly great pickles deliver a balanced yet complicated taste package. Here are the three main ways to turn cucumbers into addictively delicious pickles.

Refrigerator or freezer pickles. Making a few batches of these easy pickles will teach you so much about basic pickling that you will be ready to move up to canned pickles next time you have a bumper crop. Then again, after trying the recipes below, you may be so happy with your freezer pickles that they become family favorites.

Vinegar-brined pickles preserved in a water-bath or steam canner are fun and easy to make, and strong vinegar brines make the risk of spoilage in properly sealed jars almost nonexistent. Even first-time pickle makers can expect success with bread-and-butter pickles, which use both vinegar and sugar to preserve the cucumbers. Just don't get too carried away and make too many, because canned pickles often start softening after a year.

Salt-fermented dill pickles are fascinating to make and delicious to eat, but you must have flawless cucumbers of uniform size to make them. Kinked or oddly shaped cucumbers are fine for pickles that are cut into pieces, but with fermented ones you want only the best. Follow the step-by-step instructions for fermenting vegetables given on pages 40–41 when fermenting cucumbers. For truly fine-flavored pickles, include a grape leaf in the fermentation container along with plenty of fresh dill flowers or green seed heads and split cloves of garlic.

> **For truly fine-flavored pickles, include a grape leaf in the fermentation container along with plenty of fresh dill flowers or green seed heads and split cloves of garlic.**

Saving Cucumber Seeds

To save seeds from open-pollinated varieties, allow perfect fruits to ripen until they become large and develop leathery yellow or brown rinds. Slice away the rinds without cutting into the seeds, and use your fingers or the tip of a knife to remove the largest, plumpest seeds. Allow to dry at room temperature for 1 to 2 weeks before storing the seeds in a cool, dry place. Many gardening sources recommend fermenting cucumber seeds, but this step is not needed when you work with fully mature seeds. When given good storage conditions, cucumber seeds usually stay viable for 5 years or more.

Refrigerator and Freezer Pickles

Refrigerator Pickles

Making refrigerator pickles is a simple matter of mixing up a brine and pouring it over cut cucumbers. These pickles are ready to enjoy starting the day after they are made, and they will keep in the refrigerator for a month. Don't worry if the liquid does not quite cover the cucumbers at first. Overnight, the cut pieces will release juices that will raise the level of the brine.

For sweet refrigerator pickles, make a brine of 1 cup vinegar, ¼ cup water, ½ cup sugar, and 1 teaspoon salt. Heat the mixture just enough to dissolve the sugar. Pour over 2 cups cut cucumbers, or a mixture of cucumbers and thinly sliced onions. If desired, add a light sprinkling of mustard seeds or red pepper flakes. Makes 1 pint.

For dill refrigerator pickles, make a brine of 1 cup vinegar, ¼ cup water, ¼ cup sugar, and 1 teaspoon salt. Heat the mixture just enough for the sugar to dissolve. Pour over 2 cups cut cucumbers, and add 1 teaspoon dill seeds or several dill leaves or flower heads, along with 2 cloves peeled garlic. Makes 1 pint.

Freezer Pickles

Freezer pickles have more pickle flavor compared to refrigerator pickles, and you can eat them for months after they are made. You must pre-salt the cut cucumbers, but you can experiment freely with flavor accents such as herbs, horseradish, or celery seeds. Sliced onions or peppers also can be added as long as they are included in the pre-salting procedure to enhance their texture.

Cut clean cucumbers into uniform pieces and place them in a large bowl. Sprinkle with 2 tablespoons salt. Top with six or so ice cubes, and cover with a cloth. After a minimum of 3 hours, or a maximum of 10, drain the cucumbers in a colander and rinse very well with cold water to remove excess salt. Allow to drain while you make the brine.

For sweet freezer pickles, make a brine of 1 cup vinegar, 1 cup sugar, and ¼ cup water. Heat the mixture just enough to dissolve the sugar. Cool before pouring over 2 cups rinsed and drained cucumbers. If desired, add a light sprinkling of mustard seeds, celery seeds, or red pepper flakes. Pack into freezer containers. Freeze at least a week, and thaw overnight in the refrigerator before serving. Makes 1 pint.

For dill freezer pickles, make a brine of 1 cup vinegar, ¼ cup sugar, and ¼ cup water. Heat the mixture just enough to dissolve the sugar. Pour over 2 cups rinsed and drained cucumbers, and add 1 teaspoon dill seeds or several dill leaves or flower heads, along with 2 cloves peeled garlic and a light sprinkling of red pepper flakes. Pack into freezer containers. Freeze at least a week, and thaw overnight in the refrigerator before serving. Makes 1 pint.

GARLIC

(Allium sativum, A. ampeloprasum)

HOW MUCH
30 to 50 plants per person

- -

STELLAR VARIETIES
'Music', 'German Red', and 'Inchelium Red'

- -

BEST WAYS TO PRESERVE
Place in cool storage, dry, or pickle

Garlic is the first vegetable in which many gardeners become self-sufficient. There is plenty of time and space available for planting big cloves in the fall, the best season for planting, and few crops are as easy to store. When properly grown and cured, garlic bulbs kept in a cool, dry room will easily store for months, with some types willing to stay dormant until spring.

Gardeners can grow a different and much more varied assortment of varieties than what is available in stores, which makes growing your own garlic even more rewarding. Fresh garlic is a culinary treat, too, because of the complex flavors and apple-crisp texture found in a newly harvested crop. Once you get started with garlic, it is easy to keep your favorite strains going by planting cloves from your best bulbs in the fall. When planted in prepared beds in October, every garlic clove you plant will grow into a beautiful bulb the following summer.

Best Garlic
FOR THE
Homegrown Pantry

One of the best ways to get started with garlic is to try varieties sold at local farmers' markets. Garlic for eating and seed garlic are the same, though garlic bulbs sold for planting are usually bigger. Here are the three major types.

Softneck garlic (*Allium sativum* var. *sativum*) is the type of garlic sold in stores. The bulbs are comprised of elongated cloves, smaller in the center, with mild to moderately spicy flavor. The softneck types grow best where winters are mild, though some tolerate cold to Zone 5. These varieties do well in warm climates, and they are great for braiding. Many softnecks will keep for 8 months or more under cool, dry conditions.

Hardneck garlic (*A. sativum* var. *ophioscorodon*) are so named because their symmetrical cloves form a circle around a hard central stalk. These gourmet-quality varieties often have complex, spicy-sweet flavors, and in addition to bulbs they produce edible scapes. Storage time ranges from 3 to 8 months.

Elephant garlic (*A. ampeloprasum* var. *ampeloprasum*) is actually not a true garlic and is closely related to leeks. It produces baseball-size bulbs with four to six big cloves. Elephant garlic is hardy to Zone 5 if given deep winter mulch, but it is most commonly grown in Zones 7 and 8, where it sometimes forms wild patches. The large, upright plants with strappy leaves need wide, 12-inch spacing.

softneck garlic

hardneck garlic

elephant garlic

HOW MUCH TO PLANT?

Depending on how much cooking you do, estimate 30 to 50 plants per person for a year's supply. This includes ample seed garlic for planting in the fall.

HOW TO
Grow Garlic

When: In fall, plant cloves in well-drained beds after the first frost has passed and the soil is cool. Cloves can also be planted in late winter as soon as the soil thaws, but fall-planted garlic produces bigger, better bulbs.

- -

Where: Choose a sunny site, and loosen the planting bed to at least 12 inches deep. Thoroughly mix in a 1-inch layer of mature compost. In acidic soil, also mix in a light dusting of wood ashes. Garlic roots are concentrated in the area just below the bulbs, so it's a good practice to lay down a balanced organic fertilizer in a band at the bottom of V-shaped planting trenches. This technique places fertilizer exactly where it needs to be for this crop.

Planting: Wait until just before planting to break bulbs into cloves, and do not remove the peeling — it protects the clove until it turns into a plant. Poke the cloves into the ground 4 inches deep and 6 to 8 inches apart, with their pointed ends up. Cover the planted area with 3 to 5 inches of organic mulch, such as shredded leaves.

Where winters are cold, expect to see a few green shoots in fall, which will likely be nipped back by frigid weather. Don't worry — in spring, new shoots will push up through the mulch. In milder climates, garlic often stays green through winter, but it makes little growth when days are short and cool.

Garlic Pests and Diseases

Onion root maggots. Garlic plants that stop making new growth and unexpectedly turn yellow may have been hit by onion root maggots — tiny beige worms (fly larvae) that eat garlic roots and cloves. To reduce the likelihood of these maggots, plant your garlic in soil that has not been planted with onion family crops in the past 2 years. If you often see this pest, dust the area around plants with diatomaceous earth in late spring, which is when the egg-laying females are most active.

Onion thrips. These tiny black elongated insects rasp pale grooves in garlic leaves, but they have many natural predators. Keep areas near garlic and onions mowed to reduce the weedy habitat thrips prefer. Monitor populations with sticky traps, and use a spinosad-based biological pesticide to control serious infestations.

Root rot diseases. When they are hit with a root rot disease, garlic plants usually turn yellow before they wilt and die. Prevent fusarium and other soilborne root rot diseases by growing garlic in well-drained, fertile soil and rotating the planting space with nonrelated crops. Avoid injuring the roots when weeding, because diseases often enter plants through broken root tissues.

HARVESTING AND STORING
Garlic

When: Onions can sometimes be left to die back on their own, but not garlic. If you harvest garlic when it is still half green and then slowly cure it for several weeks, the bulbs will dry nice and tight, with plenty of papery outer scales to protect the cloves from spoiling. Here are three ways to tell when garlic is ready to harvest:

- Bulbs will be ready to dig about 20 days after most scapes are cut from hardneck varieties, give or take a few days for weather variables.

- When the three lowest leaves turn yellow and tan, but the three highest leaves are still green, it's garlic-harvesting time.

LEFT: Garlic is ready to dig when the plants begin to wither but are still more than half green.

RIGHT: Use a digging fork to loosen soil from the outside of the row before pulling garlic in early to midsummer.

- When 30 percent of the total foliar mass — lower, middle, and upper leaves — appear to be withering or show brown tips, this change indicates that the plants have cut back on the nutrients and moisture supplied to the leaves.

How: Use a digging fork to loosen the soil around and beneath the bulbs before pulling them, and take care to avoid bumps and bruises. It is ideal to be able to harvest garlic when the soil is dry, because you can easily shake off loose soil as you harvest the bulbs. But in very rainy years, you may be forced to pull your crop from mud. In this situation, the best way to remove excess soil from the harvested bulbs is to swish them vigorously in a bucket of water. Immediately move the rinsed bulbs to a warm, well-ventilated place where they can drip-dry.

CURING
Garlic

The curing process begins when you lay or hang the plants in a warm, dry place, with all of their leaves attached, for at least a week. During this time the plants will be quite aromatic. If you live in a dry climate, the garlic can be allowed to cure intact, but where humid conditions prevail, it is best to trim off all but about 6 inches of stem, lightly rub off excess soil from bulbs and twist soil from roots, and return the curing garlic to its drying place. Do not remove the papery outer wrappers, as these inhibit sprouting and protect the cloves from fungal invaders. Let the bulbs dry for at least 2 more weeks, and then trim off the remaining stem and roots. This is a good time to set aside the largest, most perfect bulbs as your planting stock for the next year's crop.

Commercial garlic is kept at 32°F (0°C) to preserve its shelf life, but cool room temperatures work better for most gardeners. In fact, room-temperature storage works better than refrigerated storage for garlic bulbs, which may break dormancy too soon when kept in the fridge. When kept at 50 to 60°F (10 to 16°C), hardnecks store well for only 4 to 6 months, so use them first. Softneck and elephant garlic store for 8 months or more.

Using Garlic Scapes

In early summer, hardneck varieties produce curled garlic scapes, which are immature flower buds on curling stems. When cut just as they make a full curl, garlic scapes are a delicious early-season vegetable. Removing the scapes also can increase bulb size by as much as 30 percent, because the plants don't waste energy developing flowers.

In cooking, garlic scapes are less assertive than garlic cloves, so they are ideal for dishes where you want only a hint of garlic flavor and aroma. Garlic scapes will keep in a plastic bag in the refrigerator for a month, or you can cut them into small pieces, steam blanch them for 3 minutes, and freeze them in freezer bags. In cooking, 1 tablespoon of chopped frozen garlic scapes is equivalent to 1 medium clove of garlic.

Three weeks after harvest, a collection of cured softneck garlic is ready to trim, clean, and store.

Garlic

FOOD PRESERVATION OPTIONS

Simple cool storage is the best way to store perfect garlic. If you find you have grown too much and need to preserve bulbs for longer than 6 months or so, dry some of your cloves until crisp, and store them in the freezer. Take them out in small batches, and use a dedicated coffee mill to turn them into freshly ground garlic powder.

A few half-pints of pickled garlic are cupboard treasures, and pickling tames garlic's flavors. In lucky years when you have only a few bulbs with serious storage issues that must be preserved, don't bother to seal garlic pickles in a water-bath or steam canner. Instead, let them marinate in the refrigerator for at least 2 weeks, and enjoy them as refrigerator pickles.

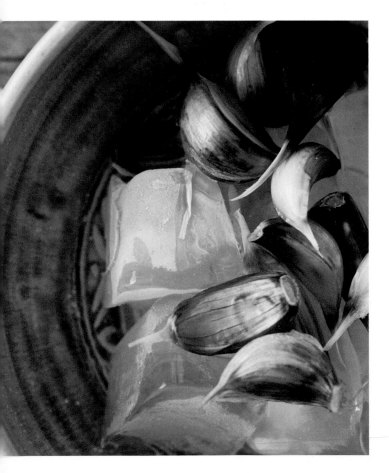

Pickled Garlic with Hot Peppers

Makes 3–4 half-pint jars

- 2 cups white vinegar
- ⅔ cup sugar
- ½ teaspoon mustard seeds
- 3 cups peeled garlic cloves
- 3 hot peppers or hot pepper strips

1 In a medium pot, mix the vinegar and sugar together and slowly bring to a simmer over medium heat. Add the mustard seeds and garlic and keep warm.

2 Place a hot pepper in each hot, clean jar, then fill with garlic and top with brine.

3 Process the jars in a water-bath or steam canner for 10 minutes.

When you need to peel a lot of garlic cloves, plunge them in boiling water for 30 seconds and then cool over ice. Many of the peelings will come away from the cloves by themselves.

KALE AND COLLARDS

(*Brassica oleracea, B. napus*)

HOW MUCH
3 plants per person in spring, 9 plants per person in fall

- -

STELLAR VARIETIES
'Red Russian', Tuscan, and 'Redbor' kale; all collards

- -

BEST WAYS TO PRESERVE
Freeze or dry

Super-nutritious and easy to grow, kale and collards are also phenomenally productive in the garden. The naturally healthy plants
resist pests and diseases better than closely related cabbage or broccoli, and because their leaves are so large and substantial, kale and
collards are the best greens to grow for freezing. Dried kale is also
tasty and useful in the kitchen, especially when you want to add a
bit of green to an almost-finished dish.

Best Kale and Collards

FOR THE

Homegrown Pantry

Kale and collards are so closely related that they can be handled as one pantry crop.

Tuscan kale, sometimes called Lacinato or dinosaur kale, has narrow, dark green leaves with a waffled texture. It is a little slower to grow than other varieties.

Curly kales look stunning in the garden, but they grow much better in fall than spring. Plantings that mature in the weeks following the first fall frost are outstanding for fresh eating and freezing.

Flat-leafed Russian kale comes in red- and white-stemmed versions, and the cold-hardy plants are fast growers with a high productive potential.

Collards can be grown in both spring and fall, with fall being the best season for freezer crops of gourmet 'Vates' or 'Champion' collards. Seedlings set out in late summer are unstoppable and rival Russian kale in terms of taste and productivity. Excellent when blanched and frozen, collards deserve wider use in gardens.

HOW MUCH TO PLANT?

Collards and kale need cool weather to grow well, so in most climates you will split your planting plans into spring and fall, using fall for your freezer crop. In spring, allow three plants per person of collards or kale for eating fresh, but triple that amount for collards or kale being grown in the fall. Each vigorous plant will produce about ½ pound per week for up to 6 weeks.

HOW TO
Grow Kale & Collards

When: In spring, start kale seeds indoors about 10 weeks before your last frost date, and set them out under tunnels or cloches when they are 5 to 6 weeks old. Start fall plants in mid- to late summer by direct-sowing seeds or starting them in containers in a protected spot.

- -

Where: Kale and collards require an abundance of nutrients, so plant them in soil that has been amended with compost and a balanced organic fertilizer.

- -

Planting: Grow young plants beneath row cover tunnels to protect them from pests and bad weather. Beautiful leaves will be ready to pick in a few weeks, but wait until after frost has sweetened the leaves to harvest kale and collards for the freezer.

- -

Maintenance: Keep the soil constantly moist, and use a biodegradable mulch to limit weeds and help keep the leaves clean.

Pests and Diseases of Kale and Collards

Cabbageworms and loopers. Kale and collards are often visited by leaf-eating cabbageworms and cabbage loopers, though the insects prefer to munch on cabbage and broccoli. Should you have so many little caterpillars on curly kale varieties that you can't hand-pick them, one treatment with a Bt or spinosad-based organic insecticide will bring them under control.

- -

Cabbage aphids. These insects are a more vexing problem because they appear in late fall, after most natural predators have retired for the season. Clusters of the gray-green sucking insects may appear on tufts of new growth. Pinch them off as soon as you see them, or give up the fight and compost the plants.

HARVESTING AND STORING
Kale & Collards

When: Starting when plants have more than seven leaves, harvest the large, older leaves from each plant when they are bigger than your hand.

How: Rinse clean in cold water, pat dry, and store in plastic bags in the refrigerator. Cook or process within 3 days.

Kale & Collards
FOOD PRESERVATION OPTIONS

You can pressure can low-acid kale and collards, but they require long processing times, which will turn them to mush. Likewise, kale fermented by itself is less appetizing than a mixed ferment that includes crunchy cabbage and carrots. When it comes to preserving collards and kale, freezing and drying are the best options.

Freezing Kale and Collards

Freezing is the best way to put by a lot of kale and collards in ready-to-use form for casseroles, soups, or eating as cooked greens. Wash the greens and cut off the thick sections of stem at the base of the leaves.

For most vegetables I like steam blanching, but with collards and kale, using boiling water is better because it removes bitter compounds from the leaves.

After blanching these greens in boiling water for 5 minutes, cool them on ice. When the blanched greens are cool enough to handle, stack three leaves together and roll them up like a cigar. Using a sharp knife, cut the roll into ½-inch slices, and then go back and cut the slices in half. Pack the greens into freezer containers, squeezing out as much air as possible. If you want small containers of frozen greens for omelets or smoothies, you can freeze the cooled greens in silicone muffin pans and move them to a freezer-safe container when they are frozen hard.

In addition to freezing chopped kale and collards, blanch and freeze a package or two of whole leaves to stuff and serve like cabbage rolls. The blanched, cooled leaves can be frozen flat, or stacked together and rolled into a newspaper-like roll and frozen as a bundle.

Kale that has been blanched and cooled can be cut into strips before it is frozen.

Drying Kale

Kale leaves can be dried plain, with no seasoning, but you can transform kale flakes into nicely flavored kale chips by tossing them with a very light coating of an oil-based dressing just before drying them (see the recipe at right). Thicker collard leaves are less pleasing and may taste slightly bitter, but flavored kale chips have a polished crispness that makes them fun to eat, and they will store for months.

Tuscan kale chips

Dried Kale Chips

Makes 1 quart dried chips

---

12 cups kale, cut into 2-inch pieces

1 tablespoon olive oil

1 tablespoon balsamic vinegar

1 teaspoon sea salt

---

1 Rinse the kale leaves well and remove the thick middle vein with the tip of a sharp knife.

2 Dry the trimmed leaves on clean kitchen towels, then cut them into pieces about 2 inches square.

3 Mix the oil, vinegar, and salt together in a large bowl, and toss with the kale leaves until they are coated.

4 Dry until crisp in a dehydrator, and store in airtight containers. You also can dry kale in a 250°F (120°C) oven, but the chips will not store well because of uneven drying. Still, they are delicious!

Best Greens

FOR

Cooking

Every gardener wants to grow greens, and every gardener should probably eat more of them. Salad greens like lettuce and arugula that are eaten raw must be included in every veggie gardening plan, but in small amounts as fits their come-and-go natures. Cooking greens are different, because having a supply of frozen and dried greens means you can make anything from spinach-stuffed pasta to a cheesy chard casserole in record time.

When planted at auspicious times, kale, collards, spinach, and Swiss chard will fill the growing season with the best greens you can eat (commercial growers often use systemic pesticides). I suggest starting in spring with kale and spinach, and growing chard through the summer. Then stock the garden with collards, turnips, and more kale for harvesting in fall, and plant more spinach for growing through winter under a protected frame. Turnips are grown as much for their storable roots as their greens, so they are covered in detail on page 227, but I wanted to include their nutrition information in this chart.

HIGH-NUTRITION GREENS

Cooked greens provide a range of nutrients that make eating some kind of greens every day a very good idea.

ONE SERVING, FROZEN	VITAMIN A (% RDA)	VITAMIN C	CALCIUM	IRON
Chard	214%	53%	10%	22%
Collards	308%	58%	27%	12%
Kale	382%	55%	18%	7%
Spinach	531%	8%	34%	24%
Turnip greens	353%	122%	32%	26%

KOHLRABI

(*Brassica oleracea* var. *gongylodes*)

HOW MUCH
5 row feet per person in spring, plus another 5 row feet per person in fall

- -

STELLAR VARIETIES
'Korridor', 'Kolibri', and 'Kossak'

- -

BEST WAYS TO PRESERVE
Freeze, dry, or ferment

One of the newest members of the cabbage family, kohlrabi was bred in Germany in the 1500s. Instead of growing a head like cabbage, broccoli, and cauliflower, closely related kohlrabi develops a rounded "bulb" in its stem, just above the soil line. With a crisp texture and sweet yet savory flavor, some people refer to kohlrabi as a vegetable apple. Growing kohlrabi is easy as long as you use the best planting dates for your climate. If you really love kohlrabi, you can grow spring and fall crops of fast-maturing kohlrabi varieties, and end the season with a few storage-type kohlrabi, which grow unusually large.

Kohlrabi is, in my opinion, one of the finest delicacies in the garden, worthy of planting two or three times each season. In the garden, kohlrabi sports a trim, upright growing habit that makes good use of space.

Kohlrabi is wonderful eaten fresh, but it also freezes well and can be dried if freezer space is tight. Kohlrabi's crisp texture is also welcome in fall vegetable ferments when mixed with cabbage, carrots, and radishes.

Best Kohlrabi
FOR THE
Homegrown Pantry

Kohlrabi varieties vary in growth rate and color. The days-to-maturity ratings on seed packets are early rather than average. Be patient and allow at least 60 days for kohlrabi to grow to perfect size; slow-maturing storage varieties need an additional month of growing time.

- **Green kohlrabi** varieties like 'Korridor' and 'Winner' are fast growers that thrive in a wide range of climates. You can plant green and purple kohlrabi together to create a beautiful bed.

- **Purple kohlrabi** varieties such as 'Kolibri' and 'Purple Vienna' are even easier to grow than green kohlrabi, because cabbageworms and other insects avoid the purple leaves.

- **Storage kohlrabi** varieties include 'Kossak' and 'Superschmelz'. When given wide spacing and regular water, these varieties produce very large bulbs to 10 inches across that will store for weeks in a refrigerator or cold root cellar.

HOW MUCH TO PLANT?

Plant 5 row feet per person in spring, and the same amount of a storage variety to be harvested in late fall. Fifteen row feet will yield about 10 pounds of kohlrabi.

HOW TO
Grow Kohlrabi

When: For your first spring sowing of kohlrabi, start seeds indoors about 6 weeks before your last spring frost date. Kohlrabi is not as cold-tolerant as other cabbage family crops, so wait until 2 weeks before your last frost date to set out seedlings. If you prefer to direct-sow kohlrabi, plant seeds around your last frost date.

Start seeds of storage varieties in midsummer, at about the same time you would sow broccoli or cabbage for fall harvest. This is usually about 90 days before your average first fall frost date.

Planting: Kohlrabi plants are heavy feeders that demand moist, fertile soil with a pH between 6.0 and 7.5. Micronutrients are important, so take the time to amend the soil with compost and a standard application of a balanced organic fertilizer before planting. Harden off the seedlings before setting them out, and cover them with row cover or tulle tunnels to exclude insect pests. Thin or transplant seedlings to 8 inches apart, but allow more space when growing vigorous storage varieties.

Maintenance: When growing kohlrabi in spring, use a row cover tunnel to protect the plants from cold winds and insects. Should the little plants refuse to grow even after the soil warms up in spring, drench them with a high-nitrogen liquid fertilizer.

Kohlrabi Pests and Diseases

Occasional cabbageworms may need plucking from your kohlrabi plants, though they much prefer cabbage and broccoli. Drying out is a more serious problem when growing kohlrabi, because the plants sit up straight and do not shade surrounding soil. A rich mulch of freshly cut grass clippings or chunky compost is therefore necessary to keep kohlrabi's root zone cool and moist.

HARVESTING AND STORING
Kohlrabi

When: Pull up entire plants when kohlrabi grow to 3 inches in diameter. Some people eat the young leaves taken from the tops of kohlrabi as cooked greens, especially in fall when the leaves tend to be sweet and tender. In summer, kohlrabi leaves taste too sharp for most palates.

How: Clip off roots and leaves, and store the trimmed kohlrabi in the refrigerator. Summer kohlrabi will keep in the refrigerator for several weeks, or you can preserve it. In fall, harvest kohlrabi before your first hard freeze and store the trimmed kohlrabi in a refrigerator or root cellar.

Kohlrabi
FOOD PRESERVATION OPTIONS

One of the great things about kohlrabi is its crisp texture, which you only get in the fresh version. Make it a priority to eat kohlrabi fresh in season, and only turn to preservation methods when you find recipes you love.

Always remove the peeling before eating or preserving kohlrabi. Coarsely grated kohlrabi makes a fabulous slaw, but the most popular way to eat kohlrabi is as oven fries — kohlrabi sticks tossed with salt, pepper, and olive oil, roasted in a hot oven for 20 minutes.

You can blanch and freeze kohlrabi in bite-size pieces, just like broccoli, or include it in mixed packets of frozen vegetables. If you have no freezer space, dry small sticks of kohlrabi that have been blanched and cooled, and use the dehydrated kohlrabi in winter soups and stews.

With the texture of water chestnuts, kohlrabi is a wonderful vegetable to add to fermentation projects. You also can ferment kohlrabi on its own, using the steps given on pages 40–41 for salt fermentation. Kohlrabi that have been peeled and cut into quarters make a great base vegetable for any fermentation project.

If you have no freezer space, dry small sticks of kohlrabi that have been blanched and cooled, and use the dehydrated kohlrabi in winter soups and stews.

'Borettana'
cipollini onion

yellow
potato onion

'Camelot'
red shallot

'Cabernet'
bulb onion

'Bridger'
bulb onion

UNIONS

(*Allium* species)

HOW MUCH
40 bulbs per person

STELLAR VARIETIES
Choose types and varieties that suit your climate

BEST WAYS TO PRESERVE
Place in cool storage, dry, or freeze

Packed with flavor and healthful nutrients, onions are a staple food in kitchens throughout the world. Familiar bulb onions are easy to grow as long as you use varieties adapted to your climate and get into the habit of starting them from seeds — the best way to have plants of regionally adapted varieties to set out at the right time. Smaller shallots can be grown from seed or from mother bulbs, and shallots are the champs of storage onions, often lasting well into spring.

It is tremendously convenient to have a store of cured bulb onions and shallots in the barn or basement, but non-bulbing onions including leeks, multiplying onions, and scallions grown from inexpensive sets can expand your fresh onion choices while easing pressure on your supply of stored onions. Diversity is key to pursuing onion self-sufficiency, so you will find coverage of shallots, leeks, and other alternative onions on page 138.

Best Onions

FOR THE

Homegrown Pantry

The key to growing robust bulb onions is to provide them with a long, stress-free growing season, because the size of the onion bulb depends on the number of green leaves the plant is able to produce. Each ring in an onion bulb is the swollen base of an aboveground leaf, so onion plants that hold plenty of big leaves produce the best and biggest onions. Changes in day length trigger the bulb-forming process, so onion varieties are sorted into four groups based on how they grow in different latitudes.

Short-day onions begin forming bulbs when days become 10 to 12 hours long, or mid- to late spring in the South and Southwest. Plants that are set out in fall and grow all winter have plenty of time to grow big fans of leaves, but spring plantings may be pushed for growing time. Short-day onions that mature before hot weather begins often taste sweet, and many of the sweetest onions are short-day varieties. Most short-day varieties also are juicy and store well for only a few weeks, even when refrigerated. Popular varieties include 'Texas 1015' and 'Granex' hybrids. Short-day onions are adapted from the 35th latitude southward.

Intermediate-day onions start bulbing when days last 12 to 14 hours long. These widely adapted varieties grow well between the 32nd and 40th latitudes, so there is some overlap with the short-day region, which is indicated in green on the map to the right. Most intermediate-day varieties are dense and pungent and store better than short-day onions. Some varieties can mature into moderately sweet onions under perfect conditions, but expect intermediate-day onions to be pungent. Most are hybrids developed by combining short-day and long-day varieties.

Overwintering onions are short-day onions with high tolerance for cold weather. Sometimes called Japanese onions, these special varieties are planted in late summer and grown through winter under a row cover tunnel as far north as Zone 5. Less prone to bolting and more dependable than intermediate-day onions, the overwintering onion plants start growing right away in early spring and produce beautiful bulb onions in early summer, a couple of months before main crop onions are ready. This can be important if you need onions for early-season pickling projects. Varieties include 'Desert Sunrise' (red), 'Bridger', and 'Keepsake' (both tan).

HOW MANY TO PLANT?

Few cooks can make it through a day without using at least one onion, but few gardens can meet this never-ending demand. Estimates of 40 bulb onions per person is reasonable if you are growing plenty of other onions, but per capita consumption of bulb onions is closer to 20 pounds per year, or 80 plants per person.

As long as the growing season lasts, try to fill some of your day-to-day onion needs with non-bulbing onions like scallions and leeks (see page 138). Grow as many bulb onions and shallots as you can find room for — keeping them together in one row simplifies rotations. If you live from Zones 5 to 7, consider including overwintering onions in your planting plan because the onions are harvested early, with plenty of time to plant another crop in the same space, and you have onions to eat through the first half of summer.

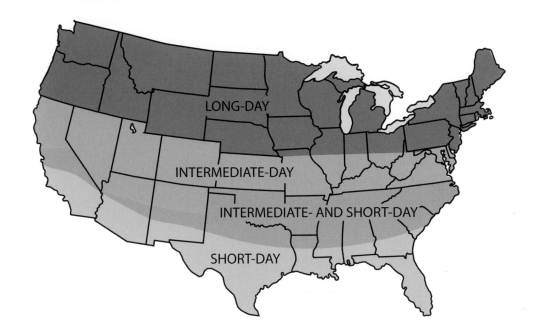

Long-day onions require 14- to 16-hour days to begin forming bulbs, so they grow best in northern regions, where there are many hours of daylight during the summer months. Long-day onions are usually dense and pungent with thick, papery skins that protect them from moisture loss, so they often store well for many months. Most long-day onions sold as plants are hybrids, but by starting from seed you can grow interesting and productive heirloom varieties and little cipollini, which have a remarkably long storage life. Long-day onions are adapted from the 38th latitude northward.

Sweet or Pungent Onions?

Onions are complex chemical organisms, and their full fury is unleashed when they are cut. As soon as the cells are opened with a sharp knife, a cascade of compounds hits the air, including tear-provoking lachrymator. If the onion is a sweet one, it won't pack much of a punch, and you'll get the most flavor from eating it raw or minimally cooked in a stir-fry. In comparison, a pungent onion will add much more body to a soup stock, but its vapors will sting your eyes, and it might give you indigestion if you eat it raw.

The sugar content of spicy storage onions is often quite high, but until the pungency compounds are broken down in cooking, you can't taste their sweetness.

As for coping with tears when you're slicing and dicing a mountain of onions for a pickling project, work outdoors if you can, and turn on a small fan to blow the onion vapors away from your face. It helps tremendously to chill the onions for a few hours before chopping, because temperatures below 50°F (10°C) suppress an onion's ability to gas off. Pungency compounds are concentrated in the root end of the bulb, so it also helps to chop it up last.

HOW TO
Grow Onions

When: You can grow onions from seeds, plants, or sets, but seeds are best because you can choose superior varieties at modest expense and control growing conditions to minimize or eliminate bolting — a big risk with sets. You can start seeds indoors very early, in midwinter, because onion seedlings grow slowly, and the upright plants are easy to hold in containers until it's time to plant them. Note that seed-sown shallots are grown exactly like bulb onions. I sow and grow bulb onions and shallots indoors at the same time, in neighboring seedling flats that must be labeled because they look so much alike.

> **It's best to grow onions from seeds because you can choose superior varieties at modest expense and control growing conditions to minimize or eliminate bolting.**

Germination: Start with fresh seeds labeled for the current crop year. Onion seeds can be kept for 2 years in a cool, dry place, but fresh first-year onion seeds germinate best. Onion germination is fastest at 68 to 77°F (20 to 25°C), with slight temperature drops at night. The tops of my fluorescent plant lights are flat, and they give off just the right amount of bottom heat needed to help onion seeds germinate quickly, or you can use the top of your refrigerator for bottom heat. To keep the seeded containers moist, enclose them in a roomy plastic bag.

Onion seedlings need bright supplemental light from the day they germinate. Position seedlings close to the bulbs to simulate sun, and keep the lights on for 12 hours a day. When the seedlings have three leaves, transplant them to containers that are at least 4 inches deep, because onion seedlings that are given plenty of vertical root space grow faster and better than those confined to shallow quarters.

As winter gives way to spring, set up a cold frame or plastic-covered tunnel outdoors, and use it as a daycare center for your onion seedlings. Onion seedlings need as much light as they can get, and the best light is outdoors. Bring the plants indoors at night as long as temperatures often drop below 50°F (10°C), and delay planting until about 3 weeks before your last spring frost.

Where: All onions grow best in fertile, well-drained soil with a slightly acidic pH between 6.0 and 6.8. Choose a sunny site, and loosen the planting bed to at least 12 inches deep. Thoroughly mix in a 1-inch layer of mature compost. Providing bioactive compost is important when growing onions, because onions take up much of the phosphorus they need through partnerships with soilborne mycorrhizal fungi.

Planting: Onion roots are concentrated in the area just below the bulbs, so it's a good practice to lay down organic fertilizer in a band at the bottom of V-shaped planting trenches. This technique places a cache of organic riches where the onions can utilize it early on, during their most active period of growth. Transplant onions to about 4 inches apart.

Maintenance: Once onion seedlings are in the ground, the war with weeds gets into full swing. Skinny onions are notoriously poor competitors with weeds, so they can't be left to fend for themselves. In addition to attentive hand-weeding with a sharp weeding tool, interplanting onions with arugula, lettuce, and other leafy greens reduces weeds between onion plants, and the greens can be pulled young, before they block light to the onions.

QUICKIE SCALLIONS. The easiest way to grow scallions is to plant inexpensive onion sets sold in spring. Simply poke them into the ground, let them grow for a month, and pull the green onions as needed in the kitchen. You can keep some sets dormant in the refrigerator and plant them in summer for fall harvest.

What to Do about Bolting Onions

Bolting is a common syndrome with onions grown from sets, or from oversize seedlings that are set out too early. Sets are a great way to grow green onions (scallions), but for a bolt-free bulb onion patch you'll need to use seedlings smaller than a pencil, set out after nighttime temperatures have warmed to above 45°F (7°C). If you are growing onions from homegrown seedlings or purchased plants and you are still having bolting problems, the next thing to try is delaying planting until warm weather arrives to stay in mid-spring. Young onion plants that are never chilled rarely bolt.

When onions do bolt, use some of the florets in salads and sandwiches, and let the others offer their nectar to bees and other beneficials. As soon as the flowers fade, lop off the blooming stalks to keep the plants from wasting energy nurturing seeds. Let the plants keep growing for about 3 more weeks, or until they show no new growth and list sideways or fall over.

> When onions do bolt, use some of the florets in salads and sandwiches, and let the others offer their nectar to bees and other beneficials.

Follow the instructions for curing onions given on page 140. A couple of weeks into the process, you should be able to see or feel a division between a lopsided but well-formed onion and the stiff base of the seed stalk. Break the two pieces apart, and compost the seed stalk after first checking to see if there is a small elongated onion hiding at its base. Continue curing the "good halves," but also eat them as quickly as is practical or use them in canning projects. Because they are missing so much of their protective outer sheaths, bolted onions do not store well.

Onion Pests and Diseases

White onion root maggots. When an onion suddenly goes weak and stops growing, gently dig it up to check for the presence of tiny white onion root maggots. The adult flies are attracted by rotting onion tissues, so discourage problems by rotating onions and composting all refuse after harvesting. Where onion root maggots are a recurrent pest, use row covers to protect your onions in spring, when the egg-laying females are most active.

Onion thrips. Thrips rasp pale grooves into leaves, but they have many natural predators. Keep areas near onions mowed to reduce the weedy habitat thrips prefer. Use a spinosad-based biological pesticide to control serious infestations.

Leaf spot diseases. As onion plants become weak with age, they become prey to numerous leaf spot diseases that are aggravated by warm, rainy weather. Warm rain also encourages pink root and several other soilborne diseases that can cause onions to rot. Use resistant varieties when you can, keep them weeded, and grow onions only in sunny, well-drained sites.

Stock Your Garden with
Alternative Onions

You will always have plenty of garden-fresh onions for everyday cooking by including some of these non-bulbing onions in your garden. Many are perennials that will come back or can be replanted for many years.

Egyptian onions (*Allium cepa* var. *proliferum*) are often called top-setting, walking, or multiplying onions. Plants develop bulblets atop tall stems in early summer and multiply by division, too. Replant bulblets in summer for fall and spring scallions. The bases of the parent plants can be divided and replanted, or you can dry and cure them like elongated shallots. These rewarding plants are hardy at least to Zone 5.

Bunching onions (*A. fistulosum* and hybrids) are more refined than multipliers. Instead of forming bulbs, these cold-hardy, disease-resistant plants multiply by division, forming clumps of scallions. Start seeds indoors in late winter, and divide established clumps in spring or fall. 'Evergreen White' is hardy to Zone 4; 'White Spear' and 'Beltsville' are hardy to Zone 5.

Leeks (*A. porrum*) are easy to grow from seed, though you should be prepared for leeks that are more slender and tender than those sold in stores. Leeks develop long white shanks that can be made longer with deep mulch. The best onions for drying, leek seedlings are tough and easy to handle. Many gardeners grow clumps of leek seedlings in containers and pop them into the garden as small spaces open up for cultivation.

Potato onions (*A. cepa* var. *aggregatum*) go by many names, including nest, hill, or pregnant onions, and they may be the ideal homesteader's onion. Planted in fall, these hardy storage onions produce a "nest" of 2- to 3-inch onions in midsummer. Potato onions are easier to grow and store than larger bulb onions and are more productive than shallots. Replant saved bulbs or make new plantings in fall or very early spring.

Shallots (*A. cepa* var. *aggregatum*, *A. oschaninii*, and hybrids) are a variable group of perennial onions, though new varieties are available that make great crops when grown as annuals from seed. Famous for flavor and long storage time, shallots look like elongated potato onions; some selections are nearly round. Shallots that show signs of breaking dormancy, like green tips or knobby root buds, can be planted in fall, like garlic. But dormant shallots set out in the fall often rot, so it is often safer to wait to plant in early spring. Whether they grew from seedlings or mother bulbs, young shallot leaves are delicious and can be substituted for scallions in any recipe.

red shallot

potato onions

leeks

scallions

HARVESTING AND STORING
Onions

With any bulb-forming onion, the rule of thumb is to wait for half of the plants to fall over, and then harvest the entire planting. This is fine if you have dry weather, but under wet conditions it's better to feel the necks of your plants for a soft spot a few inches above the onion bulb. This soft spot is a sign that the bulb has finished growing, and you can feel it a day or two before the top of the plant falls over. When rain is predicted, it's best to pull every plant that has gone soft at the neck, because moisture will cause the necks to start rotting.

Shallots and potato onions are an exception to the fall-over rule, because they often splay out over the ground as they divide into separate bulbs, but the plants continue to grow. This rather unattractive posture should therefore be tolerated until the green leaves have withered back at least halfway. Then they are ready to harvest and cure.

Curing Onions

The process of curing onions takes about a month from start to finish, but it is best not to hurry things. Pull onions, brush off excess soil, and clip off withered leaves. In wet weather or humid climates, allow the plants to rest in a warm, dry place for a few days, and then trim off leaves that have gone slimy or brown, and cut the green ones back to about 12 inches. Lightly rub off soil clinging to the bulbs, and let them cure for a couple of weeks in warm, dry shade.

Groom the bulbs a second time, using scissors to clip off roots and all but 2 inches of the withering tops. Gently wipe the curing onions with a damp cloth to clean them, and arrange them in a single layer in boxes or bins that can be brought indoors (by this time they hardly smell at all). Dry at room temperature for 2 more weeks before moving them to cooler quarters in your barn or basement. If you don't have a cool basement, look for alternative spots like downstairs closets or under your bed.

TOP: Shallots will continue to grow after their tops have fallen over.

BOTTOM: Allow harvested onions to cure in a warm, dry place before trimming and storing them.

Given the same storage conditions, some onions will break dormancy long before others. When this happens, the onions soften and a green shoot may show at the top — a sign to eat it right away. Varieties described in seed catalogs as "hard storage" onions will last until February, though they usually get eaten by then. Well-cured cipollini onions and shallots stay in good condition all the way through winter, so they take over in the kitchen when the bulb onions are gone.

Onion
FOOD PRESERVATION OPTIONS

Simple cool storage in the 40 to 50°F (4 to 10°C) range is the best way to store perfect onions and shallots. Check on onions stored in your garage or basement weekly, and look into any funky smells coming from the onion basket.

As you cure your onions, set aside those with imperfections and use them in everyday cooking or canning. Many spicy chutney recipes include onions, and thinly sliced onions are essential in bread-and-butter pickles. Also include chopped onions in vegetable mixtures that are being blanched and frozen. If you want to freeze only onions, the best course is to caramelize them first (see the recipe at right). Thinly sliced onions, including green onions and leeks, are a valuable addition to vegetable ferments.

Onions also can be dried with no blanching required, but a quick dip in simmering water helps tenderize leeks while removing bits of soil. Leeks are a dream to dry, finished in a matter of hours. Drying sliced bulb onions may be a good idea if you have more culls than keepers, but keep in mind that dried onions lack the aromatics of fresh ones, and some people find them hard to digest. Besides, let's say you want to make a warming vegetable soup. The first step is to slowly brown an onion or shallot, fresh with its sugars intact, in a small amount of fat. In this and other cases, caramelization at the bottom of the pan is essential to the dish, and for this only a fresh onion will do. Grow plenty.

Caramelized Onions

Let's say you have a hundred beautiful onions curing in the garage and a dozen flawed ones waiting in a bucket. Time to make enough caramelized onions to inspire your cooking for weeks to come. Slowly cooking the onions brings out their natural sweetness, and caramelized onions are so versatile they can be used as a foundation for rich French onion soup, slipped into a grilled cheese sandwich, stirred into mashed potatoes, or mixed with any steamed vegetable.

Makes about 2 cups

- 6 cups onions
- ¼ cup olive oil
- 2 tablespoons balsamic vinegar (optional)

1 Slice the onions vertically into thin wedges.

2 Place the oil and onions in a large skillet over medium-low heat and sauté the onions until they become translucent, about 10 minutes. Continue cooking, stirring frequently, until the onions are a rich brown color, about 25 minutes. Add the balsamic vinegar, if desired, to intensify the flavor.

3 Cool, then place in freezer-safe containers. The onions will keep in the freezer for 6 months.

PARSNIPS

(*Pastinaca sativa*)

HOW MUCH
10 row feet per person

STELLAR VARIETIES
'Lancer' and 'Andover'

BEST WAYS TO PRESERVE
Place in cold storage or freeze

One of the most vigorous root crops you can grow, parsnips will also keep through winter in the refrigerator, in a cold root cellar, or in the garden. More gardeners should grow these sturdy plants, which grow easily once the seedlings are up and going. Parsnip seeds are reluctant germinators, so the hardest part of growing a good crop is getting a good stand of seedlings. Pre-germinating seeds indoors helps to solve this problem.

Cooked parsnips have a unique creamy texture that makes them a natural addition to mashed potatoes or hummus, and there are endless variations on parsnip soup. White beans combine well in a savory parsnip soup, or you can try pear-parsnip soup made smooth with an immersion blender. Use a ribbon-type vegetable peeler to cut thick strips from large parsnips, then oil, lightly season, and bake into parsnip "bacon." It is best to precook parsnips destined for the grill.

Best Parsnips

FOR THE

Homegrown Pantry

In my experience there is little difference between parsnip varieties, so I suggest working with an open-pollinated variety like 'Lancer' or 'Andover', which allows the possibility of saving your own seeds. Parsnip plants that have been well chilled in winter will bloom and set seed in June, with the seeds ready to harvest in late July. If you don't save your own seeds, plan to buy a fresh supply every year.

HOW MANY TO PLANT?

Parsnips can be forgotten in the refrigerator for weeks at a time, which is part of their allure. Allow about 10 row feet per person, which should yield 6 to 8 pounds. Grow more if you want to try over-wintering parsnips to dig first thing in spring.

HOW TO
Grow Parsnips

When: With slow-sprouting parsnip seeds, it's helpful to do everything you can to support the germination process, starting with warm soil. Wait until the soil has lost its chill and the weather has settled to plant parsnips, usually around the time of your last spring frost date. You can wait later if you like, but don't start early and don't try transplanting parsnips. In midsummer, look for a period of cool rainy weather for planting a second crop of parsnips to harvest in late fall or leave in the ground through winter.

Pre-germinating: Begin pre-germinating the seeds 5 to 7 days before you plan to plant them. Place the seeds in a clean jar, swish them gently in lukewarm water for a few minutes, and then pour into a strainer lined with a paper towel. After the excess water drips away, place the damp towel with seeds in a food-grade container, with the lid left slightly open. Keep the container at room temperature, and check daily to make sure the seeds are nicely moist. On the fifth day, look for tiny curled "tails" emerging from the seeds. When one-third of the seeds make this much progress toward germination, plant them immediately in prepared beds.

- -

Planting: Thoroughly cultivate beds to be planted with parsnips, removing rocks and other obstructions while mixing in a generous 2-inch layer of rich compost, or compost amended with organic fertilizer. Plant pre-germinated parsnip seeds in straight rows at least 10 inches apart, spacing seeds about 1 inch apart. Even pre-germinated parsnip seeds can be slow to emerge, so it helps to reduce weed competition by covering the seeds with weed-free potting soil. After the seedlings are up and growing, thin them to at least 4 inches apart. Parsnips are big, robust plants that need ample space if they are to grow big roots.

Parsnip Pests and Diseases

Parsnips have few problems with pests, though the roots are eagerly eaten by voles. Misshapen parsnips can be caused by any disturbance to the roots, which is why parsnips are always direct-seeded and never transplanted.

It's time to plant pre-germinated parsnip seeds when one-third of the seeds have grown tails. You may not see seedlings for another week.

HARVESTING AND STORING
Parsnips

When: When older leaves begin to yellow and fail, dig a sample root to see if it has attained good size. Keep in mind that garden-grown parsnips may be larger than what you see in stores, but this is good!

Parsnips that mature in cool fall soil can be left in the ground longer, but they should be dug before the ground freezes. Leave a few plants in the ground to overwinter, and dig them first thing in spring, as soon as the little tops start to grow. If you want to save your own parsnip seeds, allow two or three overwintered plants to bolt, bloom, and produce a fresh crop of seeds.

- -

How: Before pulling parsnips, use a digging fork to loosen the soil just outside the row. Rinse harvested parsnips with cool water, or gently hand-wash them to remove clods of soil. Use a sharp knife to cut off the parsnip tops. Pat the parsnips dry with clean towels and store in plastic bags in the refrigerator or a cold root cellar, packed in damp sand or peat moss. Wait until just before using your parsnips to scrub them clean.

Parsnip
FOOD PRESERVATION OPTIONS

Parsnips will store for months in the refrigerator or in very cold storage in a root cellar or unheated basement. As long as temperatures are kept constantly cool, ideally around 40°F (4°C), parsnips packed in damp sand or sawdust will keep very well.

Use your refrigerated or cold-stored parsnips as needed in the kitchen. Should a planting have issues from root-tunneling insects that render the roots unworthy of long-term refrigeration, peel, cook, and purée the parsnips, and store the soup-ready parsnip purée in the freezer.

snow peas

shell peas

snap peas

soup peas

PEAS
(*Pisum sativum*)

HOW MUCH
15 row feet per person for snap peas, 10 row feet per person for snow peas, and 20 row feet per person for shell peas

- -

STELLAR VARIETIES
'Sugar Snap', 'Oregon Giant' snow peas, 'Green Arrow' shell peas

- -

BEST WAYS TO PRESERVE
Freeze, pickle (snap peas), or ferment (snap and shell peas)

When peas pop out of the ground in spring, the world is suddenly filled with promise. Cold-hardy peas open the season for crops you can keep, and their sweet, delicate flavor puts them on everyone's planting list. There is reason to hurry. Garden peas stop flowering and wither away when temperatures rise above 85°F (29°C), which happens in early summer in many climates. In areas where fall lasts long and winters are mild, a small fall crop of peas is often worthwhile.

Low-acid peas are poor candidates for canning because long processing times cause them to soften, but all peas are easy to freeze. If you like fermented foods, you must try fermenting snap peas or shell peas, which keep their crisp texture through the fermentation process. Snow peas cut into bite-size pieces bring color and crunch to homemade kimchi.

Best Peas

Homegrown Pantry

The most productive pea varieties share three characteristics: moderate height, determinate growth habit, and a talent for producing pods in pairs. Determinate varieties produce flowers and pods all at once after the plants reach their full height, which for the most productive varieties is between 2 and 3 feet tall.

> **You can feed four people with 1 pound of snap peas, but you will need to shell out twice as many shell peas to obtain four nice servings.**

There are four different types of peas: snap peas, snow peas, shell peas, and soup peas. Most gardeners favor snap peas because they are so productive. You can feed four people with 1 pound of snap peas, but you will need to shell out twice as many shell peas to obtain four nice servings. Snow peas fall in between.

In all pea types, very fast-maturing varieties produce small pods compared to those produced by plants that take a little longer to mature. Unless you need to grow your peas very early so they can mature before summer's heat, choose varieties that are rated at about 60 days to maturity.

Some pea varieties make beautiful edible ornamentals to grow near garden entryways or other high visibility spots. 'Golden Sweet' snow pea has buttery yellow pods; those of 'Blue Podded' soup peas are blue.

HOW MANY TO PLANT?

People can eat a lot of peas when allowed to do so, so unless you live in a very pea-friendly climate, I suggest sticking with the reasonable guideline of 15 row feet per person of snap peas (about 12 pounds), 10 row feet per person of snow peas (about 5 pounds), and 20 row feet per person of shell peas (about 8 pounds shelled). Keep records, and adjust up or down based on your family's needs.

Summer Peas for Warm Climates

When gardeners in warm climates speak of peas, they are usually talking about crowder peas (*Vigna unguiculata*), also known as field peas or Southern peas. Originating in Africa, crowder peas are a warm-weather crop planted in early summer, after tomatoes. The purple blossoms set fruit even in humid heat. You will get the most peas per square foot with semi-vining varieties like 'Pinkeye Purple Hull' or 'Mississippi Silver'. Crowder peas make great freezer crops, or you can dry them and use them like dry beans.

HOW TO
Grow Peas

When: Weather has a huge impact on the growth and productivity of peas, which can grow fast or slow, depending on how much sun and warmth the plants receive after getting a cool start. Peas definitely sprout and grow in cold soil, but they grow faster and better in springtime warmth. Start an early planting about 1 month before your last frost date, with the rest of your peas about 2 weeks later. To ensure strong germination, soak peas in water overnight before planting them.

- -

Planting: Peas like closer spacing compared to other vegetables, so plan to grow them in dense double rows on either side of a trellis. Ignore seed company claims that some varieties need no support. Even the shortest-growing peas will end up on the ground when they become top-heavy with pods, and besides, few plants are more fun to trellis than peas. Whether you use bare branches saved from tree pruning or weave a string tapestry between posts, peas eagerly grab on with their curling tendrils, and they won't let go. Do anticipate that your peas will grow slightly taller than seed catalogs say, and make a trellis for determinate varieties at least 3 feet high.

Prepare a wide planting bed by loosening the soil to at least 10 inches deep while mixing in compost. If you grew peas last year, scatter a few spadefuls of soil from the previous season's pea patch over the new planting bed. This step ensures that plenty of nitrogen-fixing bacteria are present to assist the plants in feeding themselves. It's a more reliable way to inoculate soil than using powdered inoculants, which often are stored under conditions that render them worthless. Amend the bed with a balanced organic fertilizer, using just enough to get peas off to a strong start. Poke seeds into the prepared site 2 inches apart and 1 inch deep. Thinning is rarely needed with peas.

- -

Maintenance: Water peas as needed to keep the soil lightly moist, and weed regularly until the plants develop blossoms. After the plants start blooming, try not to disturb the roots with weeding activity.

Pea Pests and Diseases

When grown in cool spring weather, peas have few insect pests except pea aphids, which can be controlled with insecticidal soap should they become numerous. Much more common is powdery mildew, a fungal disease that causes white patches to form on leaves and pods. Grow resistant varieties where powdery mildew is a recurrent problem. Resistant varieties also are available for pea enation virus, a common problem in northern climates that causes new growth to be curled and distorted. Similar leaf curl symptoms can be caused by herbicide contamination in soil or by herbicide drift.

HARVESTING AND STORING
Peas

When: Pick peas every other day, preferably in the morning. Pick snow peas when the pods reach full size and the peas inside are just beginning to swell. For best flavor and yields, allow snap peas to change from flat to plump before picking them; snap peas in stores are picked flat and underripe because they ship better that way. Gather sweet green shell peas when the pods begin to show a waxy sheen, but before their color fades. Soup peas can be left on the vines until the pods dry to tan.

How: To avoid mangling the vines, use two hands to harvest peas. Immediately refrigerate picked snow, snap, and shell peas to stop the conversion of sugar to starches and maintain the peas' crisp texture.

Crush soup pea pods in a paper bag to release the peas. After shelling and sorting, allow soup peas to dry at room temperature until they are so hard that they shatter when struck with a hammer. Store in airtight containers in a cool, dry place.

Many vegetables love being grown in soil recently vacated by peas. After old pea vines have been pulled, spinach, carrots, or fall cabbage are fine choices for follow-up crops.

LEFT: In home gardens, snap peas can be allowed to plump up fully before they are picked.

ABOVE: Shell peas put their energy into plump peas enveloped in tough, stringy pods. The pods of ripe shell peas have a waxy sheen, and the peas inside are full and round.

Pea
FOOD PRESERVATION OPTIONS

Peas are such snackable veggies straight from the garden that many of them will be eaten before they ever reach the kitchen. You'll want plenty of peas for fresh cooking when peas are in season, but hopefully you will still have some to freeze.

The standard practice is to blanch all types of peas before freezing them, which helps to preserve their color and probably protects some vitamins, too. But in the case of peas, blanching is not done for food safety reasons, so nobody will get sick if you try freezing your peas without blanching them first. Snow peas are prime candidates for raw freezing, because blanching and freezing turns them into soft, watery versions of their former selves.

Canning. Low-acid peas can be canned in a pressure canner, but the overcooked results only vaguely resemble garden peas. However, snap peas pickled in a vinegar brine need only a short processing time and produce a crisp yet earthy pickle well worth making when snap peas are in season. It is also nice that snap peas look so orderly when packed on end into half-pint canning jars. Follow the recipe for Pickled Green Beans on page 69 to make pickled snap peas.

Fermenting. Both snap peas and shell peas are candidates for fermentation, but several small details are important. First, you must use whole pods that have not had their caps removed. If the little caps are torn off, the damaged tissues are prone to going slimy in the fermentation jar. Air trapped inside the pods makes fermenting peas float, so it is best to pack them into wide-mouthed pint canning jars on end so they can hardly move, cover them with a salt brine, and exclude air with a partially filled bag of water, as shown on page 40. After about 7 days at cool room temperatures, drain off the cloudy brine, rinse the peas once or twice with cold water, and then cover them with fresh salt brine. Keep refrigerated, and eat the fermented peas as snacks. Eat only the peas from fermented shell peas.

Both shell peas and snap peas (shown here) are delicious when fermented whole, with their caps on.

Saving Pea Seeds

Peas are open-pollinated and self-fertile, so saving seeds is a simple matter of allowing a few pods from your best plants to mature until the pods dry to brown. Better yet, grow several plants in a bed dedicated to seed growing, and let the plants put all of their energy into the production of seed-quality peas. Shell the seeds and let them dry indoors at room temperature for a couple of weeks before storing them in a cool, dry place. Pea seeds will keep for at least 3 years, and often longer.

sweet pimento

green
cayenne

sweet banana

hungarian
paprika

habenero

yellow bell

jalapeño

Grow a diversity of flavorful
peppers, such as pimentos,
paprika peppers, banana
peppers, and small-fruited
bells.

PEPPERS

(Capsicum annuum)

HOW MUCH
5 sweet pepper plants and 2 hot per person

STELLAR VARIETIES
'Sweet Banana', 'Lipstick', and 'Early Jalapeño'

BEST WAYS TO PRESERVE
Freeze, dry, can, or ferment

Many people become passionate about peppers, probably because they are nutritious, beautiful, and never fail to excite the palate. These warm-natured plants can be a challenge to grow in climates with short summers, but in most areas both sweet and hot peppers are as easy to grow as tomatoes. For top flavor, peppers should be allowed to ripen until they begin to change colors. Except for a few dark green southwestern peppers such as poblanos, green peppers have fewer vitamins and lack the flavor complexities of ripe ones.

Peppers can be frozen, dried, or combined with tomatoes and other seasonings in canned salsa or pasta sauce (see the recipes on page 225). Both sweet and hot peppers make wonderful refrigerator pickles, and the types of hot sauces you can make with hot peppers are truly endless, including several fermented versions.

Best Peppers

FOR THE

Homegrown Pantry

The most versatile peppers for year-round eating are sweet peppers, plus some hot peppers that won't blow your head off, such as jalapeños. Among sweet peppers, many of the best home garden varieties have conical shapes or are smallish versions of traditional bell peppers, which grow best in warm climates. Pepper varieties that produce medium to small fruits tend to produce earlier and better than large-fruited peppers, which require a bit more patience and luck. For garden planning purposes, I divide peppers into three main groups: small sweet peppers that produce early enough to use in tomato canning projects, large sweet peppers for fresh eating and freezing, and hot peppers for canning, drying, and creative condiments. Here are some excellent varieties within each group.

> **Pepper varieties that produce medium to small fruits tend to produce earlier and better than large-fruited peppers, which require a bit more patience and luck.**

- **Small sweet peppers:** 'Sweet Banana', 'Peacework', 'Little Bells'

- **Large sweet peppers:** 'Lipstick', 'Flavorburst' (yellow), 'Carmen'

- **Hot peppers:** 'Early Jalapeño', 'Cayenne', 'Hot Banana'

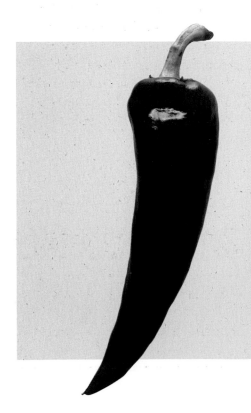

Having Fun with Specialty Peppers

The varieties listed above are productivity champs in a wide range of climates, but if you live where summers are long and warm — or have a passion for hot peppers — there are specialty peppers to fill every need. Many southwestern peppers tend to mature quite late when grown in northern latitudes, but they can be phenomenal producers farther south. Habaneros are too hot to put on the table, but if you're dreaming of making your own mango-habanero sauce, by all means make room for a couple of plants.

HOW TO
Grow Peppers

When: Plant peppers in late spring, after the soil has warmed and the last frost has passed. Start seeds about 6 weeks before your last frost date. Pepper seeds take longer to germinate compared to tomatoes, and they are prone to rot under very wet conditions. Provide very bright light, and transplant to 4-inch containers after the first true leaves appear.

- -

Planting: Prepare the soil in a sunny spot with a near-neutral pH. Scatter a sprinkling of wood ashes or ground eggshells over soil that tends to be slightly acidic. Allow at least 2 feet of space between pepper plants. Into each planting hole, mix a standard dose of balanced organic fertilizer and a heaping shovelful of compost. Set peppers deeply so that their seedling leaves are just covered, and water well.

- -

Maintenance: Peppers can tolerate high heat, but they produce best when they never run short of water. A thick mulch of grass clippings pleases most peppers. Late in the season when peppers become top-heavy with fruits, the plants are likely to fall over. Propping up fallen plants may do more harm than good, because the branches are brittle and break easily. It is best to prevent peppers from falling over by staking them early or growing them in small tomato cages.

Pepper Pests and Diseases

Tomato hornworms and swarming insects. Pepper foliage is sometimes consumed by tomato hornworms (see page 221), which are easy to spot and hand-pick from pepper plants. In some locations, swarming insects, including blister beetles and brown marmorated stink bugs, can ruin ripening fruits; the best defense is a lightweight row cover tent or tunnel installed before the hordes appear.

Viruses. Leaves that show distorted crinkles or grow into thin strings display symptoms of virus infection. Many varieties are resistant to common pepper viruses, which tend to be most common in warm climates.

Sunscald. When plants set fruit but have a sparse cover of leaves to protect them from bright sunshine, the fruits may develop patches of light-colored sunscald, which never ripen properly. Where sunscald is a chronic problem, try growing peppers in a row between rows of tall sweet corn or sunflowers. In small plantings, a shade cover made from lightweight cloth can be attached to thin stakes with clothespins.

HOW MANY TO PLANT?

A healthy pepper plant can produce more than 5 pounds of peppers, but only one or two fruits will ripen at a time, with the biggest harvest coming in the fall. Warm summer weather helps peppers produce heavier crops, while short, cool seasons mean fewer peppers per plant.

A good rule of thumb is to grow five sweet pepper plants and two hot pepper plants per pepper eater in order to have enough for eating fresh, pickling, freezing, and canning.

HARVESTING AND STORING
Peppers

When: Peppers can be harvested as soon as they begin to show blushes of red, yellow, or orange color, and then allowed to finish ripening indoors for up to 2 days.

- -

How: Use floral snips or scissors to cut peppers from the branch, leaving a short stub of stem attached. Some peppers readily break away when pulled, but others cling to brittle branches, causing the branches to break.

You can let peppers ripen on the plants in warm weather, but bring them indoors to finish ripening in the fall, when cool nights slow the ripening process. Before your first frost, gather all almost-ripe peppers (extremely underripe peppers will just collapse) and bring them indoors. They will show signs of ripening within a few days. Fully ripened peppers should be refrigerated.

After peppers start to change colors, you can let them finish ripening indoors, where they are safe from insects and stressful weather.

Pepper
FOOD PRESERVATION OPTIONS

Freezing is the easiest way to preserve peppers, because peppers cut into strips or squares don't need to be blanched first. You can dry peppers without blanching them, too, and dried peppers can be used in cooking or pulverized into concentrated powders (paprika and chili powder are made from powdered dried peppers). Many people grow peppers for making salsa, and refrigerator pickled peppers are equally popular among those who have discovered them (see the recipe on page 159). And when made with low-sugar pectin, canned pepper jelly works great as a quick base for sauces (barbeque or Asian sweet-and-sour sauces, for example). If peppers are your pride, you will eventually dabble in fermented hot sauces. Sriracha, Tabasco, and many other popular hot sauces are made from salt-fermented ground peppers to which vinegar is added as a stabilizing agent.

> When made with low-sugar pectin, canned pepper jelly works great as a quick base for sauces, such as barbeque or Asian sweet-and-sour sauce.

Freezing Peppers

The most versatile way to freeze peppers is to cut them into narrow strips and put them in freezer bags. Each time you add more to the bag, give it a shake to keep the peppers loose in the bag. I like to set aside perfect peppers, cut them in half and remove the cores and ribs, and freeze them for stuffing later. In this instance I do recommend steam blanching pepper halves until barely soft (no more than 4 minutes) before cooling and freezing them. I also blanch peppers like poblanos and Anaheims, to be stuffed as rellenos, but blanching

is not a food safety rule as much as a culinary preference. Peppers that have been roasted or grilled are great when frozen, too.

Drying Peppers

Unless you live in an arid climate, you will need a dehydrator to dry peppers. Cut clean sweet or hot peppers into strips or squares, and dry until almost crisp. Drying times will vary with pepper variety and thickness of the flesh. Spice peppers that are to be ground into paprika or other powders dry quickly, and fresh paprika is wonderful! Store your dried peppers in vacuum-sealed containers or in canning jars kept in the freezer.

One of the tastiest ways to preserve peppers is to smoke them on a covered grill before drying. Peppers pick up smoke flavors and aromas better than other vegetables, so only 30 minutes in apple wood smoke infuses them with flavor. After smoking, the peppers can be dried or frozen.

In the Southwest, thin-walled peppers often are dried whole on strings, called ristras. Chiles dried this way concentrate their flavors as they cure, but this method works best in dry climates.

Pickling Peppers

Care must be taken when canning jalapeño rings or other pepper products, which require acidification to ensure that the pH is low enough to inhibit the growth of bacteria. When canning pickled peppers or salsa, always follow a trusted recipe that includes one of three acidifying agents: powdered citric or ascorbic acid (¼ teaspoon per pint), bottled lemon juice (1 tablespoon per pint), or vinegar (2 tablespoons per pint).

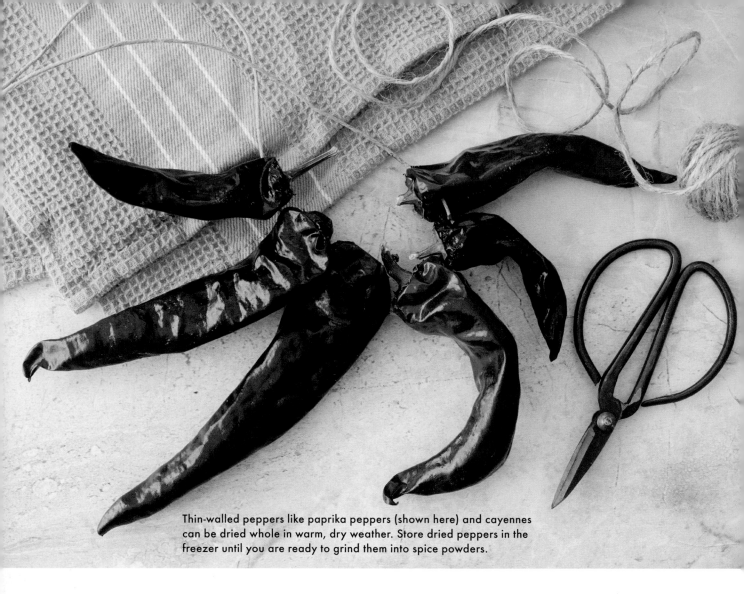

Thin-walled peppers like paprika peppers (shown here) and cayennes can be dried whole in warm, dry weather. Store dried peppers in the freezer until you are ready to grind them into spice powders.

Making Sauces with Hot Peppers

You can use salt fermentation to extend the refrigerator shelf life of firm-fleshed peppers, such as jalapeño slices. Sliced peppers that ferment for 5 to 7 days can be repacked in fresh salt brine and stored in the refrigerator for months.

Popular pepper sauces such as sriracha and Tabasco are made from peppers that are softened via fermentation, but the shorter route is to press poached or steamed hot peppers through a sieve or food mill and use the paste as a basis for unique hot sauces such as mango-habenero sauce or garlicky green jalapeño sauce. Recipes that include a high concentration of vinegar and little or no water can be canned in a water-bath or steam canner, but keep other pepper sauces in the refrigerator.

Or keep it simple. Pack small hot peppers into a jar and cover them with vinegar. After 2 weeks or so on the countertop, the vinegar will be hot enough to use as a hot sauce, and the little peppers can be chopped into recipes to add warmth and bite to cooked dishes.

Using Peppers in Salsa

The recipes for Garden Salsa and Garden Pasta Sauce on page 225 call for plenty of peppers, as do many spicy relishes. Note that when low-acid peppers are added to canned food products, proper acidification becomes crucial. Follow the recipe!

Refrigerator Pickled Peppers

Makes 3 pints

6 cups sweet and hot peppers, cut into rings and strips

3 cups vinegar

1 cup water

1 tablespoon salt

1 tablespoon sugar

1 Stuff the peppers into clean pint or quart jars.

2 Combine the vinegar, water, salt, and sugar in a large bowl and mix until the salt and sugar dissolve. Pour over the peppers, screw on the lids, and refrigerate. Start eating the pickled peppers after 2 weeks, and keep eating them until they are gone. Use opened jars within a month. Unopened jars will keep in the refrigerator for 5 to 6 months.

'Red Thumb'
pink fingerling

'All blue'
all-purpose blue

'Russian Banana'
yellow fingerling

'Carola'
all-purpose yellow

'Yukon Gold'
all-purpose yellow

'Red Chieftan'
waxy red

There are many perfect potatoes, including
yellow and pink fingerlings, all-purpose
potatoes with blue or yellow flesh, and waxy
red potatoes for boiling or roasting.

POTATOES
(*Solanum tuberosum*)

HOW MUCH
20 row feet per person

- -

STELLAR VARIETIES
'Caribe' early, 'Kennebec' midseason, and 'Russian Banana' fingerling

- -

BEST WAYS TO PRESERVE
Place in cool storage, dry, or can

Easy to grow and simple to store in a cool pantry or basement, potatoes are one of the best sources of food energy you can grow in a garden. It's also easy to save and replant your favorite strains, or you can plant purchased potatoes you like that show signs of sprouting. A single small spud can multiply itself into a cluster of fresh, juicy potatoes.

All potatoes naturally break dormancy after a few months, and by spring you may find yourself with sprouting potatoes more fit for the garden than the table. This is why it is important to preserve your imperfect or excess potatoes soon after you harvest them. Drying is the best long-term storage method. Whether you grate cooked, cooled potatoes for hash browns or cut them into slices, dried potatoes are a top convenience food in your homegrown pantry.

Best Potatoes

Homegrown Pantry

To have garden-grown potatoes on the table most of the year, you will need to grow at least two different types: early-maturing varieties to enjoy as fresh potatoes in summer and fall, and mid- or late-season varieties for storing into winter. If you have space, a planting of fingerling potatoes will bring welcome diversity.

- **Early varieties** such as 'Caribe', 'Red Gold', or 'Red Norland' grow fast and produce potatoes 90 days after planting. Early varieties have limited storage potential, so grow only enough of them to eat fresh for about 4 months.

- **Midseason and late varieties** with excellent storage potential include 'Kennebec', all 'Russet' varieties, 'Red Pontiac', and many others. These and other full-season varieties will store best if they are not harvested until 2 weeks after the vines die down. The extra time in the ground helps them to form thick skins, which enhance their storage potential.

- **Fingerlings** — including productive and waxy 'Russian Banana', red-skinned and pink-fleshed 'Red Thumb', and blue 'Papa Cacho' — are superior boiling potatoes, or you can roast them. Varieties vary in their dormancy period; late-maturing varieties like 'French Fingerling' are the best for winter storage.

HOW TO
Grow Potatoes

When: Plant potatoes 2 to 4 weeks before your last spring frost date, or when the soil has started to lose its winter chill. It is always better to delay planting until the soil warms than to plant potatoes in cold, wet soil. Plant your early potatoes first, followed by your storage crop. An unexpected late freeze will kill potato foliage back to the ground, but the plants will regrow. An old quilt or comforter spread over the little plants overnight will usually prevent freeze damage.

In hot summer climates where late-maturing potatoes are difficult to grow, make a second planting of fast-maturing potatoes in late summer. Fall potatoes will begin forming tubers when soil temperatures fall below 70°F (21°C), but the crop will be light compared to spring, when potatoes grow vigorously in response to longer days and warming temperatures.

Handling seed potatoes: Starting in late winter, place potatoes you want to grow or purchased seed potatoes in a warm, sunny spot indoors. The warmth will encourage sprouting, and exposure to sunlight makes the skins turn green and bitter, which makes the potatoes less appetizing to critters. A few days before planting, cut any seed potatoes larger than a golf ball into pieces that have at least three puckered "eyes" on each piece. Allow the cut pieces to dry, and don't be alarmed if they turn black. The darkened, leathery surfaces will resist rotting better than freshly cut ones. If you can't plant right away and need to hold cut seed potatoes, place them in a paper bag with the top folded down.

Potatoes smaller than a golf ball can be planted whole. Whole potatoes start growing faster than cut pieces, so if you plan to save and replant your own seed potatoes, set aside the small ones as your planting stock. Walnut-size potatoes are perfect for planting whole.

Planting: Potatoes grow best in rich, well-drained soil with a slightly acidic pH. Before planting, incorporate a 1-inch blanket of compost into the planting bed along with a half ration of a balanced organic fertilizer. Sawdust that has rotted to black also makes a fine soil amendment for a potato bed.

Space potatoes 14 inches apart; very vigorous late varieties may need more space. Crowding causes plants to produce numerous small potatoes, with wider spacing leading to larger spuds. Some people prefer growing potatoes in hills, with three plants per 24-inch-wide hill.

After planting potatoes 2 to 3 inches deep, you can let the soil warm in the sun for a few weeks or go ahead and mulch over the planted space. The emerging stem tips will push through any biodegradable mulch like shredded leaves or grass clippings, but you will get better weed control and warmer soil by waiting until the plants are 10 to 12 inches tall to mulch them.

- -

Maintenance: As you weed, hill up loose soil around the base of the plants. In early summer, mulch potatoes with a 3-inch-deep mulch, which will keep the soil cool and block sunlight that will turn shallow tubers green. Mulches also serve as an obstacle course to Colorado potato beetles and other insects that travel on foot. Many materials work well, including grass clippings or half-rotted leaves (straw is often laced with pesticides). Every week or so, check for gaps or thinned spots, and pile on more mulch.

Warm sunlight turns seed potatoes green and encourages them to sprout.

The color of potato blossoms reflects the variety's skin color. Red- or blue-skinned potatoes bloom pink or lavender, while the flowers borne by tan-skinned varieties are white.

Depending on your soil, chosen varieties, and the kindness of the weather, expect to produce 1 to 1½ pounds of potatoes per row foot. A 4- by 6-foot bed will produce about 25 pounds of potatoes, as will a 10-foot-long double-wide row or a 20-foot-long single row.

If you divide your potatoes into early potatoes for fresh eating and later potatoes for storage, plan on 20 row feet per person for each planting, with the goal of growing a total of 50 pounds plus per person per year, or more if you plan to share. In climates that are too cool to grow good crops of sweet potatoes (see page 207), you may want to increase the size of your regular potato plantings.

Potato Pests and Diseases

Colorado potato beetles. These are the biggest insect threat to potatoes. Start looking for the brick-red, soft-bodied larvae just as flower buds form, and either hand-pick them or treat the plants with spinosad (an organic biological pesticide). Flea beetles often make small holes in potato leaves, but they do not seriously weaken the plants.

Late blight. Extended periods of cool rain can set the stage for outbreaks of late blight, the dreaded disease that also infects tomatoes. Plants appear to melt down over a period of a few days. Promptly dig and eat any potatoes from infected plants, and compost the foliage. Do not save and replant potatoes produced in a bad blight year. Though they may seem fine for eating, they can be the source of early-season disease outbreaks when planted in the garden.

Voles. In many areas, small tunneling rodents called voles help themselves to garden potatoes. When ready-to-harvest potatoes mysteriously disappear, voles are the most likely explanation.

HARVESTING AND STORING
Potatoes

When: Harvest early potatoes when the foliage stops growing and begins to look tired and pale. Harvest storage potatoes at least 2 weeks after the tops have died back, but before the first frost. Potatoes grown in intensive beds can be gathered by hand; a follow-up light forking will turn up most of the spuds in hiding.

Cleaning and sorting: Handle fresh potatoes gently, and resist the temptation to wash them. The skins are much too fragile, but they will toughen up as they cure. Do sort through your spuds carefully, and place sound potatoes in one pile, and those with any type of issue — from green ends to unexplained holes — in another. You can trim, cook, and eat these culls, or preserve them using one of the food preservation options discussed on page 168.

Storing summer potatoes: Your first storage challenge will come in summer, when you need temporary quarters for early potatoes that won't be eaten for a couple of months. If your summer harvest is modest, cure your potatoes as described below for a few days, and then store them in boxes in the coolest place you can find. Our bedroom stays cool in summer, so I store boxes of precious summer fingerlings under my bed. Do not refrigerate potatoes, because very cold temperatures cause potatoes to convert starches to sugars, which in turn causes them to darken when they are cooked.

You can also store your summer potatoes in a trench or hole where they are covered with at least 6 inches of loose soil. Then cover the mound with several folds of newspaper to help it shed excess rain. The buried potatoes will wait out warm weather in cool, moist conditions and can be gathered as needed for use in the kitchen.

Curing for long-term storage: Flawless potatoes that stay in the ground until the plants' tops wither are the best candidates for long-term storage. Curing or drying the potatoes for 7 to 10 days further improves their storage potential. If you have clay soil, you may want to lightly rinse off excess soil, then pat the spuds dry. Lay them out in a dim room and cover them with a cloth or towels to block out sunlight. During this time, the skins will dry, small wounds will heal over, and new layers of skin will form where the outer layer peeled or rubbed off. After 3 or 4 days, turn the potatoes over so all sides can dry.

Cured potatoes can be stored in a basement, unheated garage, root cellar, or any other place where temperatures will range between 45 and 55°F (7 and 13°C). Keep them covered with a thick cloth to block light (see the seven storage ideas on page 167). Check your stored spuds every 2 weeks for signs of spoilage and, later on, sprouting. Many varieties are finished resting and ready to start growing after 3 to 4 months.

Work carefully when gathering potatoes to avoid slicing or spearing your beautiful crop.

Basement steps serve as a cool, dark storage spot for a fresh crop of potatoes.

Seven Ways

TO

Store Potatoes

1 **Place cured potatoes in a burlap bag,** tuck the bag into a plastic storage bin left open a wee bit, and keep in an unheated basement.

2 **Line plastic laundry baskets with newspapers,** with potatoes arranged in layers between more newspapers. Place the packed, covered baskets in an unheated garage.

3 **In the basement, make short towers of potatoes** by stacking them between layers of open egg cartons. Cover the towers with cloth to protect the potatoes from light.

4 **Place sorted potatoes in small cloth shopping bags that have been lined with plastic bags,** and store in a cold space under the stairs. A similar method: Sort different potatoes into paper bags, then place the bags in milk crates to prevent bruising.

5 **Use an old dresser in a cool room or basement** for storing potatoes in winter. Leave the drawers partially open for ventilation.

6 **In a shady spot outdoors, place a tarp over the ground and cover it** with an inch of loose straw. Pile on potatoes and cover with more straw, a second tarp, and a 10-inch blanket of leaves or straw.

7 **Bury a garbage can horizontally** so that its bottom half is at least 12 inches deep in the soil. Place potatoes in the can with shredded paper or clean straw. Secure the lid with a bungee cord, and cover with an old blanket if needed to shade out sun.

Potato
FOOD PRESERVATION OPTIONS

If you have little or no cool storage, or more culls than keepers, you can dry or can your potatoes for long-term storage. Freezing is not recommended, because the flesh and water separate as potatoes freeze and thaw, with unpleasantly mealy results.

Canning Potatoes

Pressure canning brings out the buttery notes in waxy potatoes, and you can process a batch at 12 pounds of pressure in 35 minutes. The pieces should be blanched before packing them into hot jars, but they need not fit tightly. Fresh boiling water amended with citric acid (to prevent discoloration) is poured over the prepared potatoes before they go into the pressure canner. *Note:* Potatoes are a low-acid food and cannot be canned in a water-bath or steam canner.

Drying Potatoes

Dehydrated potatoes are an essential ingredient in dry soup mixes, and dried potato slices make excellent scalloped potatoes or potatoes au gratin. Using the culls from the main crop, I like to dry at least one batch of potatoes each year. In spring when the fresh potatoes are gone, dried potatoes can save the day.

The most common way to dry potatoes is to dry slices. Slice well-scrubbed potatoes into uniform pieces and drop them into a bowl of cold water with a teaspoon of citric acid mixed in (to prevent discoloration). Bring a pot of water to a boil, and blanch the pieces until they are barely done, about 5 minutes. Cool slightly before arranging on dehydrator trays. Dry potato slices until hard and opaque — your house will smell like baked potatoes!

Cooked potatoes dry quickly and save preparation time when you need potatoes for soups or casseroles.

Tomorrow's Hash Browns

As you harvest your crop, set aside potatoes with cracks, sprouting ends, or other issues, and make a big batch of Tomorrow's Hash Browns, which can be dried or frozen.

Potatoes

1   Preheat the oven to 350°F (180°C).

2   Scrub the potatoes and cut away bad spots. Bake the potatoes for 1 hour, or until done. Chill overnight in the refrigerator.

3   Peel and grate the potatoes.

4   To freeze, lightly grease a cookie sheet, and shape the grated potatoes into round or oblong patties on the sheet. Freeze until hard, then transfer to freezer-safe containers.

5   To dry, spread the grated potatoes on dehydrator trays and dry until they appear translucent. Store in airtight containers in a cool, dark place. Rehydrate in warm water for 10 minutes before pan-frying your dried hash browns.

PUMPKINS

(*Cucurbita pepo, C. maxima, C. moschata*)

HOW MUCH
4 to 6 plants

- -

STELLAR VARIETIES
'Baby Pam', 'Long Pie', 'Winter Luxury', 'Jarrahdale', 'Long Island Cheese', and 'Dickinson Field'

- -

BEST WAYS TO PRESERVE
Freeze or dry

Like winter squash, pumpkins were important pantry items for many Native American tribes. Just as we might do today, cooks stirred pieces of pumpkin into porridge and dried the surplus in strips hung by the fire. Then pastry-minded colonists arrived, and the pumpkin pie was born. The culinary world was forever changed for the better.

Pumpkins come in a huge range of sizes and colors, and botanically speaking, there is no clear dividing line between pumpkins and winter squash. But as a culture, we define pumpkins as round, orange fruits with jack-o'-lantern potential. The best pumpkins for eating are small to medium in size and have dense, thick flesh enclosed in a thin skin. Pumpkins sold for carving are very different, with thin flesh and sturdy skins.

Pumpkins will keep in a cool, dry place for a couple of months, which gives you time to enjoy them in nutritious soups, pies, and baked goods. If you have a bumper crop, extra pumpkin can be dried or frozen as pie-ready purée or spicy pumpkin butter.

Depending on which varieties you choose, you can grow a few large pumpkins or a number of smaller ones. Good small pumpkins include 'Baby Pam' and 'New England Pie'. Robust 'Long Island Cheese' pumpkins need more space to produce their 6- to 10-pound fruits.

Best Pumpkins

FOR THE

Homegrown Pantry

In addition to hard rinds, most pumpkins grown to be jack-o'-lanterns have watery, weak-flavored flesh compared to varieties selected for their culinary and nutritional qualities. Small-fruited pumpkins are the best varieties for climates with short growing seasons, because they grow quickly and the fruits continue to ripen after they are harvested. In warmer climates where pest pressure is severe, pumpkins classified as *C. moschata* resist squash vine borers. Here are six good-tasting varieties, from smallest to largest.

'Baby Pam' (*Cucurbita pepo*) produces small 3- to 4-pound orange pumpkins about 95 days after planting, making it the fastest pie-worthy pumpkin you can grow. Expect four fruits per plant.

'Long Pie' (*C. pepo*) produces elongated 5- to 8-pound fruits in 104 days. A New England heirloom, it has a stackable shape that makes it easy to store. Expect three fruits per plant.

'Winter Luxury' (*C. pepo*) has round 6- to 8-pound orange pumpkins with sweet, stringless flesh. Pumpkins mature in about 100 days, but they have a short storage life due to thin rinds. Expect three to four fruits per plant.

'Jarrahdale' (*C. maxima*), the famous blue pumpkin of Australia, is much valued for its dense, dry flesh. The 6- to 10-pound pleated pumpkins are good keepers and quite decorative as well. Expect two fruits per plant. This species often develops roots where the vines touch the ground, and well-rooted plants may keep growing even after squash vine borers damage the primary crown.

'Long Island Cheese' (*C. moschata*) is so named for its squat shape, which resembles a wheel of cheese. The 6- to 12-pound fruits are mature in about 110 days and are typically borne on very long vines. Expect two fruits per plant.

'Dickinson Field' (*C. moschata*) has a long history as a commercial variety in the pre-hybrid age. Two strains have survived as heirlooms — a round form and the more authentic oblong "neck" pumpkin, which looks like a giant butternut. Both forms produce pumpkins weighing from 10 to 40 pounds, with 15 to 20 pounds most common.

> **Small-fruited pumpkins are the best varieties for climates with short growing seasons; pumpkins classified as *C. moschata* resist squash vine borers and are best in warmer climates.**

HOW MANY TO PLANT?

I like to grow one planting of a big storage pumpkin and a second planting of a variety that bears smaller fruits. In my pantry, the dream yield is four to five heavy 15-pound pumpkins for processing, and a dozen or so small pumpkins for decorating, sharing, and fresh cooking. This goal can be accomplished by growing only four to six plants of any individual pumpkin variety, because a successful vine will produce 20 pounds of fruit, or maybe twice that much! For pollination purposes you also need four to six plants of a given variety, though pumpkins classified as *C. pepo* can share pollen with summer squash, and butternuts help provide pollen for pumpkins classified as *C. moschata*.

Growing Pumpkins
FOR
Nutty Seeds

Whole pumpkin seeds consist of a hard, woody outer hull with a flattened, oblong seed inside. You can clean, dry, roast, and eat the seeds (also called pepitas) from any pumpkin, but you will get the best seeds from special pumpkin varieties grown exclusively for their dark green, oil-rich seeds. In addition to the plump pepitas, seed pumpkins bear seeds whose hulls are so thin that they fall away as the seeds dry. 'Kakai' (*C. pepo*) produces splashy green-striped orange fruits that weigh 6 to 8 pounds, usually producing two to three fruits per plant. 'Lady Godiva' (*C. pepo*) has semi-hull-less seeds. It produces 6- to 8-pound fruits in about 110 days, usually two to three per plant. Each seed pumpkin should produce a half cup of dried seeds.

Pumpkin seeds are rich in protein, manganese, zinc, and a long list of other nutrients. When pressed, they yield a delicious yet heat-sensitive oil. You can utilize the oily nature of raw pumpkin seeds by pulverizing them into a meal using a food processor. A sprinkling of pumpkin seed meal releases enough fat to lubricate a warm pan for the cooking to come.

Oil-seed pumpkins are grown just like other pumpkins, but they are processed very soon after harvesting in order to collect the seeds in peak condition. The discarded pumpkins can be composted. Like jack-o'-lantern pumpkins, they don't taste very good. The few commercial producers of oil-seed pumpkins in the United States have teamed up with farmers who feed the pumpkins to their pigs.

HOW TO
Grow Pumpkins

When: Pumpkins are planted late, after the soil has warmed, and where summers are very long they are not planted until early July for harvesting in October.

- -

Preparing seedlings: You can plant pumpkin seeds where you want the plants to grow, but you will have better control over timing and spacing if you start seeds in containers and set out 3-week-old seedlings exactly where you want them. You won't need fluorescent lights because you can grow the seedlings outdoors, in real sunlight. Pumpkin seedlings grown outdoors in 4-inch pots need no hardening off and can be set out when the first true leaf appears, when they are about 3 weeks old.

- -

Planting: Small pie pumpkins can be planted 12 to 14 inches apart, but allow more space between plants when growing hefty storage pumpkins. A well-prepared 5-foot-diameter hill will support four plants of any type of pumpkin. Enrich it first with a 2-inch layer of compost and a balanced organic fertilizer. You can set out six plants and thin back to the strongest four after a couple of weeks. Gaps in rows of early corn are another great place to slip in a few pumpkin plants. Just be sure that the corn is at least 24 inches tall before interplanting it with pumpkins.

Pumpkin Pests and Diseases

Squash vine borers. Like summer squash, pumpkins classified as *C. pepo* are at high risk for damage from squash vine borers (see page 201). Many gardeners choose *C. moschata* varieties for their main crop pumpkins because they have a very high level of resistance to this widespread pest.

- -

Squash bugs. All pumpkins can be seriously damaged by squash bugs, which suck juices from pumpkin stems, leaves, and fruits. See page 201 for strategies for controlling squash bugs in your pumpkin patch. You may be able to sidestep problems with squash vine borers and squash bugs by planting late and growing the plants beneath floating row covers until they begin to bloom heavily.

- -

Powdery mildew. As pumpkin vines age, they often become infected with powdery mildew; infected vines will produce, but the fruits may be weak of flavor. Pumpkin hybrids with powdery mildew resistance are available where disease pressure is severe. When used preventively, milk sprays (1 part any type of milk to 4 parts water) applied every 7 to 10 days from late July onward can delay the onset of cucurbit powdery mildew.

Pumpkins or Lawn?

Some gardeners don't grow pumpkins because they take up so much space, and it's true that pumpkin vines will grow anywhere from 10 to 30 feet long, depending on variety. Why not grow them outside your garden, and let the vines run over grass you would otherwise have to mow? Or on the edge of your corn patch, so the vines run among the withering stalks? You don't necessarily need a cushy garden bed, because pumpkins grow as well in hills enriched with compost as they do in the ground. Which would you rather do — grow pumpkins or mow the lawn?

HARVESTING, CURING, AND STORING
Pumpkins

When to harvest: Allow pumpkins to ripen on the vine as long as possible, at least until the vines begin to die back. The rinds should be hard enough to resist puncturing with a fingernail. Fruits of small pie pumpkins may be partially green, but they will turn orange as the fruits are cured. Ripe moschata pumpkins have no green stripes, and they turn from pinkish beige to a rich brown beige as they ripen.

> Use pruning shears to cut pumpkins from the vine, leaving at least 1 inch of stem attached.

How to harvest: Use pruning shears to cut pumpkins from the vine, leaving at least 1 inch of stem attached.

Curing: Wipe pumpkins clean with a damp cloth, then cure in a 70 to 80°F (21 to 27°C) location for 2 weeks. In late summer, this usually can be done outdoors.

Storing: Store cured pumpkins in a cool, dry place such as a basement or unheated greenhouse. Check weekly for signs of spoilage. Be watchful for mold forming around the base of the stem or soft spots anywhere on the pumpkin. Rather than take chances, eat or process pumpkins that show signs of deterioration.

Pumpkin
FOOD PRESERVATION OPTIONS

If you have a lot of pumpkin, you can put your freezer and food dehydrator to work saving your pumpkin for late-winter meals.

Freezing Pumpkin

Freezing is the best way to put by a lot of pumpkin in ready-to-use form for baked goods, pies, and soups. After wiping the pumpkin clean, cut it into chunks no bigger than your hand and scrape off the strings and seeds with a grapefruit spoon or small serrated knife. Place the cleaned pieces on their sides in a large baking dish, and roast uncovered at 350°F (180°C) for about 45 minutes, or until the pumpkin pieces soften and release their juices. Allow the pieces to cool, pour off the liquid, and scrape the cooked flesh from the rind. If the flesh is extremely drippy (this can vary from one individual pumpkin to another), drain it in a colander for an hour or so. You can freeze the cooked pumpkin in chunks, mash it with a potato masher, or purée it in a food processor before freezing it in freezer-safe containers.

Drying Pumpkin

Native Americans and early settlers preserved their pumpkins by hanging thin strips by the fire to dry. The pumpkin chips were then added to the cooking pot in winter, along with dried beans and meat. In the modern kitchen, you can quickly cut raw pumpkin into thin slices using a mandoline; the slices can then go straight into the dehydrator. Raw pumpkin chips take only a few hours to dry.

You also can steam 1-inch chunks of raw pumpkin until just done, toss them with sugar and spices, and dry the pieces until leathery in the dehydrator. The "pumpkin chews" make a great snack, and they are a tasty and nutritious addition to grain salads or oatmeal.

Make "pumpkin chews" by steaming 1-inch chunks of raw pumpkin until just done, tossing them in sugar and spices, and drying them in a dehydrator until leathery.

Making Worry-Free Pumpkin Butter

Until the 1980s, garden cooks routinely made and canned sweet and spicy pumpkin butter, a dark brown, spreadable alternative to apple butter if you have no apples. The problem is that pumpkin butter can be up to two full pH points less acidic than apple butter, making it unsafe to can in a water-bath or steam canner. Even making a hybrid apple-pumpkin butter with added lemon juice will not bring the pH of pumpkin butter down to 4.6, the safe level for jams, jellies, and fruit butters.

Even though you can't can it, pumpkin butter is still well worth making (see the Harvest Day Recipe at right). You can slather pumpkin butter over waffles or pancakes, and it makes a great filling for cinnamon rolls or crumb cakes. If you like fruit leathers, you will love "pumpkin pie jerky" made by drying sheets of pumpkin butter in a food dehydrator.

Bubbling-hot pumpkin butter is extremely dense, and I have found that when I spoon it into hot pint jars — kept waiting in a 150°F (65°C) oven — and screw on new lids, the lids seal as the jars cool. I store the cooled, sealed jars in the fridge, where they keep beautifully for a couple of months.

Or simply freeze your pumpkin butter for future use. You can freeze small portions in a silicone muffin pan, and then transfer the frozen pumpkin butter to a freezer bag for long-term storage.

Easy Pumpkin Butter

Makes 5 half-pint jars

---

6 cups pumpkin purée

1 cup brown sugar

2 teaspoons pumpkin pie spice (use commercial mix or combine ground cinnamon, allspice, ginger, and cloves)

½ teaspoon salt

¼ cup lemon juice

---

1 Combine the pumpkin purée, brown sugar, pumpkin pie spice, salt, and lemon juice in a large heavy pot with lid, and bring to a slow simmer. To control splatters, place the lid over the pot, propped open with a large cooking spoon. Cook for about 45 minutes, stirring often, and correct the seasoning by adding small amounts of white sugar or lemon juice to taste.

2 Spoon the thickened pumpkin butter into clean, warm jars, or allow to cool before storing in freezer containers.

RADISHES

(*Raphanus sativus*)

HOW MUCH
Up to 15 row feet

- -

STELLAR VARIETIES
'Champion', 'Easter Egg', 'French Breakfast', and 'Misato Rose'

- -

BEST WAYS TO PRESERVE
Refrigerate, ferment, or pickle

If you think of radishes exclusively as a salad vegetable, think again. Roasting radishes tames and mellows their flavors, so they become like savory little turnips, only with more color, and you can use radishes as stir-fry vegetables, too. Or preserve raw radishes by combining them with cabbage and other vegetables in delicious veggie ferments.

Radishes often are regarded as the perfect spring vegetable for beginning gardeners, but this is a myth. Spring's changeable weather is hard on radishes, and hungry flea beetles make things worse, so spring radishes usually need attentive help from their keeper. The story changes in the fall, when the soil is getting cooler rather than warmer. Radishes that plump up when fall weather gets nippy are always the best ones of the year.

HOW MANY TO PLANT?

Radishes mature quickly and all at once, so it is best to make multiple small sowings. In addition to growing radishes in their own row or bed, you can use them as markers between rows of slow-growing vegetables like carrots, parsley, or parsnips. We eat all of our spring radishes fresh, so those plantings are very small. Grow more radishes in fall — up to 15 row feet — to use in vegetable roasts and fermentation projects.

Best Radishes
FOR THE
Homegrown Pantry

You won't need special radish varieties for roasting or fermenting, because the same radishes that bring color and flavor to salads are great in cooked dishes or fermented with cabbage. In addition to fast-maturing round radishes, consider varieties with elongated roots, including Chinese radishes, which take less time to scrub and slice. If you love fermented foods, you will definitely want to grow big daikon radishes in the fall, too.

'Shunkyo' Chinese

'Eastern Egg' salad

'Cherry Belle' salad

'Alpine' daikon

HOW TO
Grow Radishes

When: Be patient when growing radishes in spring, and wait until 3 to 4 weeks before your last spring frost to start planting them. The best spring radishes grow when the soil is still cool but days are getting steadily warmer. In fall, start planting radishes about 8 weeks before your first fall frost.

- -

Planting: Radishes are not heavy feeders, so enrich their planting space with either 1 inch of good compost or a light sprinkling of a balanced organic fertilizer. Radish seeds are dependable germinators, but you can enhance fast, uniform sprouting by covering the seeded bed with a double thickness of fabric row cover until the seedlings appear.

- -

Maintenance: It is almost always necessary to thin radish seedlings to no less than 2 inches apart. Thin radishes early, when they have only two or three leaves, by using scissors to snip off extra seedlings at the soil line. This type of thinning minimizes disturbance to roots of neighboring plants, which is an important consideration when growing radishes. Weeding should be done early and often for the same reason.

In any season, fast-growing radishes must be kept constantly moist — a little wet is better than dry.

Consistent moisture is the essential key to growing good radishes. Radish flavor is primarily determined by variety, but hot weather and drought encourage the development of spicy flavor compounds, which are similar to those found in horseradish.

Radish Pests and Diseases

The longer radishes stay in the ground, the more likely they are to develop cosmetic problems caused by weevils, wireworms, or cracking due to changing soil moisture levels. Growing radishes quickly, in ideal weather, is the best way to avoid these problems.

Spring crops of radishes are often hit hard by flea beetles, which leave tiny holes in the leaves but do not injure the roots. You can avoid them altogether by growing radishes under row cover tunnels installed at planting time. Keep in mind that skin imperfections disappear when radishes are cut up and cooked.

All spring-sown radishes are inclined to bolt, especially if they are planted very early and exposed to cold weather. Planting later in spring reduces the likelihood that plants will bolt instead of producing plump roots. Bolting is rare with radishes grown in late summer and fall.

HARVESTING AND STORING
Radishes

When: As radish roots plump up, they push up out of the soil. Harvest radishes within a few days after the roots swell.

How: Immediately cut off the leaves with a sharp knife or kitchen shears. Wash the radishes gently to remove soil, but wait until just before using them to scrub them clean. Dry between clean kitchen towels before storing in plastic bags in the refrigerator for up to 2 months.

The
Daikon Dilemma

Oriental daikon radishes (*Raphanus sativus* var. *longipinnatus*) are one of my favorite fall crops. In addition to eating the long, lovely roots, daikons produce an abundance of foliage for composting. I plant daikon radishes for the table and for the soil, and also use them as a fill-in crop when other fall planting plans go asunder. Weeds don't have a chance once the daikons get going, and I love the way the roots push up out of the ground when they reach perfect condition for harvesting.

Daikon radishes are at peak eating quality when they are less than 12 inches long, but many varieties will continue to grow much larger if given the chance. Cold winter weather causes daikon radishes to die back and rot, but this is what you want to happen! When you use unharvested daikons as a cover crop, the deep roots create a vertical vein of organic matter in the soil. As a "bio-drill" crop to improve soil tilth and health, daikon radishes have it all — they suppress weeds, penetrate compacted subsoil, and can easily be killed by chopping off their heads in climates mild enough to permit their winter survival.

Which daikons to eat, and which to allot to the soil? The dilemma will never go away, but it is most easily handled by growing plenty of daikon radishes every fall.

Radish
FOOD PRESERVATION OPTIONS

Radishes store well in the refrigerator, but make plans for excess radishes soon after they are harvested, while they are still in perfect condition. Radishes are ideal fermentation partners for cabbage — the simple combination of shredded cabbage, sliced radishes, and salt makes a delicious sauerkraut (see page 93 for step-by-step instructions). Or ferment sliced daikon radishes with plenty of garlic for the crunchiest "pickles" of fall. Small, one-bite radishes can be pickled in a vinegar brine and kept in the refrigerator for use in salads. Processing softens radishes, but they stay crisp for weeks when handled as refrigerator pickles.

Fermented
red radishes

Radish Butter

Many people eat sliced radishes on buttered bread, which is the idea behind radish butter. This is a great use for cracked or blemished radishes.

Makes about 3 cups

2	cups clean, trimmed radishes
2	sticks softened butter (or half butter and half cream cheese)
1	tablespoon chopped fresh herbs, such as dill, fennel, or marjoram
¼	teaspoon salt

Coarsely chop the radishes in a food processor, then add the butter, herbs, and salt, and mix until combined. Store in the refrigerator for up to 3 days. Allow to soften at room temperature for an hour before serving on bread or crackers.

RHUBARB
(Rheum × hybridum)

HOW MUCH
3 plants

- -

STELLAR VARIETIES
'Victoria', 'McDonald', 'Crimson Red', and STARKRIMSON ('K-1')

- -

BEST WAYS TO PRESERVE
Freeze, can, or dry

From its Himalayan home, robust rhubarb got a lift to Europe with Marco Polo and was introduced in America around 1820. Hardy and resilient, rhubarb is now grown in temperate climates around the world. One of only a few perennial vegetables, rhubarb plants often produce for years with little care.

Growing rhubarb is easy in climates that are cold enough to grow tulips as perennials, or in Zones 3 to 7. The plants must have a cold-induced period of winter rest, and they also suffer when temperatures rise above 90°F (32°C). In the northern half of North America, rhubarb plants can be phenomenally productive, yielding stalk after stalk for pies, preserves, baked goods, and teas. Rhubarb's sour lemony flavor is due in large part to oxalic acid, which reaches toxic levels in rhubarb leaves. Rhubarb leaves should never be eaten but are perfectly safe to use as compost or mulch.

Best Rhubarb
FOR THE
Homegrown Pantry

Rhubarb varieties vary in stem color, vigor, and heat tolerance, but the differences are small.

Two older rhubarb varieties that have stood the test of time, 'Victoria' and 'McDonald', produce light green stalks tinged with red. The vigorous, disease-resistant plants are good choices for hot summer areas, though they thrive in colder climates, too.

Red stalk color is more pronounced in rhubarb varieties that can do double duty as edible ornamentals, such as 'Crimson Red' and STARKRIMSON ('K-1'). While red rhubarb is often preferred in markets, red stem color has no bearing on flavor.

If one of your neighbors is growing rhubarb, you may be able to get an excellent locally adapted strain for the asking. Most gardeners with established rhubarb plants have plenty of divisions that can be cut off and shared.

HOW MUCH TO PLANT?

For most households, three established rhubarb plants will easily produce a year's supply. More than five plants is probably too many unless you have a very large family.

HOW TO
Grow Rhubarb

When: Planting rhubarb is best done in spring, a few weeks before your last frost date, in moist, fertile soil in full sun to partial afternoon shade.

- -

Planting: Space plants 4 to 5 feet apart, or use them as focal point plants around your garden's boundary. Enrich planting holes generously with compost as well as a standard application of a balanced organic fertilizer when planting rhubarb.

- -

Maintenance: Allow a year for transplanted rhubarb to become established in the garden. Mulch to prevent weeds, and provide water during dry spells. In many areas, rhubarb plants deteriorate in midsummer and then make a comeback in fall. Rhubarb plants are killed to the ground by hard freezes, and the roots remain dormant through winter.

In late winter, rake up and compost old mulch and plant debris from your rhubarb patch, and scatter a balanced organic fertilizer over the soil. Top off with a thick organic mulch that will deter weeds until the plants leaf out.

Propagation: Established rhubarb plants multiply by division. New offshoots can be dug away and replanted or shared in late spring, when plants are showing vigorous new growth, or in late summer. Plants that have more than three crowns should have the outermost ones removed to preserve plant vigor. Use a sharp spade to sever offshoots without digging up the main crown.

Death by Rhubarb?

Rhubarb stems contain much less oxalic acid than the leaves, so they are safe to eat in reasonable quantities and provide vitamins A and C. But eating too much rhubarb too often might not be a good idea because of possible stress to kidneys, inflammation of joints, or even death. An adult would need to eat several pounds of rhubarb to feel ill effects, with 20 to 25 pounds of fresh rhubarb as a lethal dose.

Possible death by rhubarb is an entirely modern fear, because until refined sugar became cheap and widely available, rhubarb's sour flavor naturally kept people from eating too much. Limiting how much sugar you eat will limit your rhubarb intake, too. The sugar dilemma has also led me to rediscover several old uses for rhubarb, like using rhubarb juice in place of lemon juice to prevent discoloration of apples and other cut fruits. Small pieces of lightly cooked rhubarb readily give up their juice.

Rhubarb Pests and Diseases

The most common cause of holes in rhubarb leaves are slugs, which take shelter beneath the low leaves during the day. Remove withered leaves to reduce slug habitat, hand-pick the slugs at night, or put out slug traps baited with beer. In some years, Japanese beetles develop a strong appetite for rhubarb leaves, but they are easy to hand-pick into a broad bowl on cool mornings.

Leaf spots often become numerous on older rhubarb leaves in hot, humid weather, and in some seasons the plants may melt down to a few stalks in midsummer. Then the plants come back in early fall and produce a few nice young stems for eating or drinking.

HARVESTING AND STORING
Rhubarb

When: A year after planting, harvest two or three rhubarb stalks per plant weekly in late spring by twisting them away from the base. In subsequent seasons, harvest all the stalks you want for 6 weeks in late spring, and then allow the plants to grow freely. In many years, rhubarb plants may struggle through summer hot spells to the point of near collapse, and then produce lovely new stems in late summer and fall. Late-summer rhubarb is infinitely edible.

- -

How: After harvesting, cut off the rhubarb leaves. Cut the rhubarb stalks into uniform lengths and store in plastic bags in the refrigerator. To prepare rhubarb for use in recipes, remove long strings from large stalks, as you might do with celery. Slice the rhubarb into bite-size pieces, place them in a heatproof bowl, and cover with boiling water. Drain after 1 minute. This process removes excess astringency so that recipes don't require quite as much sugar.

In late spring, after the plants show vigorous growth, watch for the emergence of huge flower clusters, and cut them off to keep plants from expending energy producing flowers and unwanted seeds.

Rhubarb
FOOD PRESERVATION OPTIONS

Rhubarb is famous for producing too well, which is not a problem if you store the excess in a variety of ways. Rhubarb can be frozen, canned, or dried. Sugar is a major ingredient in most rhubarb recipes, but a few preservation methods require no sugar, such as drying small pieces of rhubarb to use in tea or freezing rhubarb juice to use as a lemon juice substitute.

Freezing Rhubarb

Rhubarb is easy to freeze, with no blanching required. However, because rhubarb softens as it thaws, it is best to remove strings and have pieces cut the way you want them before you put them in the freezer. Freeze rhubarb on cookie sheets and transfer the frozen pieces to freezer-safe containers.

Unsweetened rhubarb juice can be used in place of lemon juice in hundreds of recipes.

To save space, you can freeze unsweetened rhubarb juice, which can be used in place of lemon juice in hundreds of recipes. Cook chunks of rhubarb in just enough water to cover until soft, about 20 minutes. Mash gently with a fork. Strain the mixture through a strainer, and freeze the liquid in ice cube trays.

If you take warm rhubarb juice and mix it with an equal measure of sugar, you will have rhubarb syrup, which can serve as the base for many great drinks. Adding only a light splash of rhubarb syrup turns sparkling water into soda, or you can use it to make sweet not-really-lemonade or lemon tea. Freeze rhubarb syrup in ice cube trays, or can it in small half-pint jars. Process them in a water-bath or steam canner for 10 minutes.

Canning Rhubarb

In addition to canning versatile rhubarb syrup, many families treasure their homemade rhubarb-strawberry jam or rhubarb-ginger marmalade, which always turn out good because common recipes contain large amounts of sugar — usually more sugar than fruit. Strawberries, raspberries, or cherries bring a soft juiciness to rhubarb jam, and you can make rhubarb-and-berry jams using low-sugar pectin products.

Drying Rhubarb

Thin slices of rhubarb are fast and easy to dry in a food dehydrator. The dried rhubarb makes an excellent addition to herb teas by giving every brew a citrusy edge. And should you be making a recipe that calls for lemon and you have none, a few little nuggets of dried rhubarb can fill the need.

Candying rhubarb is a form of drying, and it is one of very few drying recipes that can be done in a warm oven that can be kept below 180°F (80°C). If you like sour candies, you will love candied rhubarb.

Chewy Candied Rhubarb

Makes about 1 quart

- 2 cups sugar
- ½ cup water
- 4 large stalks rhubarb

1 In a large saucepan, combine the sugar and water over medium heat until the sugar melts.

2 Trim the strings from the rhubarb, and either slice it diagonally into ⅛-inch slices or use a vegetable peeler to cut 6-inch-long pieces into thin strips. Place the rhubarb in the warm syrup, and toss with your hands to coat all the pieces. Allow to sit for 30 minutes to 1 hour.

3 Arrange the sugared pieces of rhubarb on dehydrator trays and dry at medium heat (125 to 135°F/50 to 60°C) for a few hours, checking them each hour. When the pieces become leathery, turn off the heat and allow them to rest for an hour before removing them from the trays. If they are entirely too sticky to handle, place the trays in the freezer for an hour, and then use a spatula to gently loosen the pieces. Store in the freezer, or dry the pieces a little more, until they are no longer sticky, and store in vacuum-sealed bags kept in a cool, dry place.

RUTABAGAS

(*Brassica napus var. napobrassica*)

HOW MUCH
10 plants

- -

STELLAR VARIETIES
'Laurentian' and 'American Purple Top'

- -

BEST WAYS TO PRESERVE
Place in cold storage, freeze, or ferment

Rutabagas rarely make it onto "most popular vegetable" lists, but they should! An ancient cross between turnips and cabbage, rutabagas have thick, dark leaves similar to those of broccoli. Although they are slow to mature, the tough plants take care of themselves, and the buttery roots are worth the wait. Rich soil, ample spacing, and protection from deer are all you need to grow these delicious roots.

When grown from midsummer through fall, rutabagas produce dense, fine-textured roots that become sweeter as the soil gets colder. Rutabagas that are harvested just before the first hard freeze will store for several months in the refrigerator or in a cold root cellar, lasting well into winter. This gives you plenty of time to use your rutabagas in fall fermentation projects, or blanch chunks to be stored in the freezer.

Best Rutabagas
FOR THE
Homegrown Pantry

I have noticed little difference when growing different rutabaga varieties side by side in the garden. It is best to bypass antique varieties, because for a while strains were selected to be good food to feed pigs in winter. Most garden seed companies sell culinary-quality varieties such as 'Laurentian', 'American Purple Top', or their descendants.

There are 'Purple Top' turnips, too, and a few turnip varieties with yellow flesh, but rutabagas are a distinctive root crop with a sweet cabbage flavor that sets them apart. The two crops also can work together in the fall garden. Rutabagas are planted a month before turnips, so you can increase the size of your turnip planting in years when you get a poor stand of rutabagas.

HOW MANY TO PLANT?

Here you must guess how many times you are likely to serve rutabagas over 3 months. About 10 big rutabagas is enough for most households, but in many climates garden rutabagas are smaller than the supermarket versions, which are grown over a long season in cool climates. Baseball-size rutabagas grown during summer's second half are quite excellent, so you may want to grow more of them. There are many ways to cook rutabaga, but the most popular ones are to make baked rutabaga "fries," to mash them with potatoes, or to include chunks of rutabaga in pans of mixed roasted vegetables.

'Purple Top' turnip

'American Purple Top' rutabaga

HOW TO
Grow Rutabagas

When: Most root crops suffer when handled as transplanted seedlings, but not rutabagas. This is fortunate, because the best time to plant rutabagas is in midsummer, when both the soil and sun may be too hot to promote good germination and early growth. Start seeds 10 to 12 weeks before your first fall frost date. If you don't have good weather for direct-seeding, simply start the seeds indoors where temperatures are constantly cool, grow the seedlings outside in partial shade for a couple of weeks, and set them out during a spell of kind weather.

- -

Where: Rutabagas like slightly acidic clay loam soil best, but they can be grown in all soil types except extreme sand. The plants have big appetites, so planting holes should be enriched with compost and a balanced organic fertilizer. Rutabagas are sensitive to boron deficiency, so also amend the bed with a light sprinkling of household borax if you often see hollow stems in your broccoli. Hollow broccoli stems are no big deal, but when interior holes develop in rutabagas, their quality is seriously compromised.

- -

Planting: Spacing directly affects the size of mature rutabaga roots. Plants grown less than 8 inches apart will tend to be elongated and small; plants grown 16 inches apart are more likely to produce large, round roots. Once the plants are set out or thinned and weeded, provide a mulch of grass clippings or other material to keep the soil cool and moist. If necessary, use a row cover tunnel to protect the little plants from grasshoppers and other summer pests.

You can get a head start with rutabagas by sowing seeds in flats and transplanting the seedlings to the garden when they are big enough to handle.

Maintenance: As nights become longer and cooler in late summer, and pests become less numerous, you can uncover your rutabagas, start giving them more water, and watch the plants explode with growth. As rutabagas grow, they often shed their oldest leaves, which you should gather up and compost. This will reduce slug problems and interrupt the life cycles of many pests and diseases.

In the weeks just before they bulb, rutabagas need soil that is constantly moist. If the soil dries out, a heavy rain can cause drought-stressed rutabagas to crack.

Rutabaga Pests and Diseases

The same pests that bother broccoli and cabbage sometimes injure rutabagas; it is seldom favored because of the plants' coarse leaves. Disease problems are rare in gardens where cabbage family crops are rotated to prevent the buildup of diseases that live in soil and infect plant roots.

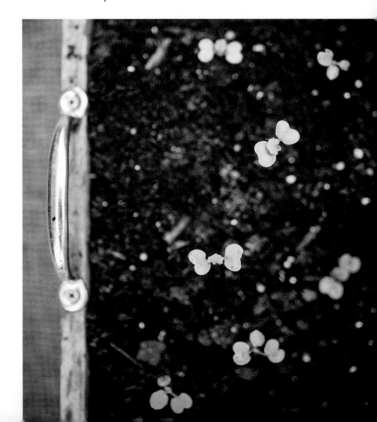

HARVESTING AND STORING
Rutabagas

When: You can start harvesting rutabagas for fresh use as soon as they reach acceptable size, but don't hurry. Rutabagas become sweeter as the temperatures fall, so wait until after your first frost to harvest the bulk of the crop. Do bring them in before a hard freeze comes.

- -

How: Immediately trim the tops back to half an inch to prevent moisture loss, and gently wash the roots to remove excess soil. Pat dry and store in plastic bags in your refrigerator, like carrots. In a root cellar, it is best to pack rutabagas in containers filled with damp sand or sawdust to delay shriveling.

Rutabaga
FOOD PRESERVATION OPTIONS

A highly nutritious food, rutabagas are an excellent source of vitamins A and C, plus potassium and fiber. Good storage conditions are essential to preserving these nutrients, so if you can't keep your rutabagas refrigerated, it's best to cook and freeze them. Peel, pare, and steam until tender, and freeze in airtight containers. Rutabagas also can be pressure canned in combination with other low-acid end-of-season veggies in soup mixes. For fabulous crunch in fall fermentation projects, cut rutabagas into thin matchsticks and ferment with cabbage and other fall vegetables.

For fabulous crunch in fall fermentation projects, cut rutabagas into thin matchsticks and ferment with cabbage and other fall vegetables.

SPINACH

(Spinacia oleracea)

HOW MUCH
5 row feet per person in spring, 10 row feet per person in fall

- -

STELLAR VARIETIES
'Tyee', 'Winter Bloomsdale', and 'Space'

- -

BEST WAYS TO PRESERVE
Freeze or ferment

Spinach gets the prize for the most cold-tolerant of salad greens, so it occupies a special place in the garden as a fall-to-spring crop. Spinach that is planted in fall and protected through winter beneath a tunnel or rigid cold frame grows very little while days are short and dim, and then comes back to life in spring and produces large amounts of crisp, sweet leaves. You can grow spinach in spring, too, though spring-grown plants promptly bolt when days get long in early summer.

Most gardeners blanch and freeze their excess spinach. When thawed and drained, frozen spinach is ready to use for dips, stuffed pasta, or creamy casseroles.

[
Spinach gets the prize for the most cold-tolerant of salad greens.
]

Best Spinach

FOR THE

Homegrown Pantry

Sometimes called winter spinach, varieties with dark green, crinkled leaves like 'Tyee' and 'Winter Bloomsdale' hold up well to cold temperatures, so they are the best types to grow through the winter.

Smooth-leafed varieties like 'Space' are a lighter shade of green, and the plants tend to grow upright, making the leaves easier to clean. Fast and easy to grow, smooth-leafed spinach is ideal as a spring salad spinach.

HOW MUCH TO PLANT?

Spinach does not hold very long in the garden when grown in spring, so keep plantings small, to less than 5 row feet per person. You will probably have extra to freeze. In fall, plant as much spinach as you can keep covered through winter, up to 10 row feet, or about 20 plants per person. Like other greens, spinach is harvested over a period of weeks or even months in the case of fall-to-winter spinach. Use my numbers as a starting point, and keep records of your plantings to find the right amount to grow for your household.

'Space'   'Tyee'

HOW TO
Grow Spinach

When: Make your first sowing of the year in late winter by starting a few spinach seeds indoors about 6 weeks before your last frost. Set out the seedlings under a row cover tunnel, and sow more seeds directly in the garden about 3 weeks before your last frost. In fall, sow spinach for fall harvest about 8 weeks before your last frost. Sow spinach for growing through winter about 1 month before your first fall frost date.

- -

Planting: Prepare the planting bed by loosening the soil at least 10 inches deep and mixing in a 1-inch layer of compost and a balanced organic fertilizer. Sow seeds ½-inch deep and 2 inches apart in rows spaced at least 8 inches apart. As the plants grow, gradually thin them so the leaves of neighboring plants barely overlap.

Prime Your Spinach Seeds

Spinach seeds can be spotty germinators, but you can improve their sprouting rate by priming them, a simple procedure that takes only a few days. About a week before planting, soak spinach seeds in room-temperature water for 24 hours. Place the wet seeds on a paper towel and allow to dry at room temperature for a day or two. Shift the seeds to an airtight container, and keep the seeds in a cool place for no more than a week before planting them. The primed seeds will retain enough moisture to complete the first stages of germination. After planting, primed spinach seeds germinate in only 5 days, compared to 10 days or more for seeds straight out of the packet.

Maintenance: In spring, fertilize overwintered plants with a thorough drench of a liquid organic fertilizer after they show new growth. Overwintered spinach often starts growing before the soil is warm enough to release enough nitrogen to meet the plants' needs.

Spinach Pests and Diseases

Moist conditions can set the scene for mildews and leaf spot diseases, so keep plants spaced wide enough apart to permit good air circulation. Aphids and leaf-hoppers can transmit viral diseases to spinach, so pull up plants that show distorted new growth and yellowing of older leaves.

Leaf miners, the larvae of a small fly, sometimes make meandering trails in spinach leaves. Gently squash them with your fingers, or remove affected leaves. Where leaf miners are a common pest, use row covers to exclude them from your spinach patch.

HARVESTING, STORING, AND PRESERVING
Spinach

When: Start pinching outer leaves when the plants are about 6 weeks old. New leaves will grow from the plants' centers.

- -

How: Rinse the leaves clean, spin or pat dry, and refrigerate immediately.

Food Preservation: Spinach is easy to blanch and freeze in small containers. I like to blanch it in steam for a minute or two, but some people use their microwaves to steam blanch spinach (allow 1 to 2 minutes, depending on your microwave). You can also include spinach in mixed fall ferments that include radishes, carrots, and garlic.

Spinach will stay productive for weeks if you harvest a few leaves at a time from the outside of the plants. New leaves emerge from the plants' center.

'Benning's Green Tint'
patty pan

'Early Prolific'
straightneck

'Zephyr'
straightneck

'Dark Green'
zucchini

'Gold Rush'
yellow zucchini

SUMMER SQUASH
(Cucurbita pepo)

HOW MUCH
4 plants per person

- -

STELLAR VARIETIES
'Yellow Crookneck', 'Raven' zucchini, and 'Sunburst' pattypan

- -

BEST WAYS TO PRESERVE
Dry, freeze, or can

Few crops express the exuberance of summer like summer squash. The oversize, overlapping leaves make efficient solar collectors, which energize fast growth and early maturation in this variable group of edible gourds.

Summer squash come in so many shapes, sizes, and colors that you can have great fun experimenting with different varieties. When you use up a seed packet, replace it with something slightly different — for example, a yellow zucchini in place of a green one. Different summer squash varieties happily pollinate one another, so you can grow a mixture of varieties in one row or bed without worrying about compatibility issues.

Summer squash makes its crop all at once, so be ready with plans to preserve big batches. Squash should be cooked before it is frozen, but it can be dried raw. You can also use your summer squash to make delicious canned relishes.

Best Summer Squash

FOR THE
Homegrown Pantry

You probably like some types of summer squash better than others, but it pays to diversify into unusual forms, shapes, and colors. When it comes to summer squash, diversity in the garden prevents boredom at the table, in the dehydrator, and in the canning jar!

- Long, straight varieties like zucchinis and yellow straightneck squash are the easiest types to slice or grate using a mandoline or spiral slicer, which is hugely important when you are making relishes or filling a dehydrator.

- Small pattypans and round zucchinis are perfect for hollowing out and using as single-serving stuffed squash. These can be prepped, steam blanched, and frozen for making stuffed squash in winter.

- Consider colors when deciding which summer squash to grow in any given season. A three-way mix of one dark green, one light green, and one bright yellow–fruited variety makes a pleasing combination in the garden and on the plate.

Some varieties grow into tight bushes, while others will sprawl 6 feet or more. Keep notes on how various varieties perform in your garden and whether their growth habit works well for you. In my experience, it's worth tolerating the chaos of varieties that develop long vines because they produce so many squash. Many times I will pull out bush types that have gone buggy and continue harvesting squash from sprawling varieties for 2 or 3 more weeks.

HOW MUCH TO PLANT?

Use four plants (yielding roughly 50 total pounds of squash) per person as a starting point for growing enough frozen, dried, and pickled squash to last a year, and adjust up or down based on how well summer squash produces in your garden and how much you like the preserved versions. For pollination purposes, six plants give bees plenty to work with during bloom season. A good average yield is 10 to 15 pounds per plant, or more for zucchini.

HOW TO
Grow Summer Squash

When: Plant summer squash in late spring, after the soil has warmed and the last frost has passed. You can direct-sow the seeds into prepared beds, but you will have better control over timing and spacing if you start seeds in containers and plant the seedlings exactly where you want them. You won't need fluorescent lights, because by late spring you can grow the seedlings outdoors, in real sunlight. I use 4-inch square containers filled with ordinary potting soil, keep the pots indoors until the seeds sprout, and immediately move them to a sheltered spot outside. Squash seedlings are ready to set out as soon as the first true leaf appears, when they are about 3 weeks old.

- -

Planting: Allow at least 2 feet of space between robust summer squash plants — 3 is even better. Mix a handful of a balanced organic fertilizer into each planting spot, and then go back and bury a heaping shovelful of compost in each planting hole, too. Do not skip the compost with this crop, because summer squash roots form dynamic partnerships with microcritters in the compost, which in turn makes a huge difference in the health and vigor of the plants.

No-Surprises Squash Seeds

Start with summer squash seeds from a reputable supplier. Cucurbit seeds are often offered at seed exchanges, but because different types of summer squash cross-pollinate with such enthusiasm, off-types are common in casually saved seeds. Buying summer squash seeds grown by professionals is money well spent.

Summer Squash Pests and Diseases

Summer squash are the favorite host plant of two widespread pests: squash bugs and squash vine borers. The easiest way to sidestep these pests is to keep squash plants covered with floating row cover until they start blooming and need to be visited by bees.

- **Squash bugs** are gray bugs with flat backs, about the size of a fingernail. They suck juices from squash stems, leaves, and fruits, which would not be so bad if there were only a few of them. But squash bugs lay many clusters of glossy brown eggs on leaves, and once those hatch you have a problem. Delaying planting until late spring can help manage squash bugs, but you should still plan to hand-pick squash bugs and their egg clusters from your plants.

- **Squash vine borers** are the larvae of a fast-moving moth that lays eggs on the squash plant's thick stem, and the hatchlings bore into the stem and feed there. When you remove the row covers, loosely cover the base of each stem with aluminum foil to reduce or delay plant death due to borers.

You may see yellow and black cucumber beetles chewing on squash flowers, too, but they are usually a minor pest on this crop. As squash vines age, non-resistant varieties may show white patches of powdery mildew. Where powdery mildew is a persistent problem, make use of the many resistant varieties available.

Hand-Pollinating
Summer Squash

Summer squash develops male and female flowers, and pollen from the male flowers must make its way to receptive females. Males often appear first, ready to attract pollinators, so by the time female blossoms open, the planting should be buzzing with bees during the morning hours. If few pollinators show up, you can do the job yourself. To hand-pollinate squash, use a feather or a dry artist paintbrush to wipe up pollen from inside male flowers, and then dab it inside female flowers. Male flowers are borne on straight stems, while there is always a tiny squash in place of a stem on the females. Pollinate random flowers for several minutes, just like a bee. The best time to hand-pollinate squash blossoms is midmorning, just after the flowers open and the pollen is fresh.

HARVESTING AND STORING
Summer Squash

When: Summer squash can be harvested as babies, with the blossoms attached, for a beautiful show at the table, but the best squash for putting by are fully grown fruits at their peak. The skin should still be tender, with the gloss of youth, and inside the seeds should be barely formed and quite soft. When your squash is in full production, harvest daily to keep from missing perfect specimens.

How: Use a sharp knife to cut squash from the stem. Sometimes they will twist off, but using a knife is better for the squash and the plants. Immediately bring the squash indoors, wash them in cool water, pat dry, and refrigerate in plastic bags until you are ready to cook or process them. Hold summer squash in the refrigerator for no more than 5 days.

Summer Squash
FOOD PRESERVATION OPTIONS

You will need more than one preservation method to do justice to prolific summer squash. Drying squash is fast and easy if you have a dehydrator, and some of your summer squash can go into canned pickles and relishes, too. Do freeze some of your crop, particularly little squash that are the right size for stuffing. Frozen single-serving squash take up freezer space, but in winter they emerge as stars in any meal.

Freezing Summer Squash

You can simply blanch, cool, and freeze sliced or cubed summer squash, but grilling or roasting gives you a chance to flavor up your squash before it goes into the freezer. For example, you can marinate ½-inch-thick slabs of squash in an Italian dressing for an hour before grilling them until halfway done. When cool, freeze singly on cookie sheets before transferring to freezer-safe containers.

Another way to prepare summer squash for freezing is to roast 2-inch chunks in a large roasting pan. First sprinkle the pieces generously with sea salt and various dried spices — cumin and chili powder, paprika and turmeric, or a curry blend — and then toss them with 1 tablespoon or so of olive oil. Bake uncovered at 375°F (190°C) for 20 to 25 minutes. The sizzling-hot pieces lose moisture as they steam, which helps to concentrate their flavor. Pack into freezer-safe containers when cool.

You also can roast summer squash with savory vegetables like onions, garlic, and peppers. This mixture will cook down into a tasty veggie spread or dip perfect for freezing in small packages.

1. Wash the squash well, and cut across the blossom end to help the squash sit flat. When preparing elongated squash for stuffing, cut them in half lengthwise.

2. Use a small knife to cut out the outline for the part of the squash to be scooped out. Use a melon baller or grapefruit spoon to carve a bowl into the squash, being careful not to cut through the bottom.

3. Steam blanch the prepared pieces for about 6 minutes, or until they are brightly colored and barely done. Cool on ice, then allow to drain on clean towels for a few minutes. Freeze in freezer bags.

Drying Summer Squash

Food preservation experts do not agree on whether or not summer squash requires blanching before it is dried. Having tried both methods, drying raw ¼-inch-thick slices is fast and easy, and the chips taste like what they are — condensed summer squash. Blanched slices take twice as long to dry, and go through a messy goo period halfway through when they cannot be touched. On the plus side, pre-blanched dried squash slices are better for snacking because they are easier to chew.

Note that you can dry summer squash in various shapes — including cubes, matchsticks, or even noodles cut with a spiral slicer made for veggies. Thin pieces dry very fast and also rehydrate quickly, so experiment with your mandoline or other cutting equipment to see what you like best.

I store my dried squash in the freezer, which means I can dry them to the leathery stage and not worry about spoilage from excess moisture. If you store your dried food under warmer conditions, dry your squash until it is hard but not cracker crisp, and use a vacuum sealer as an additional safeguard against spoilage.

Canning Squash Pickles and Relishes

In poor cucumber years, summer squash does a fantastic job filling in as a pickle ingredient as long as the recipe is well endowed with vinegar and sugar. Most recipes for bread-and-butter pickles can be made with summer squash, but I think the best use for a tabletop covered with summer squash is Zucchini and Friends Relish (page 206). As long as you don't change the brine mixture, you can vary ingredients slightly according to what you have coming from the garden.

Dry squash in different shapes for various recipes — thin ribbons for pasta, shreds for baking, or slices for soups and casseroles. Roasting squash before freezing it adds flavor and saves time.

Zucchini and Friends Relish

Makes about 5 pints

- 8 cups finely chopped or coarsely grated zucchini or other summer squash
- 2 cups finely chopped onions
- 2 carrots, grated
- 1 ripe bell pepper, chopped

  About 5 tablespoons pickling or sea salt
- 2 cups white vinegar
- 3 cups sugar
- 1 teaspoon mustard seeds
- 1 teaspoon ground turmeric

1 Combine the squash, onions, carrots, and pepper in a large bowl and sprinkle the salt over them. Place a few ice cubes on top, cover with a clean cloth, and let stand 6 hours or overnight.

2 Drain the vegetables in a colander, and rinse thoroughly with cool water to remove excess salt. Then rinse again. The rinsed pieces should taste pleasantly salty.

3 Combine the vinegar, sugar, mustard seeds, and turmeric in a large pot and bring to a simmer over medium heat. Add the vegetables and return to a simmer. Cook for 5 minutes.

4 Pack the mixture into hot pint jars, leaving ½ inch of headspace. Process in a water-bath or steam canner for 10 minutes, as described on pages 36–37.

SWEET POTATOES

(*Ipomoea batatas*)

HOW MUCH
12 to 14 plants per person

STELLAR VARIETIES
'Covington' orange, 'O'Henry' white, and 'Violetta' purple

BEST WAYS TO PRESERVE
Place in cool storage, freeze, or dry

Sweet potatoes have long been a staple crop in climates with warm, muggy summers, but modern varieties have helped to push the growing range for this super-nutritious root crop all the way to Ontario. Few crops keep as well as sweet potatoes, which can be stored for months at cool room temperatures. Unlike many other crops, the quality of sweet potatoes improves in storage. Sweet potatoes taste best about 2 months after they have been dug.

In the garden, sweet potatoes make beautiful edible ornamentals because of their lush summer growth. An ideal crop to grow on a gentle slope, vigorous sweet potato vines knit themselves together into a tangle of foliage that shades the soil and suppresses weeds. A warm-season crop, sweet potatoes are planted in early summer, after tomatoes, and stay in the ground until early fall. Sweet potatoes grow best in warm, well-drained soil with a slightly acidic pH.

Unlike many other crops, the quality of sweet potatoes improves in storage.

Best Sweet Potatoes

FOR THE

Homegrown Pantry

Sweet potato varieties vary in the color of their flesh and skins, as well as in their leaf shape, texture, and vine length.

- **Orange-fleshed sweet potatoes** are the most popular and nutritious type, and some short-vined varieties such as 'Georgia Jet' grow fast enough to make good crops where you have only 100 days of warm summer weather. Productive, disease-resistant varieties such as 'Covington' or 'Beauregard' deserve a trial in any garden for their uniformity and fine eating quality. The cooked flesh of most orange sweet potatoes is very soft and moist.

- **White-fleshed sweet potatoes**, including Japanese varieties, are as easy to grow as those with orange flesh, and popular favorites like 'O'Henry' and 'Sumor' mature in only about 100 days. Fun to use in the kitchen, the cooked flesh of white sweet potatoes is distinctly creamy, making it a favorite for soups or baby food. Easier to grow and store in warm climates compared to regular potatoes, white sweet potatoes make excellent potato salad.

- **Purple-fleshed sweet potatoes** need a long, warm season to produce good crops, but the starchy, deep purple roots of varieties like 'Violetta' and 'All Purple' are worth the 120-day wait. The dry flesh of purple sweet potatoes makes them perfect for baking or frying, and the purple pigments also enhance their nutritional value with increased antioxidants.

Japanese 'Murasaki'

'Covington'

'O'Henry'

HOW MANY TO PLANT?

Climate and growing conditions influence sweet potato productivity, which ranges between 1 and 2 pounds per plant. Estimate 12 to 14 plants per person for eating fresh and storing, which should produce about 25 pounds per person.

Growing sweet potatoes begins with rooted stem cuttings, called slips, which sprout from the ends of stored tubers. If you want to grow your own slips, you can start with sweet potatoes you grew the previous year, or work with purchased sweet potatoes you would like to grow.

Where: Choose a site with fertile, well-drained soil in full sun. Where summers are short, use black or clear plastic to warm the soil where you want to grow sweet potatoes. Row-cover tunnels (see page 7) also can be used to give sweet potatoes the early-season warmth they crave.

Planting: Sweet potatoes benefit from a generous helping of fully rotted compost dug into the soil before planting, along with a light application of a balanced organic fertilizer. Space slips at least 12 inches apart, with at least 3 feet between rows. Plant sweet potato slips diagonally in prepared soil, so that only the top two leaves show at the surface. Water well. In hot, sunny weather it helps the slips tremendously to cover them with upturned flower pots or other shade covers for a few days after planting. With adequate moisture and protection from searing sun, sweet potato slips that look shabby usually recover quickly and make good crops.

Maintenance: Sweet potatoes do not need mulching because their vining foliage does such a good job of covering the ground. Do keep them weeded for the first few weeks after planting. As sweet potatoes mature in late summer, water them as needed to keep the soil from drying out. Heavy rains that follow dry spells can cause sweet potatoes to crack.

Sweet Potato Pests and Diseases

Slightly acidic soil helps to suppress sweet potato diseases, and many good varieties provide genetic resistance to common sweet potato problems. Sweet potatoes are members of the tomato family, and rotating them with non-related vegetables helps prevent problems, too. Avoid growing sweet potatoes in new garden areas previously covered with grass, because ground-dwelling grubs and wireworms (click beetle larvae) chew holes and grooves in sweet potato tubers, and they are often numerous in soil covered with grass and weeds. Deer love to eat sweet potato leaves, so row covers, fences, or other deterrents may be needed, especially in late summer. Only very hungry deer eat squash foliage, so interplanting pumpkins or butternut squash with sweet potatoes helps to deter casual browsing. Stored sweet potatoes are a great favorite of hungry mice.

Growing
Sweet Potato Slips

1 In early spring, move the parent potatoes to a warm, sunny room such as your kitchen.

2 A month before your last frost date, soak the tubers in warm water overnight. The next day, plant the tubers sideways or diagonally in shallow containers, covering them halfway with potting soil. Keep indoors, in a warm, well-lit place, and maintain even moisture to encourage the formation of sprouts.

3 Move the plants outdoors after danger of frost has passed. When handled this way, slips will emerge from both ends of the sweet potato, with each potato producing six or more slips. When the stems are more than 4 inches long and the weather is warm and settled, break off the sweet potato slips from the mother potatoes and plant them. If the soil is still chilly, you can pot up your slips and grow them in small containers until the weather warms.

HARVESTING AND STORING
Sweet Potatoes

When: Begin checking the root size of fast-maturing varieties 3 months after planting. If left in the ground too long, some early varieties will produce seriously oversize roots. Most varieties can be left in the ground as long as the vines are still growing and nighttime temperatures are above 50°F (10°C). Sweet potatoes left to sit in cool, moist soil are prone to developing skin issues.

- -

How: Some sweet potato varieties develop a cluster of tubers right under the plants, but others may set roots 2 feet from the mother clump. Begin digging from the outside of the row, loosening soil with a digging fork before pulling up plants by their crowns. Place the potatoes in a laundry basket and clean off soil with a strong spray from your hose, but do not scrub. Place the rinsed potatoes in a shady spot to dry.

Curing Sweet Potatoes

Fresh sweet potatoes need to be cured in a warm place for 2 to 3 weeks. During this time, wounds to the skin heal over, and the flesh becomes sweeter and more nutritious.

Arrange harvested sweet potatoes in a single layer in a warm, humid place where temperatures can be raised above 80°F (27°C) during the day for 7 to 10 days. In warm climates, a well-ventilated outbuilding is ideal. In cooler climates, a bathroom or closet with a space heater makes a good curing place. After curing, sort through your sweet potatoes and move the most perfect ones to any dry place where temperatures will stay above 55°F (13°C). The flavor and nutritional content of sweet potatoes improves after a couple of months of storage.

Sweet Potato
FOOD PRESERVATION OPTIONS

Sweet potatoes are so easy to keep in their raw, whole state that they are preserved only to cope with culls or to pre-cook them in the interest of convenience. Uncured sweet potatoes with minor issues should be set aside and allowed to dry indoors for at least a week; whatever problems they have will not get worse and may get better.

Cooked sweet potatoes give good results when frozen — whether sliced, mashed, or kept whole. Bake or steam sweet potatoes until just barely done before cooling and freezing them. Be careful with purple sweet potatoes, which bleed unless they are cooked whole, in their skins.

> **Cooked sweet potatoes give good results when frozen — whether sliced, mashed, or kept whole.**

Sweet potatoes also can be dried, and there are two ways to do it. For future use in soups or casseroles, steam slices or cubes until barely done before drying in the dehydrator. Raw slices can be dried, too, but they must be kept quite thin. In addition, you can cut raw sweet potatoes into long, ¼-inch-thick strips and dry them as dog treats.

Savory Sweet Potato Chips

These wavy chips are good for slow snacking, so vary the seasonings to your taste. For best results with this recipe, use a mandoline slicer to cut sweet potatoes into uniform ⅛-inch slices.

Makes about 3 cups

2	tablespoons lemon juice
3–4	sweet potatoes
3	tablespoons melted coconut oil
1	teaspoon sea salt
1	teaspoon paprika
1	teaspoon dried pulverized rosemary

1 Place the lemon juice in a large bowl. Slice the sweet potatoes into ⅛-inch-thick rounds and toss the slices with the lemon juice as they are cut. Add the oil, salt, paprika, and rosemary, and gently toss until the slices are uniformly coated.

2 Place the potato slices on dehydrator trays and dry at medium heat (125 to 135°F/50 to 60°C) until the chips are dry and curled. Store in airtight containers.

SWISS CHARD
(*Beta vulgaris ssp. cicla*)

HOW MUCH
4 plants per person in spring, plus 4 plants per person in fall

STELLAR VARIETIES
'Fordhook Giant', 'Bright Lights', or 'Silverado'

BEST WAY TO PRESERVE
Freeze

Gardeners often show great enthusiasm for crops that they are not used to eating very often. The best example of this is Swiss chard, a workhorse cousin to spinach and beets. Of all the good greens you can grow in your garden, chard is the best one for keeping its eating quality through the hot summer months. Happy chard plants can be phenomenally productive, plus their upright growth habit helps them makes excellent use of space.

You can substitute cooked chard for spinach in recipes, or use chard leaves as a substitute for pastry crust when making quiches or vegetable casseroles. Simply oil the baking dish before arranging large chard leaves on the bottom and sides, and then pour in the filling. When frozen, chard retains its savory succulence but loses its stained-glass beauty.

Best Chard

Homegrown Pantry

If you want only a few plants from which to pick fresh leaves for cooking, choose a white-stemmed variety like 'Fordhook Giant' or 'Silverado'. White-stemmed varieties are not as showy as those with colored stems, but they consistently outperform their more colorful counterparts in terms of productivity and bolt resistance.

Brightly colored chards are the queens of edible ornamentals. Varieties bearing red, pink, yellow, or orange ribs are available individually or in mixtures. If you want to buy only one packet of seeds, you can start with a mixture like 'Bright Lights' and select for color after the seedlings are up and growing. By the time chard seedlings have leaves, you can tell their mature colors.

HOW MUCH TO PLANT?

For fresh eating and casual freezing (for example, when you include chopped chard in frozen packets of summer squash or snap beans), grow about four plants per person in spring, and another four plants per person in the fall. You can grow more for freezing, but don't get carried away if you are also growing collards, kale, or other cooking greens for putting by. Over time, a healthy chard plant easily produces more than 2 pounds, but it is over a period of weeks or months, with two to three big leaves harvested per week.

HOW TO
Grow Chard

When: In spring, either direct-sow or set out seedlings about 2 weeks before your last spring frost to ensure steady production. Chard seedlings that get well chilled often bolt, while those that experience only passing cold continue to produce leaves all summer. For a fall crop, start seeds about 10 weeks before your first frost date, and set out the seedlings when they are 4 weeks old. Chard often survives winter from Zone 7 southward, but the plants make little new growth while days are short, cold, and cloudy. Overwintered chard plants promptly bolt in the spring.

- -

Where: Prepare a rich, fertile bed by mixing in a 2-inch layer of compost and a balanced organic fertilizer applied at label rates.

- -

Planting: Plant seeds ½ inch deep and 3 inches apart. You can also start seeds indoors under bright lights and set out the seedlings when they are about 1 month old. Thin newly germinated seedlings with cuticle scissors instead of pulling them out. Like beets, chard seed capsules often contain two or more seeds. Snip off all but the strongest sprouts at the soil line. Thin or transplant chard to 12 inches apart.

- -

Maintenance: As the plants grow, mulch between them to keep the soil cool and moist and to reduce splashing of soil onto leaves. Provide regular water to encourage strong, steady growth.

Chard Pests and Diseases

Slugs. Holes with smooth edges that appear overnight in the leaves are the work of slugs, which also may rasp grooves into the stems. Trap them by nestling shallow containers baited with beer into the soil, or mulch between plants.

- -

Viral diseases. These cause new leaves to be small or distorted, with unusual crinkling. Plants sometimes outgrow infection, but chard showing viral symptoms should be pulled out if the plant fails to perk up after a couple of weeks.

- -

Leaf spot diseases. Sometimes prolonged periods of warm rain can lead to outbreaks of cercospora leaf spot or other leaf spot diseases that cause leaves to shrivel as the fungi take hold. Remove affected leaves, and keep plants widely spaced to promote good air circulation.

- -

Deer. Chard must taste like candy to deer, because it ties with beets as their favorite garden crop. If you cannot fence out your deer, you may need to use row covers to keep them from seeing your chard. If they can't see it, they won't eat it.

HARVESTING AND STORING
Chard

When: Twist or cut off individual outer leaves as you need them in the kitchen. Three to five leaves can be picked from mature plants at a time, but be sure to leave the growing crown intact.

How: Immediately refrigerate in plastic bags. You can wait until just before cooking or freezing chard to wash the leaves.

About once a week, remove older leaves that have lost their sheen and compost them. If you can't stand throwing away all those second-rate leaves, dry them on cloths spread out in a parked car on a sunny day, and feed the dried greens to your chickens in winter. Thin chard leaves dry very quickly, and when offered the dry greens in a separate bowl, my chickens gobble them up.

Chard
FOOD PRESERVATION OPTIONS

Cooked chard can be substituted for spinach in any recipe, so it's great to have several packets of frozen chard in the freezer. You can freeze chard in small batches, but I like to save up leaves for a few days and work with a sink filled with beautiful leaves. Thoroughly wash the chard leaves and shake them dry. Use the tip of a sharp knife to cut out the ribs, then coarsely chop the leaves into pieces about 3 inches square. When you have set aside several ribs, pull off any long strings from the outside of each one, and chop each rib into 1-inch pieces. Place the chopped ribs and leaves in a large pot, add 1 cup of hot water (just enough to provide steam), and bring to a boil. Stir once or twice, and turn off the heat. After about 3 minutes, pour out the cooked greens into a colander. When cool enough to handle, pack the steamed chard into freezer-safe containers.

When you have set aside several ribs, pull off any long strings from the outside of each one, and chop each rib into 1-inch pieces.

'Opalka'

'Amish Paste'

'Cherokee Purple'

'Striped Roman'

'San Marzano'

'Dad's Sunset'

'Stupice'

'Sun Gold'

TOMATOES

(Solanum lycopersicum)

HOW MUCH
6 plants per person

STELLAR VARIETIES
'Sun Gold' yellow cherry, 'Stupice' early, 'Roma' paste, and 'Brandywine' slicing

BEST WAYS TO PRESERVE
Freeze, can, or dry

A good tomato crop makes a happy gardener, in part because many people become food gardeners so they will have homegrown tomatoes. But tomatoes need a lot of precious space in the summer garden, so it's important to think strategically as you plan a patch that will produce fabulous fresh tomatoes and productive processing tomatoes for putting by.

In most gardens, a mix of heirlooms and disease-resistant hybrids is a sure route to success. Many traditionally bred hybrid varieties are available as organic seeds, and hybrids like 'Roma' or 'Plum Regal' produce bigger crops because they stay healthier longer. You should still save room for a few fresh eating tomatoes chosen for flavor.

Try to match your variety choices with what you plan to do with the crop. Firm and fleshy paste tomatoes yield thicker sauces and salsas than juicier slicing tomatoes, which work well when dried, and cherry tomatoes make a fine dehydrator crop, too. There are many reasons to plan your tomato plot with the end in mind.

> **Drying concentrates the exquisite flavors of juicy cherry tomatoes and big slicers like 'Cherokee Purple', but paste tomatoes such as 'Amish Paste' or pepper-shaped 'Opalka' produce the best canned sauces.**

Best Tomatoes

── FOR THE ──
Homegrown Pantry

A tomato planting plan designed to produce fresh and preserved tomatoes involves a mix of specialized varieties. You will want a few early tomatoes and some round summer slicers for the table, but for canned goodies like tomato sauce, salsa, or marinara sauce, you will get the best results with comparatively dry-fleshed paste tomatoes. With hundreds of choices, selecting varieties can get confusing quickly. The varieties named here are reliable producers in a wide range of climates, so they are a good place to start.

- **Cherry tomatoes** are vigorous and easy to grow, and they set fruit under extreme cold or hot conditions. Yellow 'Sun Gold' has a sweet, fruity flavor that has helped it win numerous taste tests. A heart-shaped red cherry, 'Tomatoberry Garden', makes a wonderful companion to 'Sun Gold', or you can try blight-resistant 'Mountain Magic' in climates where late blight is a serious late-summer threat.

- **Early tomatoes** are essential because they ripen weeks ahead of other varieties. Early-maturing varieties like 'Glacier' and 'Stupice' set fruit in cool weather, so they play an important role in the mid-summer food supply.

- **Paste or canning tomatoes** are by far the best varieties to grow for making into salsa or sauce. The fruits have thick walls and small seed cavities and tend to be uniform in shape and easy to peel. Determinate varieties that produce all at once over a 3-week period are best for canning. Good varieties include widely adapted 'Roma', early-maturing 'Nova', heirloom 'Amish Paste' and 'Opalka', and blight-resistant 'Plum Regal'.

- **Full-season slicing tomatoes** are so big and beautiful that it is tempting to plant a lot of them, which is fine if you have the space. The pink-fleshed form of 'Brandywine' is justifiably famous for flavor, and orange 'Kellogg's Breakfast' has a large and loyal following. Yellow tomatoes like 'Persimmon' or dark-fleshed 'Cherokee Purple' are fun to grow, too. All are easy to dry.

HOW MANY TO PLANT?

There are no standard numbers on pounds of tomatoes produced per plant because yield varies with climate and variety. Warm summer weather helps tomatoes produce heavier crops, while short, cool seasons mean fewer tomatoes per plant.

In a climate that is moderately kind to tomatoes, estimate three plants per person for fresh eating, or six plants per person if you are canning, drying, and freezing your tomatoes. It is also important to grow the different types in proper balance. For example, a two-person household might grow 12 plants, divided as follows:

- 2 early tomatoes for fresh eating and drying

- 2 cherry tomatoes for fresh eating, freezing, and drying

- 6 paste tomatoes for canning

- 2 slicing tomatoes for fresh eating and drying

HOW TO
Grow Tomatoes

When: Plant tomatoes in late spring, after the soil has warmed and the last frost has passed. Start seeds of early varieties 8 weeks before your last frost date, with others 2 weeks later (6 weeks before your last frost date). Provide very bright light, and transplant the seedlings to 4-inch containers after the first true leaf appears. As they gain size, move early tomatoes to dark-colored gallon pots, which provide extra warmth to the roots on sunny days.

- -

Planting: Allow at least 2 feet of space between tomato plants. Into each planting hole, mix a standard dose of a balanced organic fertilizer and a heaping shovelful of compost. Set tomatoes deeply so that their seedling leaves are covered, and water well.

- -

Maintenance: Tomatoes are vining plants that require support. You can buy wire cages or make your own from concrete reinforcing wire. Tomatoes also can be trained to grow on a fence, or they can be tethered to multiple sturdy stakes. The higher tomato foliage is held above the ground, the less the risk of diseases that thrive on damp leaf surfaces.

Tomato Pests and Diseases

Tomato foliage contains nicotine-like compounds that are poisonous to people and shunned by most mammals, but tomatoes are the preferred host plant for leaf-eating tomato hornworms. Hornworms are easy to hand-pick, or you can control them with a *Bacillus thuringiensis* biological pesticide. Aphids and birds are occasional bothers, but by far the greatest threats to tomato health are diseases. Fusarium and verticillium wilts lurk in the soil, aphids and thrips spread devastating viruses, and damp weather invites a host of leaf spots and blights.

Good resistance to many of these diseases is easily available by choosing appropriate varieties; better seed catalogs list which forms of resistance various varieties offer. If your tomatoes (or those of your neighbors) are often hit by a certain disease, try both hybrid and heirloom varieties that offer some level of resistance.

Also keep in mind that young tomatoes are naturally vigorous and healthy, while older plants can't stand up to trouble. Strive to grow your tomato crop quickly, get it put by, and then move on to your second season with cool-weather crops. In climates with very long, hot summers, give yourself a break and grow tomatoes in spring and fall.

HARVESTING AND STORING
Tomatoes

When: Tomatoes can be harvested as soon as they begin to show blushes of color, and then allowed to finish ripening indoors at warm room temperatures. Or you can let them ripen fully on the vine. Much depends on weather conditions and predator pressure like birds pecking holes in tomatoes or squirrels stealing the crop. Cool nights can slow the ripening process, and heavy rains can cause almost-ripe fruits to split. Err on the side of safety by harvesting tomatoes promptly, and discard tomatoes that have gone soft.

When night temperatures regularly fall into the 40 to 50°F (4 to 10°C) range, gather all green tomatoes that might be close to ripe and bring them indoors. Very immature specimens should be composted, but those that show signs of ripening can be eaten fresh or made into relishes or chutneys.

- -

How: Never subject ripening tomatoes to chilling. Keep them at room temperature until they show full color, and then process them for long-term storage.

Easy-Peel Tomatoes

Tomato skins slip off easily if you drop the fruits in boiling water for about 30 seconds. Scald tomatoes in small batches, waiting for the water to come back to a boil between each batch.

Tomatoes that are frozen whole split their skins as they expand. Instead of blanching them, let them thaw for about 10 minutes, and then peel the frozen tomatoes under warm running water.

Tomato
FOOD PRESERVATION OPTIONS

In a good tomato year, you can stock your pantry with an assortment of ready-to-eat tomato products. Freezing should be your backup plan, with most of your preservation time spent canning sauces and drying tomato slices and tomato "raisins" — halved cherry tomatoes dried to the texture of raisins. If you add one new tomato food preservation skill each season, it won't be long before you are growing and preserving all the tomatoes you will need for a year, in ways that suit your style of cooking.

> **Most of your preservation time should be spent canning sauces and drying tomato slices and tomato "raisins" — halved cherry tomatoes dried to the texture of raisins.**

Freezing Tomatoes

Whole, well-washed tomatoes of any size can be tossed into freezer bags and stored frozen until they are needed for cooking. This is practical for a gallon or two of cherry tomatoes or small slicers, but few freezers have space for a bumper crop of tomatoes. You can save some space by cutting tomatoes into pieces and warming them to a simmer before packing the stewed tomatoes into freezer containers. Better yet, roast extra tomatoes with garlic, olive oil, and fresh herbs, and freeze the roasted tomatoes.

Drying Tomatoes

The notion of dried tomatoes may be new to you, but drying tomatoes requires much less kitchen time compared to canning because the tomatoes are sliced and dried raw, with their skins intact. A dehydrator takes care of the rest. You can add the dried bits to soups, stews, casseroles, salad dressings, and pasta dishes.

All types of tomatoes can be dried, and drying is the best way to capture and condense the flavors of sweet cherry tomatoes or heirloom slicers. Once you get used to having dried tomatoes in your pantry, you will miss them when they're gone!

Tomatoes contain a lot of water, so you will need a dehydrator to dry them. Tomatoes destined for drying need to be clean, but you don't need to blanch or peel them. Cherry tomatoes must be cut into halves or quarters and are best dried until they are leathery yet soft. This may take 8 hours or more. Expect ⅜-inch tomato slices to stick to the trays as they dry — don't try to move them during the drying process. When tomatoes are dry enough to store, they will lift off easily in one piece. Store your dried tomatoes in vacuum-sealed containers or in bags or canning jars kept in the freezer.

Canning Tomatoes and Special Sauces

Care must be taken when canning tomatoes and tomato products, which require acidification to ensure that the pH is low enough to inhibit the growth of bacteria. The three choices for acidifying agents are powdered citric acid (¼ teaspoon per pint), bottled lemon juice (1 tablespoon per pint), or vinegar (2 tablespoons per pint). Citric acid or lemon juice are usually better in tomato sauce or canned tomatoes because they affect flavor less than vinegar. However, vinegar can enhance the flavor of some tomato sauces, as it does in the Garden Salsa recipe below.

If you have a food mill or sieve, you can make a smooth, seedless sauce — or thick tomato juice — from tomatoes that have been cut into pieces and simmered slightly to soften them. You also can put tomatoes through a juicer to get a seedless juice.

Of all the canned tomato products you might stock in your pantry, diced tomatoes are probably the most versatile in the kitchen. Peel and dice paste tomatoes, then bring them to a simmer before canning them (with acidification) in a water-bath or steam canner for 20 minutes. Processing times are longer for tomatoes and tomato sauces than for other vegetables in order to kill microorganisms known to survive when the jars do not heat through completely.

In addition to plain sauce and diced tomatoes, most gardeners make some version of the standby recipes on page 225 for salsa and pasta sauce. Note that when low-acid ingredients like onions and peppers are added to these food products, proper acidification becomes even more crucial. In the recipes on page 225, do not increase the amount of non-tomato ingredients, and don't forget the vinegar or lemon juice!

HARVEST DAY RECIPE

Garden Salsa

Makes about 5 pints

- 8 cups peeled, diced paste tomatoes
- 2 cups chopped peppers (mixture of sweet and hot)
- 2 cups chopped onions
- ½ cup cider vinegar
- 1 tablespoon finely chopped garlic
- ¼ cup chopped fresh herbs (oregano, cilantro, parsley)
- 1 teaspoon salt
- 1 teaspoon ground cumin
- 1 teaspoon chili powder

1 In a large pot, mix the tomatoes, peppers, onions, vinegar, garlic, herbs, salt, cumin, and chili powder, and slowly bring to a simmer over medium heat. Cook for about 10 minutes, until the onions are translucent and some of the liquid has evaporated.

2 Spoon the simmering salsa into clean, hot jars. Process pints in a water-bath or steam canner for 20 minutes.

HARVEST DAY RECIPE

Garden Pasta Sauce

Makes about 5 pints

- 10 cups peeled, diced paste tomatoes
- ½ cup chopped onions
- 1 cup chopped sweet peppers
- 1 tablespoon finely chopped garlic
- ¼ cup chopped fresh herbs (oregano, basil, parsley)
- 1 teaspoon salt
- 4 tablespoons lemon juice
- 2 tablespoons brown sugar (optional)

1 In a large pot, mix the tomatoes, onions, peppers, garlic, herbs, salt, lemon juice, and brown sugar, and slowly bring to a simmer over medium heat. Cook for about 10 minutes, until the onions are translucent and some of the liquid has evaporated. If you want a thicker sauce, gently simmer the mixture for an hour longer, stirring occasionally to keep it from sticking to the bottom of the pot.

2 Spoon the simmering pasta sauce into clean, hot jars. Process pints in a water-bath or steam canner for 20 minutes.

'Purple Top White Globe'

'White Egg'

TURNIPS

(*Brassica rapa* var. *rapifera*)

HOW MUCH
12 medium-size turnips

- -

STELLAR VARIETIES
'Purple Top White Globe', 'White Egg', and 'Amber Globe'

- -

BEST WAYS TO PRESERVE
Place in cold storage, freeze, pickle, or ferment

Turnips have been feeding people since prehistoric times, and they deserve star status in the fall garden. No other vegetable gives you super-nutritious greens and crisp roots that rival carrots for crunchiness, all in less than 60 days. An ideal crop for fall, turnips make easy follow-up crops to plant after beans or summer squash. Turnips grow so quickly that little or no weeding is required to establish a pretty bed.

When harvested just before the first hard freeze, turnip roots will keep in the fridge or root cellar through the first half of winter. Turnips are great veggies for adding to fall fermentation projects, and they bring spunky flavor to pans of roasted winter vegetables. You can blanch and freeze extra turnip greens.

Best Turnips
FOR THE
Homegrown Pantry

Turnip varieties have distinct talents, and those described as salad turnips are best for fresh eating and pickling. Salad turnips like 'Hakurei', 'Oasis', and 'White Egg' are harvested when the roots are the size of a golf ball. Because salad turnips are harvested young, in about 50 days, the greens can be harvested in one fell swoop, at the same time as the roots.

All-purpose turnips take longer to mature than salad turnips, about 60 days, but the roots are larger, with a finer texture. The greens produced by these stalwart plants are delicious, but it is best to not pick greens from plants intended to produce big roots. Make an extra planting if you want to grow enough turnip greens for fresh eating and freezing.

HOW MANY TO PLANT?

Turnips, rutabagas, kohlrabi, and radishes are similar as cooked vegetables, so consider them as a group when estimating yields. Beyond what you might eat fresh in late fall, a dozen medium-size turnips, or a few more if they are small, are enough to last most households through the first half of winter.

All-purpose turnips take longer to mature than salad turnips, but the roots are larger, with a finer texture.

HOW TO
Grow Turnips

Where: Turnips grow best in fertile, well-drained soil with a pH between 6.0 and 7.0. They are a good crop to plant in space vacated by early potatoes or peas, or you can grow them between rows of harvested sweet corn as a "mop up" crop to utilize leftover nitrogen. If you are planting turnips after a heavy-feeding crop, mix a light application of a balanced organic fertilizer into the planting bed as you prepare it for seeding.

- -

Planting: Sow turnips for fall harvest 60 to 70 days before your first fall frost. Hot weather can present challenges, because the seedbed must be kept constantly moist for about 3 days. In sunny weather, erect a cloth shade cover over the newly seeded bed to keep it from drying out in midday.

- -

Maintenance: After 10 days, thin seedlings to at least 3 inches apart in all directions. Wide spacing leads to bigger roots, so go back after a couple of weeks and pull up half the seedlings so that the remaining ones are 4 to 6 inches apart. These thinnings should bear tender greens big enough to eat.

Water as needed to keep the soil lightly moist — the best way to grow big turnips with no splits and cracks. As the plants grow, pull off older leaves that turn yellow or show brown spots to reduce problems with pests and diseases.

Turnip Pests and Diseases

Gather outer leaves from turnips to interrupt the life cycles of various leaf spot diseases and insect pests. Watch for outbreaks of aphids. If an aphid problem does develop, remove any badly infested leaves and compost them before dousing plants with water to dislodge wanderers. Do not use insecticidal soap unless you do not plan to eat the greens, which can taste slightly soapy no matter how well they are washed.

Flea beetles and other small insects may make small holes in young turnip greens, but the plants are so vigorous that they quickly outgrow the damage. Sometimes wet weather causes leaves to erupt with leaf spot disease. Seriously troubled turnips can often be rejuvenated if you cut all foliage back to 2 inches from the crown.

Overwintering Turnips

Mature turnips are surprisingly cold hardy. I have had roots survive at 0°F (−18°C) under snow, even when nibbled by deer. Turnips that survive winter promptly produce sprays of yellow flowers in spring. Both the unopened flower buds and the green seedpods are edible and make interesting additions to soups and salads. Honeybees love the flowers.

HARVESTING AND STORING
Turnips

When: Turnips get sweeter as the weather gets colder, so it's best to harvest them after a few light frosts but before your first hard freeze.

- -

How: Handle turnips gently to avoid bruising, and trim back tops to just above the crown. If you plan to store your turnips in the refrigerator, wash the roots in cool water to remove excess soil, pat dry, and store in plastic bags. Do not wash turnips that will be stored in damp sand in a root cellar, because the idea is to trick the roots into thinking they are still growing in a garden.

Turnip
FOOD PRESERVATION OPTIONS

If you're out of cold storage space for turnips, there are several ways to preserve them for later consumption, including freezing and fermenting, or you can turn them into pickles. Don't wait until the roots start to soften to take action. It is better to work with fresh turnips in food preservation projects.

I freeze a few packages of steamed turnip greens, and I always include bite-size chunks of turnip roots with the greens to provide contrast in texture. Turnips work well in vinegar-brined canned pickles, too, and you can turn them red and savory by including sliced beets and red onions in the vegetable mix. But if food fermentation interests you, use turnips generously in creative krauts, kimchis, or other fermentation projects with cabbage, radishes, and other fall vegetables. Cut into sticks, squares, or wedges, fermented turnips retain their crisp texture as natural microorganisms transform them into a spunky, probiotic food.

Turnip Green Cuisine

The world seems divided into people who love or hate turnip greens, though many haters change their minds after tasting young, garden-grown turnip greens. Turnip leaves smaller than your hand are ideal for quick stir-fries, and they can stand in for spinach in calzones, casseroles, and many other cooked dishes. To freeze turnip greens, steam them until they are thoroughly wilted (about 5 minutes), then cool and freeze.

> **When freezing steamed turnip greens, I always include bite-size chunks of turnip roots with the greens to provide contrast in texture.**

WINTER SQUASH

(*Cucurbita pepo, C. maxima, C. moschata*)

HOW MUCH
4 to 6 plants per household

- -

STELLAR VARIETIES
'Waltham' butternut, 'Burgess' buttercup, and 'Honey Bear' acorn

- -

BEST WAYS TO PRESERVE
Place in cool storage or freeze

When you're gardening to put nutritious food on the table, easy-to-store winter squash should be near the top of your planting list. One of the most nutritious crops you can grow, winter squash holds its vitamin A and other healthy riches even when stored for months at cool room temperatures. Food storage simply does not get easier than this.

Winter squash come in a huge range of sizes, shapes, and colors, and flavor varies from spicy and nutty to almost fruity. If you are new to winter squash, purchase different types at a fall farmers' market and see which are your favorites. The goal is finding winter squash that please your tastes and fit your cooking habits — an enjoyable quest that may take several seasons of squash growing and eating. All winter squash grow best under warm conditions, in fertile, well-drained soil with a pH between 6.0 and 6.5.

Best Winter Squash

Homegrown Pantry

Where you garden will affect your choice of which winter squash to grow, because climate influences their overall health and vigor. Here are the six most popular types, listed from smallest to largest.

Delicata Squash (*C. pepo*)

Also called sweet potato squash because of the loaf shape, exuberant delicata vines produce striped oblong fruits weighing 1 to 2 pounds each. The fast-growing vines can be trained to tumble over a fence or low trellis, or you can let them run on the ground. Delicata squash are ready to harvest in about 90 days, and the cured fruits will store in a cool place for 3 to 4 months. These squash are usually served stuffed or cut into rings that are baked or grilled (the skins are edible).

Acorn Squash (*C. pepo*)

Compact acorn squash plants quickly produce heavy crops of pleated, heart-shaped squash weighing 1 to 2 pounds each. More pest tolerant than summer squash, heirloom acorn varieties famous for flavor deserve consideration. Acorn squash mature in about 90 days and store for 3 to 4 months. Acorn squash are most often roasted or stuffed.

Spaghetti Squash (*C. pepo*)

Prolific and easy to grow, the fast-growing plants produce heavy crops; fruit size varies with variety. Widely adapted in a range of climates, spaghetti squash mature in about 90 days and store for 3 months. The tender strings of cooked spaghetti squash resemble pasta because of their unique texture and mild flavor. Flesh from the cooked fruits is used as a pasta substitute in hot dishes and casseroles.

Butternut Squash (*C. moschata*)

Bulbous, smooth-skinned butternuts are resistant to squash vine borers and are non-preferred by squash bugs, which makes them easy to grow. Butternuts need 100 to 110 days of warm weather to produce a good crop, so they may not ripen fully in cool climates. Where they grow well, butternuts become staple crops in most homegrown pantries because they are easy to grow, versatile in the kitchen, and can store for 6 months or more. Moist butternut flesh works well in soups, pies, and purées.

Buttercup Squash (*C. maxima*)

Bred to be a sweet potato substitute in northern climates, long-vined buttercup squash plants run 12 to 15 feet and produce blocky fruits weighing 2 to 5 pounds. Buttercups are moderately susceptible to common squash pests, and the fruits mature in about 100 days. Buttercups store for 4 to 6 months. Similar to Japanese kabocha squash, the dense, dark orange flesh of buttercup squash becomes flaky when baked, like starchy potatoes, so they are often regarded as the best winter squash for pies.

Hubbard Squash (*C. maxima*)

Prized for their dry, light orange flesh and stability in storage, long-vined hubbard squash grow best in the cool, moist climates of the Northeast and upper Midwest. Depending on variety, the fruits can weigh 5 to 15 pounds, with rinds that may be blue-gray, green, or red. Unfortunately, hubbard squash are attractive to all squash pests. Most varieties mature in about 100 days, and the fruits store for 6 months. These varieties are valued for baking and pies, but they do not have the deep orange flesh color of butternuts.

Hubbard

Delicata

Acorn

Spaghetti

Butternut

'Honey Nut'

Kabocha

HOW TO
Grow Winter Squash

When: Sow seeds in prepared beds or hills in late spring, after your last frost has passed. You also can start seeds indoors under bright lights and set out the seedlings when they are about 3 weeks old. In most climates, there is no need to rush, and delaying planting may help with the management of squash bugs and other common pests. In Zone 6 and warmer, you can plant more winter squash in early summer, using space vacated by fall-planted garlic or early spring lettuce. Transplant container-grown seedlings to help get midsummer plantings growing in a hurry. Stop planting winter squash 14 weeks before your first fall frost date.

- -

Where: Choose a sunny site with fertile, well-drained soil. Prepare planting hills within wide rows, or position them along your garden's edge. Space 3-foot-wide hills 5 to 6 feet apart.

- -

Planting: Loosen the soil in the planting sites to at least 12 inches deep. Thoroughly mix in a 2-inch layer of mature compost and a light application of a balanced organic fertilizer. Water well. Plant six seeds per hill, poking them into the soil 1 inch deep. Ten days after sowing, thin seedlings to three per hill. If using seedlings, set out three seedlings per hill. Where wild pollinators are plentiful, you will need five to six plants of the same species to get good pollination.

Winter Squash Pests and Diseases

Powdery mildew. Among diseases, powdery mildew is a common problem best prevented by growing resistant varieties, which often have the letters *PMR* (for powdery mildew resistant) after their variety name. In addition, a spray made from 1 part milk to 4 parts water can suppress powdery mildew if applied every 2 weeks during the second half of summer.

Squash bugs, squash vine borers, and cucumber beetles. Winter squash often face challenges from insects, including these three. For gardeners in the eastern United States, where squash vine borers sabotage both summer and winter squash, butternuts are preferred because borers usually leave them alone. Winter squash varieties that are susceptible to borers can be protected with aluminum foil shields crumpled around their bases. Better yet, start plants indoors to give them a strong, pest-free start, and then grow them beneath row covers until the flowers open and need visits by bees to complete pollination.

Big, healthy plants will produce well despite pest challenges. In addition to using row covers to protect young plants, these techniques can keep pests at a manageable level:

- Delay planting your main crop until early summer, after wandering squash bug and cucumber beetle adults have found other host plants.

- Grow squash in an area where chickens or other poultry range. Chickens won't control big infestations, but they will nab many insects in search of host plants. Chickens do not eat squash foliage or fruits.

- Some varieties are so attractive to pests that they can be used as trap crops — blue hubbard winter squash and yellow straightneck summer squash can be used as trap crops for squash bugs and borers.

- Check often for the brown egg clusters of squash bugs, and rub them off leaves with a wet finger or a cloth dipped in water. Trap squash bugs by placing small boards under plants during periods of cool weather. First thing in the morning, quickly brush squash bugs hiding under the boards into a bucket of soapy water.

Winter squash are such productive plants that it is possible to grow too many. Most gardeners grow only two or three varieties per season — for example, a small variety for stuffing and a larger butternut or buttercup for long-term storage. When planning for winter squash, consider your expected harvest from other orange-fleshed storage vegetables, particularly pumpkins and sweet potatoes. You can only store and eat so many orange veggies before you burn out.

You will need to grow four to six plants of any winter squash variety to ensure good pollination. Small-fruited acorns and delicatas will produce many small squash, while larger-fruited types will produce fewer but larger squash. In general, a successful winter squash plant will produce about 20 pounds of fruit, or two to five squash per plant, depending on fruit size.

HARVESTING, CURING, AND STORING
Winter Squash

When to harvest: Winter squash fruits are ripe if you cannot easily pierce the rind with your fingernail and the stem near the fruit becomes woody and brown. Many varieties also show a change of color. Do not hurry to harvest winter squash, because immature fruits do not store well. Unless they are threatened by pests or freezing weather, allow the fruits to ripen until the vines begin to die back.

- -

How to harvest: Use pruning shears to cut fruits from the vine, leaving 1 inch of stem attached.

- -

Curing: Clean away dirt with a soft, damp cloth, and allow the fruits to cure in a warm, 70 to 80°F (21 to 27°C) place for 2 weeks. Sun will not hurt the curing squash, and many cool-climate gardeners use their greenhouses as curing chambers.

- -

Storing: Store cured squash in a cool, dry place such as your basement or a cool closet. Check every 2 weeks for signs of spoilage. See page 13 for a quick reference to how long different squash and pumpkins can be expected to store.

CUTTING UP WINTER SQUASH. To make large fruits easier to cut, use your sharpest, heaviest knife to lop off a slice from one side of the squash to create a flat surface, then roll the squash onto the flat side. To cut into squash with very hard rinds, you may need to tap on the back of a sturdy knife with a mallet.

Sticky Fingers from Cutting Squash

Cutting up raw winter squash has a surprising side effect: it leaves your hands coated with a sticky substance that feels like thin, fast-drying glue that won't wash off. Don't worry, you probably are not having an allergic reaction, though this is a remote possibility. You are simply a victim of the squash trying to defend its valuable cache of seeds.

Squash plants use gluey juices in various forms to protect themselves from insects and other predators. Known to botanists as phloem latex and apoplastic fluids, these plant-produced glues are intended to shut down insect mouthparts, like built-in sticky traps.

As for the garden cook, you can protect your skin with gloves, or be prepared to deal with the aftermath with packing tape. When you're finished cutting squash for the day, dry your hands well and make a loop of 6-inch-long packing tape, adhesive side out. Use the loop of tape to strip off the gluey residue if you don't want to wait for it to wear off naturally, which usually takes several hours.

Winter Squash
FOOD PRESERVATION OPTIONS

Cool storage of winter squash is so easy that you should rarely need to preserve it in other ways. The fundamental challenge is finding different ways to cook winter squash so that you use up your homegrown supply in a timely manner. Toward this end, I suggest roasting some of your winter squash every week or two, making a major dish like a batch of squash-apple soup, and putting the rest into the refrigerator. Even if you just peel and chop the squash and store it raw in the refrigerator, you are more likely to cook with winter squash that's two steps away in the fridge than to take on a whole one from the basement.

You can use winter squash in any recipe that calls for pumpkin and in many recipes that use sweet potatoes. Grated winter squash can sometimes pass for carrots, especially when lightly cooked.

Old-fashioned squash pies laced with cinnamon and ginger will never go out of style, but newer trends in winter squash cuisine include savory risottos and creamy squash-stuffed ravioli. Sage is a great accent herb for winter squash, and many cooks brush chunks of baked or grilled squash with maple syrup or honey toward the end of cooking to get a caramel glaze.

Squash soup brings endless possibilities because you can take the flavor in any direction you like. Indian curries, Mexican chilis, and creamy cheese soups can be interpreted using winter squash as a major ingredient. Chickpeas or lentils work well for boosting the protein in squash soup to make it into a more satisfying meal. To reduce cleanup, try using an immersion blender rather than your food processor to purée cooked winter squash.

> **Grated winter squash can sometimes pass for carrots, especially when lightly cooked.**

FRUITS

FOR THE

Homegrown Pantry

If you want to save money while eating better fruit than you can buy, the simple answer is to grow a selection of fruits and berries suited to your climate. You don't have to worry about spray residues on raspberries or pears you grew yourself using organic methods, and the purity issue carries over into the kitchen, too. From apple jelly to blackberry wine, stocking your pantry with treasures made from homegrown fruits is serious fun for self-provisioning gardeners.

Selected fruits can do double duty in the landscape, for example you might use a thicket of prickly blackberries or raspberries as a deer-deterrent hedge, or let a pair of dwarf cherry trees anchor an ornamental bed in a sunny front yard. Strawberries are often happy to grow on slopes or along the base of a fence, and you can use grapes as arbor plants to create shade during the summer months.

Where should you begin? Berries make fabulous foundation plants in an edible landscape and often begin bearing at a young age, so start by finding sweet spots for these forgiving plants. Next, move on to tree fruits, and check with your extension service for tree fruits recommended for your area. Plant the best adapted, most disease-resistant cultivars you can find. With a solid investment of follow-up care and patience, you will soon be enjoying the best fruits in the world.

BERRIES

ANY TEACHER OF PERMACULTURE will quickly point out that the edges of wooded land, where the shady canopy opens to sun, have the capacity to produce a diversity of useful plants, with berries leading the pack. Easy to grow and naturally resistant to diseases, super-nutritious berries are the best fruits to grow organically in most climates. Enriching the boundaries of your property with berries is one of the wisest landscaping decisions you will ever make.

Some berries start producing fruit in as little as a year after planting, and they rarely lose their newly fertilized flowers to late-spring freezes, as often happens with fruit trees. Whether you want fresh raspberries for your breakfast cereal or strawberries for smoothies, the goal is to match talented berries to the sites you have to offer. As you add to your collection of berries, choose species or varieties that bear at different times, from late-spring strawberries to fall raspberries.

Begin by choosing one or two berries you're willing to pay dearly for at the farmers' market, like strawberries or raspberries. Any berries grown by local farmers will grow at your place, too. Plenty of sun brings out the best flavor in most berries, but they also like a few hours of afternoon shade where summers are hot, which brings us back to the woodland edge, or maybe your backyard fence. Boundaries and berries go together.

> **Enriching the boundaries of your property with berries is one of the wisest landscaping decisions you will ever make.**

BLUEBERRIES
(*Vaccinium* species)

HOW MUCH
5 or 6 plants

- -

STELLAR VARIETIES
Varies with climate, and a mix of varieties improves pollination

- -

BEST WAYS TO PRESERVE
Freeze, can, dry, or ferment

Native to moist, acid soils in North America, various types of blueberries have been improved to the point where some type of blueberry can be grown in almost any garden. In addition to producing delicious berries that can make you healthier and smarter, blueberry bushes look good in every season of the year — spring flowers give way to clusters of purple berries in summer, and the leaves turn bright red in fall. In late winter, the new stems often turn shades of red and purple, bringing subtle color to a snow-covered garden.

Blueberries take time to pick, but once gathered they can be stashed in the freezer until you are ready to make preserves, dried blueberries, or even blueberry wine. Freezing and thawing softens blueberries, which prepares them nicely for long-term preservation.

Best Blueberries

FOR THE

Homegrown Pantry

Climate and soil are major factors to consider when choosing blueberries for your garden. The various types are descended from native species, so they are not easily tricked into changing their soil preferences or their tolerance of winter cold.

In cold winter climates, choose northern lowbush varieties like 'Bluecrop' or petite, half-high 'Northblue'. These sturdy little plants can survive temperatures to −40°F (−40°C), and their compact size makes them easy for kids to pick.

In temperate climates, try northern highbush blueberries, which are descended from strains that grow wild in the eastern mountains. This group of slow-growing but productive blueberries is generally rated as adapted in Zones 5 to 7. There are dozens of varieties, and pollination is enhanced if you plant more than one variety. Check with your Cooperative Extension Service for varieties recommended for your area.

In warm climates, rabbiteye blueberries are among the easiest fruits to grow organically. They make a lovely edible hedge, and they bear heavy crops every year. In some areas, southern highbush types are recommended to extend the season. Known for their exceptional heat tolerance, southern highbush blueberries ripen earlier than the rabbiteye types.

Once established, blueberry bushes will bear for decades.

HOW TO
Grow Blueberries

When: Set out purchased plants in spring, 4 to 6 weeks before your last frost, when the plants are emerging from dormancy. As long as they are kept watered, blueberry plants purchased in containers can be set out until early summer.

- -

Planting: Blueberries cannot take up nutrients unless the pH is quite acidic, below 5.5, so most gardeners need to amend planting holes with leaf mold, yard waste compost, or other acidic amendments when setting out blueberries. Light dustings of garden sulfur will also keep the pH down in the blueberry patch, as will acidic mulches like pine needles, rotted wood chips, or sawdust.

- -

Maintenance: Blueberries also need constant moisture, but not too much. Plan ahead to use soaker hoses or another efficient watering method to provide water to plants during droughts. Young plants are easily lost by letting them run dry.

In late winter, top-dress established blueberries with a balanced organic fertilizer before renewing the surface mulch. Again, sawdust or wood chips make great mulch for blueberries. A second light fertilization in late summer (and more mulch) will support the plants as they develop latent buds for the following season.

Pruning Blueberries

Until they are 6 or 7 years old, blueberries need pruning only to remove dead and damaged wood and to keep the plants shapely. After that, periodic pruning to rejuvenate plants is in order, but you need not do it every year. Blueberries that are trimmed yearly to keep them tidy can be pruned only every other year, and they will do just fine.

When you do prune, do it in late winter, before the plants emerge from dormancy. Count the number of new canes that survived from the previous season — they will look greenish. Prune out the same number of old canes by cutting them off near the base. Also top back the new canes by about half their length to encourage them to develop lateral branches.

Blueberry Pests and Diseases

Blueberries are naturally slow-growing plants, but they have few serious problems with insects and diseases when they are grown in favorable soil and kept nicely mulched. Watch blueberry foliage for little moths or other web-making creatures, and remove them by hand. Blueberry maggots, the larvae of a small fly, can cause yucky problems in ripe fruit. In small home-size plantings, yellow sticky traps set up in late June can help monitor and capture the flies before they lay eggs on ripening blueberries.

As the blueberries begin to ripen, expect to see birds coming for breakfast. You can use pieces of wedding net (tulle) fastened in place with clothespins to deter most bird feeding, though some birds will get underneath the covers and jump up to get berries. Some gardeners build enclosures made from chicken wire to keep birds off their berries, but I don't recommend using bird netting unless you are prepared to deal with panicked hummingbirds who become ensnared in it.

Blueberries are generally happiest growing in patches, as they do in the wild. Plants usually do not start producing until they have been in the garden for a few years, but once established, the bushes will bear for decades. At maturity, petite northern lowbush varieties should produce about 3 pounds per plant. The other types grow into bigger plants, with 6 to 8 pounds per plant a realistic figure for mature highbush and rabbiteye blueberries.

Not all of these berries will make it into the picking basket, so don't be afraid to start out with five or six blueberry plants in a compatible mix of varieties. There is no harm having a few extra blueberry plants, because once you have picked all you want, birds will harvest the rest.

HARVESTING AND STORING
Blueberries

When: Blueberries ripen over a period of 4 to 6 weeks, so plan to pick your berries at least every other day for a month. In peak season, pick every day, preferably in the morning when the berries are cool. To pick with two hands, modify a milk jug by cutting a roomy opening in the top, but leave the handle intact. Loop the handle through a belt, or tie it to a belt loop, and you have an unbeatable container for harvesting blueberries.

Blueberries are ripe when they turn dark, show a dusty "bloom" on their skins, and come away from the stem easily when picked. Berries that feel soft are overripe — compost them.

- -

How: If you don't have time to rinse and freeze your blueberries right away, place them in rigid containers in your refrigerator so they won't get smashed. A cooler kept chilly with frozen water bottles wrapped in towels is a good way to cool down large harvests that won't fit in the refrigerator.

Blueberries are ripe when they turn dark, show a dusty "bloom" on their skins, and come away from the stem easily when picked.

Freezing and thawing softens blueberries, which prepares them nicely for drying or making into blueberry preserves or wine.

Blueberry
FOOD PRESERVATION OPTIONS

You can use fresh or frozen blueberries to make jams, syrups, or homemade wine. Always take the time to thoroughly rinse blueberries in cool water before freezing them (birds are messy visitors). Place the berries on a clean kitchen towel and pat them dry with another towel before freezing them. Blueberries that are dry when frozen do not stick together.

Preserves

Blueberry preserves made with low-sugar pectin are fabulous on toast, pancakes, ice cream, and much more, so use part of your crop for preserves. If you want to use your blueberries in smoothies but don't have freezer space, can pints in a water-bath or steam canner, using reconstituted white grape juice or pineapple juice in place of a sugar syrup. Blueberries tend to float unless they are canned in a heavy syrup or thickened pectin, but floating berries don't matter when the contents of the jar are going into the blender. To get a denser pack, soften the blueberries in boiling water for 30 seconds, and then mash them slightly as you push the berries firmly into hot canning jars.

Dried Blueberries

Blueberries take a long time to dry, so expect to spend a couple of days dehydrating them in 4-hour sessions. Freezing and thawing blueberries before drying them helps them to collapse and dry a little faster, and helps tenderize the skins, too. Dried blueberries can pass for sprightly raisins in baked goods and hot and cold breakfast cereals.

Blueberry Wine

There is one special trick to turning a gallon of fresh or frozen blueberries into a gallon of wine: you must use at least half fruit juice (rather than water) when creating a batch to get a flavorful wine with solid character. Good choices include white grape (my favorite), red grape, apple, or pineapple juices. The amount of sugar needed will vary slightly with your choice of juice, but this is true of all country wines.

Follow the basic recipe and wine-making directions given on pages 46–47. Place fresh or thawed blueberries in a fermentation bag, and once it is in the primary fermenter, mash it well with your hands or a potato masher. As the wine progresses, rack as needed to eliminate sediment — usually about every 6 weeks. Blueberry wine tastes best when it has aged at least 1 year.

EASY BAGGING. Because round blueberries roll so well, you can gather up the edges of a kitchen towels and pour the berries into a freezer bag through the open side of the bundle.

Double Blueberry Vinegar

Blueberries and raspberries infuse inexpensive vinegar with flavor and aroma like magic, and the surprising colors of berry vinegars are beautiful, too. If you like, include herbs such as basil, sage, or thyme in your berry vinegars, which are perfect for salad dressings or mixing with olive oil for dipping with bread.

Makes about 3 cups

- 2 cups white or cider vinegar
- 1 tablespoon sugar or honey
- 2 cups fresh blueberries, rinsed and patted dry

1 Place the vinegar, sugar or honey, and 1 cup of the blueberries in a saucepan. Mash the berries with a potato masher or fork, and bring the mixture to a simmer.

2 Strain the mixture into a clean quart canning jar. Add the remaining 1 cup blueberries to the vinegar, screw on a lid very loosely, and place in a cool, dark place for 2 to 3 days.

3 Strain the mixture again before storing it in clean vinegar bottles.

'Interlaken'

'Flame'

'Mars'

'Summit' muscadines

GRAPES

(*Vitis* species and hybrids)

HOW MUCH
3 plants per household

STELLAR VARIETIES
Climate specific, based on chill hours, disease pressure, and personal preference

BEST WAYS TO PRESERVE
Dry, can, freeze, or ferment into wine

The most valuable fruit for making juice, long-lived grapes can be grown in most climates provided that appropriate varieties are chosen. Cold hardiness and disease tolerance vary widely across grape varieties. Some varieties bred in Minnesota can survive temperatures to −30°F (−34°C), while disease-resistant muscadine grapes excel in warm climates with limited winter chilling. Growing grapes is easiest in fertile soil with a near-neutral pH. Growing grapes organically is easier in the arid West than in the humid East, where disease prevention is a high priority.

Grapes ripen all at once in late summer or early fall, and fresh grapes can be frozen until you are ready to process them. It takes only a little time to turn grapes into juice for jam, drinking, or making into wine. Perfect seedless grapes dry into big, beautiful raisins.

Best Grapes
FOR THE
Homegrown Pantry

Seedless table grapes produce clusters of juicy, thin-skinned berries great for eating fresh, drying into raisins, or making into juice. Grapes may be red or blue or light green (called white grapes), depending on variety. Best adapted in Zones 5 to 7, varieties like red 'Canadice', blue 'Mars', or white 'Himrod' may develop a few small seeds, but not nearly as many as fully seeded grape varieties. These and similar seedless varieties do well when grown on a head-high arbor.

Juice and jelly grapes are the survivors of the grape world, in part because their genetic background includes native American species. Most varieties produce downward-facing shoots, so they need a high trellis or an arbor. Dark blue 'Concord' and red 'Delaware' are hardy to Zone 4, while white 'Niagara' and 'Ontario' are slightly less cold hardy. In addition to using these trouble-tolerant varieties for juice and jelly, they make a decent country wine.

> **Juice and jelly grapes are the survivors of the grape world, in part because their genetic background includes native American species.**

Muscadine grapes are easy to grow in warm, humid climates where other grapes succumb to diseases. The sweet berries have a robust, musky flavor that makes them good for fresh eating, juice, jelly, or wine. The thick skins are too tart for some tastes, but they contribute mightily to the flavor of muscadine juice or jelly. Muscadine fruit clusters are small compared to other grapes, but the berries are large and easy to pick.

White wine grapes created by crossing European and American grapes can be grown organically in hospitable sites. Compared to red wine grapes, the whites mature earlier, and several have been bred with short summer climates in mind — for example, 'LaCrosse' and 'Louise Swenson', which are both hardy to Zone 3. New York–bred 'Cayuga White' and 'Traminette' need a longer season, but they are among the most adaptable white wine grapes in Zones 5 to 7.

All of these grapes require close management and a two-tiered trellis to support growth from the upward-facing buds.

Red wine grapes such as merlots take a long time to ripen, though early-maturing varieties are available for cold climates. When grown in warm, arid climates such as the California wine country, red wine grapes can produce yields in excess of 30 pounds per plant. Newer hybrids have high productive potential when grown where summers allow complete ripening, which is critical for good flavor. The vines tend to be very vigorous, and varieties with upward-facing shoots require a firm two-tiered trellis. 'Chambourcin' is a good choice where summers are warm and humid. 'Cynthiana' and 'De Chaunac' are hardy to Zone 4.

HOW MANY TO PLANT?

Grapes are long-lived plants that produce best when they are more than 3 years old. Yield varies with variety and how the grapes are grown, but generally it ranges between 15 and 30 pounds per plant. For home gardeners, three plants of any given variety is a good start. Varieties vary in disease resistance, so separating them on different trellises or arbors gives you a safety margin in the event that one variety runs into trouble.

Grow Grapes

When: Set out newly purchased plants in spring, 4 to 6 weeks before your last frost. Grapes grown in containers can be set out until early summer.

- -

Where: Grapes require a sunny, well-drained site with no fences or other structures nearby that block air movement. Without abundant sun, grapes will not develop their full sweetness or flavors.

- -

Planting: Before planting, dig out all perennial weeds and amend the soil with at least 2 inches of mature compost or other high-quality organic matter. If your soil tends to be acidic, use light applications of lime or wood ashes to raise the pH to between 5.6 and 6.2. Most grapes are planted 7 to 9 feet apart, with a trellis or supportive arbor installed at planting time. After planting, water thoroughly and mulch the area beneath the plants with 2 to 4 inches of wood chips or another organic mulch that will suppress weeds. When allowed to grow around the base of the plants, weeds can increase problems with disease.

Trellising and Pruning Grapes

To maximize productivity and prevent disease, match your trellis design and pruning practices to the natural growth habit of your grapes. In general, 'Concord' grapes and other juice and jelly varieties produce downward-facing branches from long canes that form a cascade of foliage, so they do best on a high trellis or arbor. Similarly, muscadine grapes are easiest to manage on an overhead rectangular trellis, sometimes called an X trellis. With these vigorous grapes, pruning is directed toward preserving two to four 6-foot-long canes while trimming out excess growth.

Most table and wine grapes produce upward-facing shoots, so they do best on a two-tiered trellis that supports the branches as they gain height. Tight wire trellises are preferred because they do a good job of supporting the vines when they become heavy with fruit. You must aggressively prune table and wine grapes and remove all old growth except selected fruiting spurs. However, when growing table grapes on an arbor, you can prune a little less in order to get a thick cover of foliage.

Prune grapes in late winter, before the buds begin to swell. The first year after planting, concentrate on helping young plants grow straight, sturdy trunks. Begin training side branches in the second year. Buds are ready to bear fruit 3 years after planting. Each grape variety you grow will respond differently to various pruning practices, so be prepared to fine-tune your methods.

Some of the best sites for trellised grapes provide shade for the roots while the vines scramble up into the sun.

Grape Pests and Diseases

Diseases are a constant threat to grapes, and prevention should first be directed to attentive trellising, pruning, and mulching. In all areas, powdery mildew (evidenced by whitish patches on leaves) can weaken plants and reduce grape flavor. Minimize problems with preventive sprays of 1 part milk to 4 parts water.

Brown rot. Rare in the West, this fungal disease is a serious problem with eastern grapes. Regular sprays with organic copper-based fungicides are often needed even when disease-tolerant varieties are grown. Microbial fungicides based on *Bacillus subtilis* (such as Serenade) also can offer significant protection.

- -

Beetles and birds. Grapes are among the favorite foods of Japanese beetles. Early-season hand-picking is essential for good control. Grapes are a favorite food of many wild birds, too. Use bird netting or tulle netting to protect your crop. Tulle netting also can help protect plants from Japanese beetles.

HARVESTING AND STORING
Grapes

When: Grapes are ripe when they taste sweet and have mature seeds inside. Early-maturing white or red varieties may be ready to pick a month before later-maturing blue or black grapes. Allow grapes to stay on the vine until the berries show a whitish bloom on the skins, but bring them in should a period of wet weather be predicted. If not rescued, ripe grapes often crack after heavy rains.

How: Store clusters of unwashed grapes in the refrigerator, in plastic bags that help retain humidity. Wash thoroughly before eating or preserving.

Grape
FOOD PRESERVATION OPTIONS

Fresh or frozen grapes can be made into juice, jelly, or wine, and seedless grapes can be dried into raisins. If some of your seedless grapes are sweet and tender enough for fresh eating, freeze them whole on cookie sheets, then store them in freezer-safe containers. Grapes split as they freeze, which makes them easy to peel for use in special dishes.

Raisins. Seedless grapes can be slowly dried into raisins in a dehydrator. First, the clean berries should be "checked," a process whereby they are dunked in boiling water for 30 seconds and then cooled over ice. Grape skins seem to be smooth, but they are actually composed of thousands of waxy little plates. Checking helps to create openings in the grape skin through which moisture can escape, so it is not to be skipped when drying grapes into raisins.

Juice. Grapes of all types easily give up their juice when barely heated to a simmer before being crushed and drained. Refrigerate grape juice for at least 24 hours to allow it to clear, then pour off the juice and discard the tartaric acid crystals in the bottoms of containers to avoid grittiness. Grape juice can be canned or frozen, with or without sugar, or made into delicious jelly.

Wine. Grape wines develop flavors from the juice, skins, and seeds of grapes, and the best way to start is with fresh grapes, well crushed by hand, by feet, or in a grape crusher. If you have no time to make wine but your grapes are ready to harvest, simply stash them in the freezer. To save space, remove the stems and smash the grapes into freezer-safe containers.

HARVEST DAY RECIPE

Canned Grape Drink

For many families, it is a yearly tradition to put up quarts of this delicious drink in late summer and let the colors and flavors develop until the winter holiday season. Strain out the grapes before serving.

Makes 6 quarts

6 cups washed, clean grapes

3 cups sugar

5 quarts hot water

1 Sterilize 6 quart canning jars with lids.

2 Place 1 cup of the grapes in each jar, followed by ½ cup of the sugar. Add hot water to within ½ inch of the rims.

3 Wipe the rims clean, screw on the lids, and process in a water-bath or steam canner for 20 minutes.

Red raspberries from cultivated plants are twice as big as wild black raspberries, which are concentrated little packages of raspberry flavor and aroma.

RASPBERRIES

(*Rubus* species)

HOW MUCH
Six plants, to start

- -

STELLAR VARIETIES
'Nova' summer red, 'Jewel' black, and 'Anne' fall-bearing yellow

- -

BEST WAYS TO PRESERVE
Freeze, can, or ferment into wine

Juicy, sweet, and pleasingly seedy, raspberries make a valuable addition to landscapes intended to produce good things to eat. In areas with cold winters and warm summers, you can grow summer-bearing red, black, or purple raspberries, which ripen in early summer, before most vegetables need harvesting. In warm climates, you can grow fall-bearing raspberries, which bear their crop after summer's worst heat has passed.

Raspberries and other bramble fruits make excellent boundary plantings, and they love colonizing open fences. A dense thicket of raspberries 8 to 10 feet wide can serve as a living fence to deter deer or other intruders. Prickly raspberries also can help protect young trees from deer damage.

Most gardeners freeze their raspberries for use in baked goods and smoothies, but freezing is only the beginning of what you can do with a bumper crop of raspberries. Either fresh or frozen raspberries lend their unique flavors to juices, jams, syrups, homemade wine, and fragrant raspberry vinegar.

Best Raspberries

FOR THE

Homegrown Pantry

Consider the ripening times of other fruits you are growing when choosing raspberries to grow in your garden, so you won't be overwhelmed when it comes time to harvest. Early-bearing red raspberries ripen before blueberries beg to be picked, but later-maturing varieties may leave you pressed for picking time. In temperate climates, fall raspberries ripen at the same time as apples and pears.

Summer red raspberries (*Rubus idaeus*) bear clusters of plump berries in early to midsummer on canes that grew the season before. The best type for freezing or canning, summer-bearing red raspberries are stiff enough to grow on a modest trellis. Because these varieties get on with the business of fruiting soon after they emerge from winter dormancy, they are easy to manage as compact bushes tethered to posts or fences. Popular varieties include 'Nova', 'Latham', 'Boyne', and 'Taylor'.

Black raspberries (*R. occidentalis*) grow wild in many areas, and they can be grown as cultivated plants in Zones 5 to 7. Black raspberries are packed with nutrition and wild berry flavor, so they are valuable in making juices, wines, and jellies.

Purple raspberries combine the productivity of red raspberries with the flavor and vigorous growth habit of black raspberries. Like black raspberries, the purples produce heavy crops that ripen all at once in early summer.

Fall-bearing raspberries produce berries from midsummer to fall on the new season's growth. Some varieties produce golden berries with unusually sweet flavor. If you have no tree fruits that fill your time in September, by all means give autumn raspberries a place in an airy corner of your yard. Because fall-bearers produce on the current year's growth, the plants can be cut back to stubs in winter, making them easy to manage as landscape plants.

HOW TO
Grow Raspberries

When: Set out purchased plants in spring, 4 to 6 weeks before your last frost, when the plants are emerging from dormancy. Raspberry plants purchased in containers can be set out until early summer.

- -

Where: A few hours of afternoon shade benefit raspberries grown in hot climates, but in most areas full sun is key to growing raspberries with rich, sweet flavor. Raspberries can produce for 10 years or more when grown in deep, fertile soil that drains well.

- -

Planting: Before planting, dig out all perennial weeds and amend the soil with at least 2 inches of mature compost or other high-quality organic matter. Raspberries have shallow root systems, so a deep year-round mulch is the best way to keep them happy. A mulch of straw, weathered sawdust, grass clippings, or wood chips will suppress weeds, help maintain soil moisture, and serve as a barrier between the soil and raspberry leaves and fruit. In late winter, top-dress established raspberries with a balanced organic fertilizer before renewing the surface mulch.

Pruning Raspberries

In midsummer, pinch back new cane tips at 4 to 5 feet to stimulate the growth of heavy-bearing lateral branches. Fall-bearing raspberries can be tip-pruned in midsummer to delay the fall crop until after hot weather passes.

When a raspberry cane finishes producing fruit, it sends leftover nutrients back to the roots and then dies. To keep a clean patch with good air and sun penetration, remove old canes in winter by cutting them into pieces with pruning loppers. Fall-bearing raspberries are usually mowed to 4 inches high in late winter, just before new growth begins.

Raspberry Pests and Diseases

When individual raspberry canes wilt, the problem is usually due to feeding by cane borer larvae. Cut back wilted canes to 6 inches below the damage to prevent further injury.

Black raspberries are a favorite food of many species of birds. Use tulle netting to protect your crop. Birds rarely bother yellow raspberries, but red raspberries sometimes require protection. Tulle netting also can help protect plants from Japanese beetles.

HOW MANY TO PLANT?

Summer red raspberries can produce up to 20 pounds of fruit from a 25-foot row, or you can estimate about 1½ quarts per plant. Black, purple, and fall-bearing raspberries usually produce slightly less. Raspberries spread naturally by sending up new shoots from root buds, so you can start with a small planting of five or six plants and expand it by digging and moving new plants to where you want them to grow.

HARVESTING AND STORING
Raspberries

When: Raspberries are ripe when they show good color and come away from the stem freely when picked. Daily harvesting is best, because hot sun can scald ripe raspberries, and prolonged rains can cause them to rot. If hot weather strikes just as your raspberries are ripening, cover the plants with old sheets during the day to prevent sunscald.

How: Harvest raspberries in shallow containers, piling them no more than three berries deep. Refrigerate picked berries immediately, and eat or process within 3 days. Wait until just before eating or freezing raspberries to rinse them clean with cool water.

Raspberry
FOOD PRESERVATION OPTIONS

You can use fresh or frozen raspberries to make jams, syrups, or batches of raspberry lemonade or homemade wine.

Frozen. To freeze raspberries, rinse the berries with cool water and place on a clean kitchen towel. Pat dry before freezing in bags or containers. Raspberries won't stick together if you freeze them on a shallow pan covered with waxed paper for an hour, and then transfer the frozen berries to freezer-safe containers.

Juices, wines, and teas. Black and purple raspberries produce an aromatic, tart juice that can be added to a variety of drinks from homemade sodas to herb teas. Home winemakers value black and purple raspberries for the complexity they bring when blended with other wines — for example, wines made from apples or pears. Perfect fresh or dried raspberry leaves, harvested when they are a deep green color, can be included in herb teas, too.

Vinegar. Finally, you can use a few of your most perfect berries to turn ordinary vinegar into sprightly raspberry vinegar for splashing on salads or sharing with friends.

When allowed to marinate for a week or two, raspberries transform ordinary white vinegar into a flavorful base for marinades and salad dressings.

Gardeners can grow strawberries with great flavor, which is at its peak when the berries ripen in the first warm days of summer.

STRAWBERRIES

(*Fragaria × ananassa*)

HOW MUCH
25 plants

STELLAR VARIETIES
'Earliglow', 'Jewel', and 'Sparkle'

BEST WAYS TO PRESERVE
Freeze, can, dry, ferment

As the first fresh fruits to ripen in early summer, strawberries are much beloved despite the fact that you must get close to the ground to pick them. Strawberries are also easy to grow organically when you work with the plant's natural cycles of growth and rest. Cold hardy and adaptable, strawberries have two limitations — they require acidic soil with a pH between 5.5 and 6.5, and new plantings are easily overtaken by weeds. If you have alkaline soil, grow strawberries in containers filled with acidic compost. Commit to a zero-tolerance policy for weeds in your strawberry patch.

Several simple food preservation methods work well with strawberries. Strawberry jam and preserves are easy to make, whether you start with fresh berries or berries stored in the freezer. Drying strawberries to the leathery stage concentrates the berries' colors and flavors, and few snacks are as nutritious as chewy dried strawberries.

Best Strawberries

FOR THE

Homegrown Pantry

The two types to consider are June-bearers, which produce their crop over a 3-week period in late spring or early summer, and everbearers, which bloom and set fruit from spring to fall.

June-bearing varieties in general produce better-quality, more flavorful berries, so they are the top choice if you want a lot of berries for freezing or making into jam or wine. The plants produce many runners, so you can grow them as a ground cover or matted row, or use them as edging plants. Cold and heat hardiness vary with variety, so check with your Cooperative Extension Service for recommended varieties for your area that are also resistant to common diseases. Ripening times vary, too. 'Earliglow' ripens 2 weeks or more ahead of 'Sparkle', so growing more than one variety extends your harvest season.

Everbearing strawberries (also called day-neutral strawberries) are fun to grow, but they are more valuable for fresh eating than for freezing and canning. These varieties often produce a heavy set of berries in early summer, followed by several more lighter flushes in late summer and fall. Cool night temperatures below 65°F (18°C) and regular fertilization are needed to keep the plants productive. These are excellent strawberries for large containers or raised beds, where they can be given attentive water and regular feeding, but everbearers won't produce the concentrated crop needed for preservation purposes.

HOW MANY TO PLANT?

A planting of 25 June-bearing strawberry plants grown in a 30-square-foot bed will produce about 25 quarts (30 pounds) of strawberries annually for 3 to 4 years. Diseases develop over time in any strawberry planting, so it is a good idea to start a new strawberry bed every 5 years, starting with certified disease-free plants.

HOW TO
Grow Strawberries

When: Strawberries are best planted in early spring, up to 6 weeks before your last frost. Plants also can be set out in fall, which is a common practice where winters are mild. Finding plants for sale in autumn can be difficult, but gardeners often have plants to share from thinning or edging their strawberry beds.

Where: Choose a sunny, fertile site that is free of perennial weeds for growing strawberries. Enrich the site with plenty of rich compost or rotted manure, and add some rotted-to-black sawdust if you have it. Growing strawberries in raised rows or beds ensures good drainage and makes the berries easier to pick.

Planting: New plantings are usually made from dormant plants, which are sold in bunches. Spread out the bundled plants and trim off any dead leaves and roots. Find the central crown, and transplant so that the base of the crown rests at the soil line and the roots are spread out and covered with soil. Mulch between plants with pine needles, chopped leaves, weathered sawdust, or another mulch that supports acidic soil conditions.

Following spring planting, pick off flowers that form during the first season. Also pinch off about half of the runners to help the mother plants concentrate on the following year's crop. If you don't need more plants, you can help the plants produce better the next year by removing all runners.

Maintenance: Do your best to keep your strawberries weeded at all times. If you cannot adequately control weeds with hand-weeding and mulch, you might try using roll-out sheet mulches made from paper, plastic, or other manufactured materials to prevent weeds from sprouting.

Fertilize established strawberries in early spring, just as the plants show vigorous new growth, using a balanced organic fertilizer. In late summer, mow or cut back old leaves 4 inches from the ground, fertilize again, and mulch with an acidic material such as sawdust or pine needles. Strawberry plants often become semi-dormant in hot summer weather and perk up when nights cool down in the fall.

Strawberry Pests and Diseases

Slugs, snails, and birds. As soon as strawberries start to ripen, expect these visitors to arrive. Slugs and snails chew rounded holes in fruits at night and hide in mulch during the day. Control them by hand-picking, temporarily pulling back mulch, and capturing them in traps (see page 215). Use featherweight covers made from wedding net (tulle) to keep out birds.

Diseases. Strawberries can be weakened by a number of leaf spot diseases, which are interrupted by mowing or cutting off the foliage in midsummer. Soilborne diseases build up over time, so it is best to start a new bed in a fresh site every 5 years, but pay attention to what your plants tell you about how often they want to be renewed. Especially in mild winter climates, plants set out in late summer or early fall keep enough green growth through winter to be ready to bear the following spring. But because of disease pressure, the planting may not produce well for more than a couple of years.

HARVESTING AND STORING
Strawberries

When: Pick strawberries when they become fully colored but are still firm, and harvest at least every other day.

How: Harvest in the cool of the morning, and place berries in shallow containers or boxes, piling them no more than three deep. Refrigerate immediately. Wait until just before eating or preserving to wash strawberries under cool running water and remove their green caps. Preserve extra strawberries within a day after picking.

Strawberry
FOOD PRESERVATION OPTIONS

You can use fresh or frozen strawberries to make smoothies, desserts, or strawberry preserves — a family favorite in many households. Strawberries also can be dried or made into wine.

Jams and preserves. These are two of the best ways to put by these highly perishable berries. Both jams and preserves can be processed in a water-bath canner, since strawberries' natural pH is quite acidic, below 4.0.

Frozen. To freeze strawberries, rinse the berries with cool water and place on a clean kitchen towel. Pat dry before freezing in bags or containers. If you want frozen strawberries that don't stick together, freeze individual berries on a shallow pan covered with waxed paper for an hour, and then transfer the frozen berries to freezer-safe containers. Take the opposite approach when freezing strawberries to use as dessert toppings. Slice the berries and sprinkle with sugar before freezing them. Sugar has a tenderizing effect on frozen strawberries and helps preserve their bright color.

Dried. If you have a bumper crop and limited freezer space, drying some of your strawberries is a good plan, too. Strawberries have such tender skins that they dry better than other berries, especially when cut into uniform pieces. Watch the temperature closely and try to keep it around 120 to 130°F (50 to 55°C). Because of their high sugar content, strawberries are prone to going moldy so they must be dried quickly.

Fermented. Fresh or frozen strawberries make an aromatic, ruby-red wine perfect for sipping cold on a summer evening.

Dried strawberries

TREE FRUITS

THE MOST PRODUCTIVE food plants you can grow are fruit trees — something you already know if you have mature fruit trees on your property. If you have no trees or not enough, the right fruit trees will add beauty and value to your land, and they will keep you well stocked with organically grown fruits for year-round eating.

Not that fruit trees are always a sure thing. Modern disease-resistant varieties take a little of the worry out of growing fruit trees, but unless you live in an ideal fruit-growing climate, expect the unexpected where tree fruits are concerned. Late frosts frequently kill the fertilized blossoms of species that bloom early, resulting in fruitless years, and sometimes fruit trees drop their fruit for no apparent reason. Fair enough, because in most years the harvest from mature trees will be measured in bushels, and you will have more than enough delicious homegrown fruit to put by and share.

Best Fruit Trees for the Homegrown Pantry

The following fruit tree groups have their own profiles starting on page 267: apples; cherries; pears and Asian pears; and plums, peaches, and nectarines. When the right cultivars are grown in hospitable climates and given attentive care, each of these fruits stands a good chance of producing quality crops under organic management. And because they bear at different times of year — for example, cherries ripen in early summer, followed by summer plums, peaches, and nectarines, and apples and pears in the fall — it's a nice base group for a self-sufficient homestead.

Where should you start? When your purpose is to fill your pantry, make it a priority to select and plant apples and pears, which are easier to grow organically compared to other tree fruits. They become kitchen mainstays because they can be dried, canned, frozen, or fermented into wine.

The "stone" fruits — cherries, plums, and peaches — bear earlier, but they are more likely to run into problems with pests and diseases. However, all of the stone fruits can be purchased grafted onto dwarfing rootstocks. It's easier to monitor dwarf trees for problems and to use organic sprays or traps to keep the trees healthy.

Glean Fallen Fruits

If growing fruit trees is but a dream for you, you can still become rich in canning-quality fruit by helping friends or neighbors with their harvest. Picking and sorting apples is hard work, and most tree owners are happy to share imperfect fruits that need to be attended to quickly in exchange for a few hours of work.

How Many Fruit Trees Do You Need?

Although some varieties of some tree fruits are described as "self-fertile," pollination and fruit set are generally enhanced when two trees of the same species are grown together. When planning space, think in terms of compatible pairs.

Next, consider ripening times — cherries and plums will be but a memory when the first apples ripen. Let your tastes and climate guide you as you select trees. Five or six trees you decide you cannot do without is a good place to start. Fruit trees require ongoing care, and taking on too many may not leave you time to attend to proper pruning and maintenance. It is better to succeed with a few fruit trees than to fail with many.

How to Grow Fruit Trees

When: Set out new trees in mid-spring, after the soil has thawed and the whole world is emerging from dormancy.

Where: Choose a sunny, well-drained site that is not in a low spot where frost is likely to linger in spring.

Planting: Clear away weeds and grasses, and dig a planting hole that is twice the size of the rootball of the tree. If you can choose between sizes, buy a big tree, ideally 5 to 6 feet tall. Set the tree in the prepared hole, and backfill soil as needed to plant the tree at the same depth it grew at the nursery. Make sure the graft union, which looks like a swollen area on the main trunk, is high enough so that it will never be covered by soil or mulch. Water well, then finish filling the hole.

Err on the side of safety by installing a trunk guard made of spiral plastic or fine mesh hardware cloth. A trunk guard protects newly planted trees from insects, rodents, sunscald, and physical injuries that often happen with mowers and string trimmers. Finally, stake the tree to hold it steady in the wind, and mulch the root zone with wood chips, sawdust, or other slow-rotting mulch that makes poor mouse housing.

Maintenance: One year after planting, remove the stakes and trunk guard from the tree. On a dry day, paint the trunk with white latex paint to protect it from winter injury. Sand added to the paint may deter nibbling by rabbits and voles. For the first 10 years, fertilize fruit trees annually in early spring by scratching a balanced organic fertilizer into the soil surface (follow application rates on the product's label). After that, fruit trees have such extensive roots that they can usually forage for themselves, but they may need deep watering during dry periods.

Caring for established trees: The fruit tree year starts in late winter, when the trees are dormant but days have begun to lengthen. Get out on mild days to trim off dead wood and knock down mummies (shriveled fruit from last year), studying each tree for its pruning needs. The goal of pruning fruit trees is to manage limb structure so that come summer, each leaf and fruit will be bathed in light and fresh air. The ideal branching pattern varies with species, and some apples and pears can be pruned into wall-hugging espaliers to save space. Begin pruning fruit trees to shape them in their first year, and then prune annually in late winter, before the buds swell. With mature trees, aim to remove up to 20 percent of the limbs to sculpt an open canopy. Pruning a little too much questionable growth is better than removing too little.

You can mulch beneath trees with wood chips or sawdust, which looks nice and reduces the chances that the trunks will be injured by lawn mowers or string trimmers. Or let the ground become colonized by a mixture of grasses and clovers, which should be mowed only every 2 to 3 weeks. Lush vegetation that is cut high provides habitat for ground beetles and other active predators that help control fruit pests that spend part of their life cycle in the ground.

Thinning fruits: Many fruit trees set too much fruit in good years, with many fruits in clusters and few spaced 3 inches apart, so the excess should be thinned using a small pair of scissors. Thinning helps to prevent alternate bearing, in which trees fall into the habit of bearing every other year. Wait until the green fruits grow to the size of a dime, and shake a few limbs to see if the tree shows signs of shedding excess fruits on its own (sometimes they do). If the tree insists on holding far too many closely spaced fruits, clip off the smallest ones and those that are misshapen or show blemishes. Then do your best to thin fruits to at least 3 inches apart.

Citrus Fruits for Tropical Climates

Citrus fruits (*Citrus* hybrids), including kumquats, Satsuma or mandarin oranges, and 'Meyer' lemons, are among the easiest fruit trees to grow organically in Zones 8b to 10. Fragrant oils in citrus leaves and rinds provide protection from pests, but citrus fruit can't take much cold. The hardiest of them — 'Owari' satsuma, 'Nagami' kumquat, and 'Meyer' lemon — may occasionally need to be covered with blankets on cold nights, but winter harvests of homegrown citrus fruits are worth the trouble.

APPLE MAGGOT TRAP. From apple maggots to cherry fruit flies and peach tree borers, many small insects that injure fruits can be monitored or controlled with the right traps. When you have only a few trees and notice recurrent pest problems, the right traps can quickly help turn things around. Here, a small vial of pheromone lure attracts apple maggot adults to a fake red apple covered with sticky glue. Covering the trap with a plastic bag makes it reusable.

APPLES
(*Malus domestica*)

HOW MUCH
3 or 4 dwarf, or 2 or 3 standard

STELLAR VARIETIES
Climate specific based on chill hours and disease-resistance needs

BEST WAYS TO PRESERVE
Dry, freeze, juice, can, or ferment

Everybody eats apples, and if we all ate one organically grown apple a day, we would certainly be healthier for it. Growing your own apples calls for patience and dedicated effort, but it is well worth the work.

As with all fruit trees, you never know what the harvest will be from your apple trees. In a good year, you may easily accumulate a year's supply of applesauce, juice, jelly, and chewy dried apples, but in other years you will be lucky to make two pies. Be prepared to forgive these hardworking trees, and trust that they have their reasons for taking a rest. Even in years when they don't make a crop, apples serve as well-behaved landscape trees that offer fragrant flowers in spring and cooling shade in summer.

The flavor of many apples improves after a couple of weeks in refrigerated storage, so you can take your time preserving them using several different methods. Blemished apples that need immediate attention can be canned as applesauce, or you can pare and freeze them for processing later. Apples dry beautifully, and they can be fermented into a light white wine or kicky apple cider.

Best Apples

Homegrown Pantry

When choosing apple trees to grow, your first concern should be finding cultivars with strong resistance to common apple diseases, including apple scab, fire blight, cedar-apple rust, and powdery mildew. You will also need to check a variety's cold-chilling requirements to make sure it is a good fit for your climate. For example, you would need a low-chill variety rated at only 400 chill hours in some parts of the South, but in the North, 1,400 chill hours might be a better match. Your Cooperative Extension Service can provide you with a list of apple varieties that are locally adapted and offer various forms of disease resistance.

Next, look at ripening times. Early-ripening summer apples are nice to have, but they store under refrigeration for only a few weeks, so you may need to process them at the same time you are coping with the year's crop of tomatoes and peppers. Apples that ripen in September and October are better candidates for extended cold storage, which gives you more time to get them preserved. And this is true: a couple of weeks of post-harvest chilling in the basement or fridge improves the flavor and juiciness of many mid- and late-season apples.

If you have a couple of productive trees, you will probably preserve your apples in numerous ways — including freezing, drying, juicing, and water-bath or steam canning as jelly, chutney, spiced rings, or applesauce. Some apples are better for specific uses, but you will need to experiment with the apples available to you to discover their preservation secrets. For example, my Rome-type apple is the best one for drying, but another tree with Macintosh background makes better applesauce. For juicing and wine making, my favorite is a nameless, decades-old tree that grows in a neighbor's yard and bears small yellow apples.

HOW MANY TO PLANT?

Once you have settled on a couple of disease-resistant varieties, you will need to choose between dwarf trees, which have been grafted onto special rootstocks that keep the trees small, at 15 feet or less, or full-size trees, which are grafted onto rootstocks chosen only for added vigor. Sometimes semi-dwarfs (larger than dwarfs and smaller than full-size trees) are available on special rootstocks. Dwarf apples are best for small properties and are easier to care for, but semi-dwarfs and standards make better long-lived landscape trees, and in good years they will bury you in fruit.

The choice is yours, and you can mix things up if you like. When planning a mixed orchard, I suggest including a couple of dwarf apples and one standard tree. Keep in mind that the harvest times for traditional and Asian pears overlap with apples, so in the interest of delicious diversity, save space in your planting plans (and preservation time in your kitchen) for pears.

HOW TO
Grow Apples

Where: These adaptable, long-lived trees need a sunny, well-drained site with slightly acidic to near neutral soil. Newly planted apple trees often need to be protected from deer and drought. Wood chip mulch is often useful for maintaining soil moisture for young apples.

- -

Maintenance: Apple trees need attentive pruning every year. Prune young trees to shape them, and prune older trees to remove "suckers" and tall branches that are hard to pick. When managing established, vigorous semi-dwarf apple trees, expect to remove 10 to 20 percent of the tree's canopy every year. The best time to prune is early spring, at the same time that yellow forsythias bloom.

Apple Pests and Diseases

In addition to the routine care described on page 265, apples must be protected from cedar-apple rust, which is hosted by junipers and cedars. These landscape shrubs and trees can give rise to outbreaks that cause orange spots and galls on apple leaves, which can seriously weaken the trees.

Most apples need to be thinned, and all trees should be monitored for apple maggots (the larvae of a small black fly) and codling moths (a moth larvae that tunnels into fruits). Pheromone-baited sticky traps are available for both pests.

Apples that fall to the ground often attract yellow jackets and other stinging insects. Prevent unpleasant encounters by picking up fallen fruit with a gloved hand in the cool of the morning.

Clusters of closely spaced apples ripen unevenly and give pests a place to hide. Start thinning clusters by removing the smallest fruits when they are the size of a quarter.

HARVESTING AND STORING
Apples

When: There are several ways to judge the ripeness of apples. Pick a sample fruit in which the "under-color" in the palest areas has changed from green to yellow. This is hard to spot in some varieties, so cut the fruit in half to look at the seeds and the starry halo around them. In an underripe apple, the seeds will be light brown and the halo will be green. Ripe apples have dark brown seeds, and the halo changes from green to cream. With some varieties, you won't have to guess; the trees start dropping their fruit when the apples are ready.

- -

How: To pick apples, you will need an orchard ladder, a long-handled fruit picker, and an apron or bag for the collected fruit. On the ground, you will need three baskets, boxes, or other containers — one for perfect fruits, one for slightly bruised and blemished ones, and one for the culls. Working with a helper is always a good idea where ladders are involved, and a helper makes apple picking go faster, too.

Immediately move your harvested apples to a cool place like a basement or the coolest room in your house. Next, sort through your best apples, wiping each one with a damp cloth, and set aside any imperfect fruits — those with bruises or worm holes — and preserve as soon as possible. If the weather is warm, store your perfect apples in perforated plastic bags in the refrigerator. In cooler weather, you can keep apples in a chilly basement or outdoors in coolers kept in the shade. Flawless apples can be stored in the refrigerator for 3 months or more. They do best in loosely closed plastic bags.

underripe

ripe

Underripe apples have blond seeds, and you can see a green halo around the seed cavity. Ripe apples have dark seeds and no green halo.

Apple
FOOD PRESERVATION OPTIONS

Apples can be preserved in numerous ways, including drying, freezing, juicing, and water-bath canning as jelly, chutney, chunks, or applesauce. Below I will walk you through how apple processing proceeds at my house. Try a couple of new projects each year, and you will gradually learn which apple products your family likes best.

Sour, barely mature apples blown to the ground in storms are naturally high in pectin, so early green apples are often preferred for making jelly. You can add frozen blackberries, raspberries, or grapes to the pot to change the color and flavor of your mostly-apple jelly.

As the harvest picks up, use the bruised fruits (with bad parts cut away) to freeze enough cinnamon-spiced apples to use in pies and cakes. For this use, it is best to simmer peeled, sliced apples in a spiced syrup until done, about 5 minutes, and then freeze them when they are cool.

> **Sour, barely mature apples blown to the ground in storms are naturally high in pectin, so early green apples are often preferred for making jelly.**

Make Fruit Nectar

Each time you pare a quantity of apples — or pears or stone fruits, for that matter — for a preservation project, simmer the leftover cores and fleshy trimmings in water, then strain and chill the resulting liquid. Thick with natural pectins, apple "nectar" can be drunk straight up or sweetened to taste with sugar, honey, or stevia. As long as you have room in the freezer, freeze your excess nectar in clean canning jars or freezer jars filled three-fourths full to allow room for expansion.

applesauce

plain dried apples

apple-tomato ketchup

canned apple slices

spiced dried apples

Drying Apples

Apples are among the few dried foods that taste good without being rehydrated, and they are easy to cook with, too. Some people steam blanch ½-inch-thick apple slices before drying them, which gives you the kind of soft, chewy apple bits you get in processed foods. But apples that are dried raw are quite good, and if using organically grown apples, you can leave the peels on for added fiber and nutrition. To dry a batch of apples, first prepare a big bowl with acidified water (see page 23). In a second, smaller bowl, place a small amount of brown sugar and "apple pie" spices. As you pare the apples, place them in the acidified water. Drain, then toss the slices with the sugar and spices. Dry apples until leathery, and store them in airtight containers in your freezer. If you need small pieces of apple for a recipe, use scissors or kitchen shears to cut your dried apples to size.

Making Apple Juice

Apples are considered a "dry" fruit because they contain little juice compared to, say, blackberries or peaches. But apples will give up a modest amount of juice. Using the most efficient do-it-yourself equipment (an apple mill that shreds the apples into pieces, after which the pieces are pressed to push out the juice), a bushel of apples will produce just over 3 gallons of juice.

Use a mill and press. In many communities, you can network to get access to an apple mill and press, and crude but effective home-built models go back hundreds of years. Once pressed, raw apple juice must be immediately consumed (with gusto!), frozen, fermented into cider or wine, or heated to the point of sterilization and canned. In the latter case, you should add a dash of lemon juice (per pint) to make sure the canned product is adequately acidic.

Freeze. Lacking the use of an apple mill and press, you can pare washed apples into chunks, removing only the cores and bad places, and freeze them in large freezer bags. When thawed, sufficient tissues will have broken down to create a flow of juice. If you transfer frozen and thawed apple pieces to a jelly bag, massage it with your hands to break up the pieces, and patiently twist and push to coax out the juice, you can obtain great gulps of fresh, raw apple juice from frozen apples. The browned thawed apple gook left behind is worth a quick simmer in water kicked with cinnamon or other spices. Strained and sipped warm, you have a refreshing apple toddy.

Steam. A final option is to steam the juice from your apples, which requires a three-section basket steamer. Clean apples that have been trimmed to remove rot spots can go into the steaming basket whole, but it takes a while for the juice to flow (40 minutes to 1 hour). After the juice is collected, the steamed apples can be put through a food mill or sieve to make a smooth applesauce.

Creative garden cooks can choose from a dozen different ways to store a bumper crop of apples.

Apple Cider or Apple Wine?

Apple cider and apple wine are easy to make with homegrown apples. Historically, hard apple cider is made by allowing the natural sugars in raw apple juice to ferment into alcohol, using the natural yeasts present on apples. Depending on the sweetness of the apples used, a natural cider will yield a beverage that is 4 to 6 percent alcohol. In the old days, this naturally made cider was kept in a cool cellar until it was consumed. I suggest making a faster-starting, more predictable version by gently heating the juice to 130°F (55°C) to kill most wild yeasts and bacteria, and then using a champagne yeast to ferment the juice.

If you add sugar, honey, or a mixture of the two to apple juice and then ferment it, you can make a very nice cider or white wine. Cider has a lower alcohol content compared to wine, so it is not as stable after bottling. See page 44 for information on making your own wine. Or skip the juice-making altogether and make wine from chopped apples enclosed in a fermentation bag. Either fresh or frozen apples are fine, and berries such as blackberries or raspberries can be added to vary the wine's color, aroma, and flavor. Apple wine ferments somewhat slowly, and you'll need to rack it several times before it is still, clear, and ready to bottle; I figure on 8 months from start to bottling. After bottling, apple wine needs to age for at least 1 year, but it is worth the wait.

Canning with Apples

Apple products from applesauce to jelly can be canned in a water-bath or steam canner as long as they are slightly acidified from citric acid, lemon juice, vinegar, or a high concentration of sugar.

Sweetened preserves. Low-sugar pectins work great with apples, so you can make cinnamon-apple chunks in light syrup or low-sugar jellies using half the sugar present in commercial products. Not that all sugar is bad. I think a small amount of sugar gives applesauce a sheen and helps counterbalance the bitterness of cinnamon and other spices, and in some recipes, such as apple chutneys, a sharp balance between sugar and vinegar is what makes the concept work.

Applesauce. To make a smooth applesauce or apple butter, cook the apples long enough to soften them, about 10 minutes, then put them through the same type of manual food mill used for tomatoes. To make chunky applesauce, peel and core the apples before cooking them in just enough water to steam the pieces.

Flavored ketchup. The natural runniness of homemade tomato ketchup can be remedied by including about one-third applesauce in your ketchup. Applesauce, puréed jalapeños, and mature green tomatoes make a delicious green ketchup, too.

Spiced apples. Apples studded with cloves and preserved in a vinegar brine are another of many possibilities for preserving apples in canning jars.

CHERRIES

(*Prunus avium* and *P. cerasus*)

HOW MUCH
1 standard tree or 2 dwarf trees

- -

STELLAR VARIETIES
Sweet cherries for Zones 5 to 7 include 'Stella' and 'Lapins'; sour cherries for Zones 3 to 8 include 'Montmorency' and 'North Star'

- -

BEST WAYS TO PRESERVE
Freeze, dry, or can

Cherry trees are breathtaking when they are in bloom, and juicy, sun-ripened cherries are so packed with antioxidants and other nutrients that they almost qualify as medicine. If other gardeners in your area successfully grow cherries, put them on your planting list. The earliest-bearing of all fruit trees, cherries ripen in early summer, when there is plenty of time to harvest and store them.

The freezing process tenderizes cherries, and even cherries that are to be dried benefit from being frozen first. Freezing also helps cherries release their nutrient-rich juice, a delight to drink in early summer. Dried cherries are delicious by themselves, or you can use them in baked goods and cooked cereals.

Best Cherries

FOR THE

Homegrown Pantry

There are two types of cherries to consider for your garden: sweet and sour. Most fresh cherries sold in supermarkets are sweet cherries (*Prunus avium*), while most dried and canned cherries are tart or sour cherries (*P. cerasus*). Sour cherries often contain as much sugar as sweet cherries, but they have more acids that contribute to their tart taste. Instead of putting flavor first, consider these horticultural differences between the types:

Sweet cherries have problems with extreme cold and heat, so they grow best in Zones 5 to 7, which is a rather limited geographical range. Most varieties are not self-fertile, so you need two trees, and sweet cherries bloom so early that the fruit is often nipped back by late freezes. Even on dwarfing rootstocks, sweet cherries grow 15 to 20 feet tall.

HOW MANY TO PLANT?

A single standard cherry tree would be a valuable addition to any landscape, but a pair of dwarf trees will be easier to maintain. At full maturity, a standard cherry can easily produce 150 pounds of fruit, while a mature dwarf tree can be expected to produce between 30 and 40 pounds of cherries in a good year.

Sour cherries can take more cold and heat, with some varieties hardy to Zone 3 and a few are capable of prospering in Zone 8. Most sour cherries are self-fertile, and their extended bloom time gives them a better chance of producing a crop in years with cold spring weather. Dwarf forms can easily be kept to 12 feet tall, making them easy to maintain.

Sour cherries often contain as much sugar as sweet cherries, but they have more acids that contribute to their tart taste.

HOW TO
Grow Cherries

Where: Site selection is crucial to growing good cherries, which need fertile, well-drained soil with a near-neutral pH. Cherries also need regular water, so plant them within easy reach of your hose. Planting cherries close to your house makes it easier to keep an eye on young trees, which need close monitoring during the first few years after planting.

Maintenance: Cherries are at high risk for developing trunk issues, so avoid any small scrape or cut to the main trunk. Instead of using a rigid trunk guard, wrap the trunk of newly planted trees with mosquito netting or window screening to deter borers and protect it from injury. If you do see oozing holes in your cherry tree's trunk, poke a needle in the hole to kill the borer or beetle responsible for the damage.

Cherry Pests and Diseases

Brown rot. A fungal disease called brown rot causes cherry fruits to become covered with brown fuzz just as they ripen. Pruning to keep the tree open to sun and fresh air is your best defense; commercial growers use intensive fungicide sprays to manage this disease.

Fruit flies and birds. Cherries that have little worms inside have been visited by cherry fruit flies. Sticky traps can help monitor and control this pest. As cherries approach ripeness, most gardeners need to protect their crops from birds with bird netting or tulle covers, held in place with clothespins.

HARVESTING AND STORING
Cherries

When: Pick cherries in the cool of the morning.

How: Dwarf trees can be picked by hand, but to harvest cherries from a large tree, spread tarps or sheets on the ground, and shake the limbs to make the ripe fruit drop. Historically, this was done by the child in the house most adept at climbing trees.

Lay the harvested cherries out in shallow boxes or bins in the shade, or place them in a cooler with a couple of frozen water bottles that have been wrapped in kitchen towels. Gently rinse cherries clean with cold water and pat dry. Keep chilled in perforated plastic bags, and preserve within 2 days.

A cherry pitter makes fast work of preparing cherries for eating fresh, cooking, or food preservation projects.

Cherry
FOOD PRESERVATION OPTIONS

If you own a productive cherry tree, you need a plunge-powered cherry stoner. Once the stones (pits) have been removed, you can freeze, dry, or process your cherries into preserves or syrup.

Freeze. If you're short on time, simply freeze your pitted cherries. When you want to make wine, juice, or jelly later, thaw some cherries and you're ready to go. If you plan to make smoothies or decorate plates with some of your cherries, freeze them on a cookie sheet and transfer to bags when they are frozen hard so they won't stick together.

Dry. To prepare cherries for drying, freeze and thaw them to tenderize the fruit. Squeeze the thawed cherries slightly to remove excess juice before placing them in the dehydrator. Be sure to save the juice for drinking. Cherries are best when dried only to the leathery stage, so store dried cherries in the freezer. Dried cherries are great for baking as well as eating out of hand, or you can rehydrate them and add them to sauces or smoothies.

You can enjoy super-nutritious cherry juice on its own or combine it with other fruit juices.

Cherries dry better and are more tender when they are frozen first.

PEARS AND ASIAN PEARS

(*Pyrus* species and hybrids)

HOW MUCH
1 or 2 trees

STELLAR VARIETIES
'Moonglow' and 'Potomac' pears, and 'Shinko' Asian pear

BEST WAYS TO PRESERVE
Dry, can or freeze

Of all the fruit trees brought from Europe and planted by American colonists more than 300 years ago, the lone survivor is a pear. Capable of bearing for decades, pear trees also adapt to a wide range of climates.

There are two types of pears: European (common) and Asian. The best common pears grow into standard-size trees, at least 30 feet tall and wide, but many Asian pears are semi-dwarf by nature, topping out at 12 to 20 feet. Pears are not quite as cold-tolerant as apples, with cold hardiness ending in Zone 4 for common pears and Zone 5 for Asian pears, but low-chill varieties of both types are available for warmer climates. Pears are premier fruits for canning, and perfect fruits can be held for months in the refrigerator. Once you have apples, next you need pears.

Best Pears
FOR THE
Homegrown Pantry

Common and Asian pears differ in taste and texture, and both are easy fruit trees to grow organically. I prefer traditional pears for canning, but dried Asian pears are like candy — it's hard to stop eating them.

Another big difference becomes clear at harvest time. Many pears must be picked just shy of ripe and allowed to ripen in a cool place for weeks or even months. Asian pears must be allowed to dangle from the tree until they fall into your hand, be refrigerated immediately, and kept refrigerated at all times.

When choosing which varieties to plant, look for those with good resistance to fire blight, a bacterial disease that is very common in moist climates. The number of chill hours required for good fruit production also varies with cultivar. Your Cooperative Extension Service can provide you with a list of pear varieties that are locally adapted and offer resistance to fire blight or other diseases.

> **I prefer traditional pears for canning, but dried Asian pears are like candy — it's hard to stop eating them.**

'Hosui' Asian pear

'Barlett' pear

HOW TO
Grow Pears

Where: Pears need a sunny site with good air circulation so their leaves dry quickly after rains. Soil that is well drained with a pH between 6.0 and 6.5 is ideal, but pears are pretty adaptable plants. Be patient with little trees, because they are slow growers. Mulch them with wood chips to control weeds and keep the soil moist.

- -

Maintenance: You will need to prune young pear trees to shape them, but once pear trees mature they need less pruning compared to other fruit trees. In late winter, remove branches damaged by winter weather or disease along with weak, twiggy growth.

Pear Pests and Diseases

Pear trees that sidestep fire blight and are protected from browsing deer are usually slow but steady growers. Be patient and resist the urge to over-fertilize trees planted in a good site to make them grow faster. Shoots on young trees should grow 14 to 20 inches each year.

You may occasionally see the same insect pests that bother apples in pears, including apple maggots and codling moths. Usually only a few fruits are compromised, so additional controls are not needed. Pears that fall to the ground often attract yellow jackets and other stinging insects. Prevent unpleasant encounters by picking up fallen fruit with a gloved hand in the cool of the morning.

HOW MANY TO PLANT?

Most (but not all) pears are self-fertile, so you may need only one tree. Still, I suggest starting out with two trees of each type, and taking out any weaklings later if nature does not do it for you. In abundant years, it is easy to trade pears for other things, because everybody likes pears.

Pears

With common pears, the best time for harvest varies among varieties. Fruits from most varieties are best when "mature green" — a full-size pear that is still green but with a yellowish undertone and dark seeds inside. Most trees begin dropping a few fruits when the majority of them are ready to pick. Still, it may take two or three harvesting sessions to gather all the pears from a mature pear tree.

As with apples, sort pears as you pick them and immediately begin treating the perfect ones like refrigerated jewels. Every week or so, bring out a few of your perfect common pears and let them ripen at room temperatures. These are your fresh eating pears. Meanwhile, keep imperfect pears in a cooler kept chilled with frozen water bottles, and get them canned or frozen as quickly as possible.

- -

Asian pears must be allowed to fully ripen on the tree. If you must tug to pull them from the branch, they are not ready. Ripe Asian pears will release if you rock them upward in an open hand. Refrigerate Asian pears immediately, and keep them chilled at all times. Preserve blemished fruits within a few days.

Popular pear types including D'Anjou (shown here) and Bartlett are picked at the mature green stage and allowed to ripen slowly, under cool conditions.

Dried Asian pears

Pear
FOOD PRESERVATION OPTIONS

The best way to preserve common pears is to can them in a light syrup, and the best way to preserve Asian pears is to dry them. If you have time for neither and are staring down a bushel of blemished pears, cut off the good parts and throw them in a freezer bag. When time permits, you can press out some fresh juice or ferment the pear chunks into wine.

Canning. Canning pears is quite straightforward — peel and pare ripe pears, soak the pieces in an acidic solution (see page 23), then drain and add to a pot. Add just enough water to the pot to cover the pieces halfway, then slowly heat the pears to a gentle simmer. Add spices and sugar to taste, and a generous spritz of lemon juice, and pack the simmering mixture into hot canning jars. Process in a steam or water-bath canner for 20 minutes. To thicken pear syrup without adding a lot of sugar, use a small amount of a low-sugar pectin product (about one-fourth of the standard measurement) and follow the mixing procedures on the package.

Drying. It is not necessary to peel Asian pears before cutting them into ¼-inch-thick pieces for drying. Do drop them into an acidic solution to prevent browning, but don't bother with sugar or spices — the concentrated sugars in dried Asian pears make them as sweet as raisins. Use scissors or kitchen shears to cut dried Asian pear pieces into raisin-size tidbits, and use them as raisin substitutes in recipes.

PLUMS, PEACHES, AND NECTARINES

(*Prunus* species and hybrids)

HOW MUCH
Two trees

- -

STELLAR VARIETIES
Climate specific based on chill hours and disease-resistance needs

- -

BEST WAYS TO PRESERVE
Freeze, can, dry, or ferment

Plums, peaches, and nectarines are all variations of the *Prunus* species, which includes cherries. Cherries ripen so early that they often escape problems with pests and diseases, while the later-ripening stone fruits are sitting ducks for numerous insect pests and brown rot, the fungal disease that turns fruits into fuzzy mummies just as they ripen. When grown organically, plums, peaches, and nectarines are boom-or-bust producers, blessing you with huge crops some years and giving you nothing in others.

Here are some things to keep in mind when deciding which of these fruit trees you might include in your home plantings.

early ripening peach

red Japanese plum

nectarine

European plum

yellow Japanese plum

Plums (*Prunus* species and hybrids) tend to produce fruit erratically because plum trees often lose their crop to late freezes or disease, but this is less of a problem in warm climates where spring freezes are not usually very severe. Best adapted in Zones 4 to 8, plum trees produce heavy crops of juicy fruits, which vary in color from light green to dark purple. In some areas, selected native species, such as beach plums in the Northeast or sand plums in the Midwest, may make the best homestead plums.

Cultivated plums are placed in two groups:

- **Japanese plums** ripen in early to midsummer.

- **European plums** ripen in late summer or early fall.

Because European plums spend more time on the tree, they are more likely to have bad things happen to them. Five minutes of hail that leaves tiny pock marks in the softening fruits is all it takes to lose a crop to insects or disease. This is less likely to happen with improved varieties of Japanese plums, which ripen before disease pressure becomes severe. Several varieties developed at Auburn University in Alabama provide some resistance to several common diseases.

Peaches and nectarines (*P. persica*) are on everyone's want list, but growing these fruit trees organically requires an excellent site, preventive pest management, and luck. More than other fruit trees, peach and nectarine trees need deep soil with no compacted subsoil or hardpan. Peaches and nectarines are best adapted to Zones 5 to 8, but specialized varieties can be grown in colder or warmer climates. For example, 'Reliance' peach and 'Hardired' nectarine are known for their cold hardiness, while 'Florda Glo' peach or 'Suncoast' nectarine are adapted to semi-tropical climates.

In all climates, peaches are known for being short-lived trees. Cold injury or wood-boring insects often cause peach and nectarine trees to decline at a young age, so you should plan to add new trees to your collection every few years.

A common disease called bacterial leaf spot can seriously weaken peaches and nectarines, but genetic resistance is available in several peach varieties and in one or two nectarines. And while most peaches are susceptible to brown rot, a few varieties provide some resistance. Your Cooperative Extension Service can provide you with a list of disease-resistant peach and nectarine varieties that are known to grow well in your area.

Grow Plums, Peaches, and Nectarines

Planting: Follow the instructions for planting cherries on page 277 when siting and setting out new trees. Rich, well-drained soil with a pH between 6.0 and 6.5 is ideal. Fertilize young trees with a balanced organic fertilizer in early summer and again in early fall.

- -

Maintenance: Most *Prunus* trees need aggressive pruning in late winter to remove damaged wood and open the centers of the trees to sun and fresh air. It is better to prune too much than too little. To prevent disease during the season, many organic growers use a biofungicide based on *Bacillus subtilis* as a primary defensive measure. In fall, rake up leaves and gather up fallen fruits and compost them to interrupt the life cycles of several common diseases.

HARVESTING AND STORING

Plums, Peaches, and Nectarines

When: When you notice a few fruits falling to the ground, the harvest is usually imminent. Peaches, plums, and nectarines usually ripen all at once, within a 10-day period. Pick fruit in the cool of the morning, and set aside and compost fruits with issues that make them unusable.

How: Handle fruits as gently as eggs. Immediately chill the fruit in coolers or a refrigerator. Sort through the chilled fruits, and keep the perfect ones refrigerated to delay final ripening. Keep others in a cool place indoors, arranged in shallow boxes, until you can process them for long-term storage. Fully ripe plums keep best in the refrigerator.

> **Pick fruit in the cool of the morning, handling fruits as gently as eggs.**

Peach preserves capture summer in a jar, or you can dry ripe plums (bottom) or peaches (left) to eat as healthy snacks.

Plums, Peaches, and Nectarines

FOOD PRESERVATION OPTIONS

Plums, peaches, and nectarines can be frozen, dried, fermented, or canned as preserves or fruit butter.

Frozen. Peach preserves are the pride of many cooks, but you can freeze peaches and nectarines if you don't have time to can them. To remove skins, dip fruits in boiling water for 30 seconds or so. As you pare the fruits, drop the halves or slices into an acidic solution to prevent discoloration (see page 23). Drain, pack into freezer containers, and sprinkle with a little sugar, which tenderizes the fruit and protects its color.

Dried. Ripe peaches and nectarines contain so much moisture that they are slow to dry, and the long drying times increase chances that the fruit will darken to brown. Be sure to use a strong acidic solution to pre-condition slices being prepared for drying. Dry only until leathery, and store in the freezer.

Plums are surprisingly easy to dry. Use a sharp serrated knife to cut away the two rounded "cheeks" from each plum, and dip the pieces in an acidic solution to prevent discoloration. Arrange skin side down in a dehydrator, and dry until leathery. Simmer the pits with remaining flesh attached in a little water to make a drinkable fruit nectar as described on page 271.

Canned. Peaches make elegant preserves or jam, and you can preserve whole or pitted plums by canning them in a light syrup. Peach or plum butter is delicious, too.

Wine. Plums make a spunky wine that can be drunk when rather young. Cut up plums as if you were drying them, and freeze the pieces until you are ready to make wine.

Purée. The day after harvest, when you have a quantity of bruised fruit that needs attention, a food mill can save the day. Simmer the washed, trimmed fruit for a few minutes to soften it, and then mill it into a purée. For use in smoothies, freeze the purée in ice cube trays. Use larger freezer containers if you plan to use the purée later to make a fruit butter or dry into a fruit leather.

The skins and stones from cooked, cooled plums are removed by a food mill. The purée can be frozen or used to make dried fruit leather.

purple basil

catnip

Genovese basil

dill

apple mint

rosemary

thyme

marjoram

monarda

flat-leaf parsley

HERBS

FOR THE

Homegrown Pantry

When it comes to saving money by growing your own food, herbs are big-ticket items. Dried herbs from the store are costly, and most are far from fresh. It's fortunate that many familiar kitchen herbs are easy to grow, and most can be preserved by simply drying them. When alternate methods are needed, such as with basil, they are discussed in the individual entries below.

Tea herbs grown for drinking also deserve a place in the homegrown pantry, and you may be surprised at how many plants — not all of them herbs — are safe and useful when used as tea herbs. Raspberry leaves, for example, impart the musky flavor notes of black tea, and fine bits of dried rhubarb will make any tea taste like lemon. In winter, it's great fun to get out your collection of dried tea herbs and make up blends for the coming week.

I'll cover kitchen herbs first, and then come back to herbs for tea. You can add medicinal herbs to your collection, too, but that's a subject big enough for another book. Besides, when you eat lots of fresh veggies and fruits, and then add refreshing teas made with antioxidant-rich herbs to your diet, you may not need medicinal herb plants beyond a pot of aloe stationed in the kitchen, its magic leaf gel ready to heal minor burns.

KITCHEN HERBS

It takes only a few days to make a pretty infused vinegar with red-leafed basil.

IT TAKES ONLY ONE growing season for a gardener to become hooked on the flavors and colors that culinary herbs bring to every dish they touch. This need not only be a pleasure of summer, because there are simple ways to preserve almost any herb you care to grow. Herbs in general are easy to please when grown in hospitable sites, but it may take a few seasons of trial and error to learn which herbs are the best bets for your climate and soil.

Nine wonderful kitchen herbs to grow and preserve are profiled below. While you may want to grow basil, parsley, and other favorites every year, don't feel like you must grow and store every culinary herb you want, every year. Expect variation. There will be stellar seasons for sage and banner years for basil, and these natural changes in the garden keep things from getting boring in the kitchen, too.

There are also a number of herbs that didn't make my list, for various reasons. Fennel, chives, and garlic chives are great in the kitchen, but they can be invasive in the garden unless you lop off the underripe seed heads, without exception. Except for mint (see page 297), which is worth the small trouble needed to manage it, the herbs described here can be trusted not to stage an unwanted takeover of your garden.

BASIL
(*Ocimum* species)

Basil is a warm-season annual that is grown from seed on the same schedule as tomatoes. In spring, greenhouse-grown seedlings are a good buy, because there are usually several seedlings in a pot. These can be gently repotted into individual containers and allowed to grow new roots for a week or so before being set out in the garden. Start seeds of other varieties you want to grow in late spring, after the weather turns warm.

If you plan to freeze basil pesto (the best way to preserve basil), grow three or four plants per person of a green-leaved 'Genovese' type. You will need only two plants of a red-leafed variety to make gorgeous pink-tinted basil vinegars.

To prevent diseases such as downy mildew and fusarium wilt, give basil plants plenty of space, allowing 18 inches between plants, and grow them in well-drained soil that has been enriched with a standard application of a balanced organic fertilizer. Begin pinching leaf tips when the plants are 8 inches tall, and pinch back two more times to maximize leaf production.

Harvest basil for making pesto in batches, making one cutting when the first pointed green flower buds appear, and a second one about 10 days after the first. After that, there will be no holding the plants back from flowering their heads off. Where summers are long and warm, it's a good idea to have a second or third crop of seedlings coming along for fresh use.

Basil presents unique challenges in terms of food preservation. It loses much of its flavor when dried, turns black when cut, and tends to darken when frozen and thawed, too. These issues make frozen pesto base the best way to preserve basil as a winter foodstuff. You can make other herbs into freezable pestos, too.

Growing a couple of different basils each year brings variety to the kitchen and the table.

CILANTRO
(*Coriandrum sativum*)

Cilantro is a hardy annual leafy herb that bolts quickly when sown in spring. This is not a bad thing if you want nutlike cilantro seeds, which are the spice known as coriander. If you allow three spring-sown plants to flower freely and develop mature seeds, you will have enough seeds to sow for a couple of years, lots of volunteer seedlings from shed seeds, plus crunchy coriander seeds for your spice cabinet.

The best way to have plenty of cilantro for fresh cooking is to sow a few seeds every few weeks. Late summer is the best time to grow a large crop of cilantro to preserve, because plants are not as eager to bolt when days are getting shorter. Cilantro plants grown in the fall produce many more leaves per plant than those grown in spring, so you will need only about 6 plants per person. Preserve cilantro by freezing as pesto, or you can chop the herbs and freeze them in ice cubes — a great way to have cilantro for soups and Asian dishes. Plants that survive winter (common from Zone 6 southward) promptly burst into bloom in early spring, and overwintered plants are strong seed producers.

Herb Pestos for the Freezer

Frozen pesto base is a choice method if you want to preserve basil for year-round use on pizza, pasta, or even potatoes. Use a food processor to combine clean basil leaves with olive oil, allowing about ½ cup olive oil for every 2 cups loosely packed basil leaves. Add a little salt and a tablespoon of lemon juice, purée until blended, and freeze the mixture in ice cube trays or silicone muffin pans. When frozen hard, transfer the frozen pesto to an airtight container. The purée can be thawed and remade into finished pesto by adding garlic, Parmesan cheese, and nuts, or it can be taken in another direction and used to flavor Thai dishes. It is important to add garlic, cheese, and nuts *after* herb pestos are thawed to avoid unwanted flavor changes.

In addition to basil pesto, other garden herbs are prominent players in pestos from around the world. All are easy to freeze.

- Parsley and oregano purée forms the base for Argentine chimichurri sauce.

- Cilantro purée is the base for green mojo sauces from Spain.

- In the Middle East, mint pesto is a traditional accompaniment for lamb.

DILL
(*Anethum graveolens*)

Dill is a cool-season annual herb that can be started early, while cool conditions prevail. If you start a few plants indoors in early spring, and set them out under cloches a couple of weeks before your last frost date, they will be in bloom by the time cucumbers and other veggies are ready to pickle in midsummer. Allow one plant to develop mature seeds, staking it if necessary to keep the drooping seed heads high and dry. The biggest and best seeds for both cooking and replanting are produced by the second set of yellow blossom clusters produced by the plants. When the seeds in these large clusters turn brown, gather them in a paper bag, and let them continue drying indoors for a week. They should then be easy to crumble with your hands, and the heavy dill seeds will accumulate in the bottom of the bag. Dill seeds deserve much wider use as a spice, whether you knead them into dill bread or add them to a simmering pot of cabbage.

I like to start three or so more dill plants in summer so I will have plenty of fresh dill for cooking and freezing well into fall. Summer squash and other frozen veggies get a needed flavor boost from the addition of chopped dill tossed with the blanched veggies just before they are frozen. Dill foliage also can be dried, but it lacks the vibrant color and flavor of fresh dill.

MARJORAM

(Origanum majorana)

Marjoram is an oddball annual oregano that is one of the best savory herbs to grow in a container. Its strange flowers are little green balls, which you are most likely to notice when picking sprigs for cooking (yes, they are edible!). Marjoram is winter hardy only in very mild climates, but container-grown plants that are cut back and brought indoors in fall, and grown under lights or in a sunny window, often survive to face another season.

Dried marjoram holds its flavor well, which resembles oregano with a light, faintly minty finish. Three healthy plants grown in a large planter will produce about a pint of dried leaves, plus all you want for fresh cooking. To preserve marjoram's complex flavor, wait until just before cooking to crush the leaves. Marjoram is a great herb for flavoring salad dressings and makes a refreshing accent herb for roasted vegetables.

Three healthy marjoram plants grown in a large planter will produce about a pint of dried leaves, plus all you want for fresh cooking.

Managing
Your Mints

All mints are vigorous spreaders that expand their territory by developing wandering underground stems (stolons) that give rise to new plants. They have a well-deserved reputation for invasiveness, so it's important to become familiar with various mints' uses as well as how they behave in a garden.

Mints require monitoring, so it's a good idea not to take on more than you can keep up with and to grow only as much mint as you need. Areas that are bordered by pavement or mowed grass are excellent sites for mint, or you can grow mints along the edge of your garden as an edible, drinkable ground cover. Mints attract numerous bees and other pollinators when they bloom in midsummer, so avoid planting mints near entryways.

BEST MINTS TO GROW

First, let's eliminate spearmint. Tough enough to thrive in asphalt cracks, spearmint is very difficult to dig out once it is established. Besides, other mints taste much better when used in food and drinks.

For cooking. Choose from the peppermint group (*Mentha* x *piperita*), which includes chocolate mint and orange mint — two cold-hardy strains worth a trial in any garden. Both are best handled in a contained bed or large planter, but stragglers are easy to dig out or mow over. Peppermint's reddish leaves are flat and less hairy than other mints, so they are very easy to dry.

For tea. Start with upright apple mint (*M. suaveolens*), which has frosty green leaves that are fleshier and hairier than those of other mints, so they take a little longer to dry. Apple mint is a willing spreader, so you might let it make itself at home on a sunny hillside or slope you would rather not mow. If you don't have room for apple mint, peppermints make great tea.

For small spaces. If your space is limited to raised beds or large containers, try something punchy like ginger mint (*M.* x *gracilis*) or Chinese mint (*M. hapocalyx*). Originating in southwest China, the best strains of Chinese mint are so potent that a little goes a long way in recipes or tea mixtures. Chinese mint plants tend to be well behaved, forming clumps similar to those of lemon balm.

For shade. If you have pockets of shady space to fill, try American mountain mints (*Pycnanthemum* species). Many native plant nurseries sell improved mountain mints that thrive in partial shade, with leaves that make a tea loaded with woodsy undertones beneath the mint and menthol. However, as with monarda (discussed on page 307), harvesting too many mountain mint sprigs and leaves for tea means fewer lovely flowers, which provide nectar for butterflies and countless other native insects.

A leaf from a good culinary strain of oregano should feel instantly vibrant on the tongue, followed by a peppery warmth with a hint of cool mint.

OREGANO
(*Origanum vulgare*)

Oregano has been called the prince of herbs, a fitting nickname because it is easy to grow and adds savory spice to hundreds of dishes. Start your oregano adventures by buying a plant from a local greenhouse in spring. Trailing varieties are available for growing in containers or rock gardens. Taste before you buy; a leaf from a good culinary strain should feel instantly vibrant on the tongue, followed by a peppery warmth with a hint of cool mint.

Let the plant grow freely in a well-drained bed, harvesting leaf tips as needed for cooking and drying. Then see if the plant survives winter. If it does, lift and divide and replant a couple of clumps from the mother plant in spring. Oregano is generally easy to grow, but it does tend to rot out when left to sit in one spot year after year, which is why it's best to move

it around a bit. Use a sharp serrated knife to cut out chunks of green stems with roots and soil attached, and move them to a fresh planting spot intact. Two or three mounds of established oregano will provide a year's supply. When allowed to bloom, oregano attracts a variety of small beneficial insects.

Oregano can be bothered by four-lined plant bugs, which make small brown spots in the newest leaves. Shear back branches showing many spots or browned leaf edges to force out a new flush of leaves.

Harvest oregano for drying in summer, when the plants suddenly grow tall and prepare to flower. Trim stems to about 6 inches long, and dry in a dehydrator or on screens in a warm, well-ventilated place. When dried to crisp, strip off whole leaves and store in airtight containers in a cool, dark place.

PARSLEY
(*Petroselinum crispum*)

Parsley is in constant demand in the kitchen because it brings color and subtle flavor to so many different dishes. A hardy biennial by nature, parsley should be sown from seed at least twice a year so you always have young plants coming on. Plants started in early spring will produce a huge crop of leaves in early summer, and you can grow a second crop in fall by starting more seeds in late summer. In most climates, the fall plants can be nursed through winter beneath a sturdy cold frame. These plants will produce a nice flush of leaves in early spring before they bolt and burst into bloom.

Most garden cooks prefer flat-leafed parsley, but curly varieties are fun to grow, too. To grow a year's supply of fresh, dried, and frozen parsley, you will need a total of six to eight plants.

Parsley seeds can be slow germinators. To wake them up, pour very warm water over the seeds in a strainer, then let them dry on a paper towel overnight before planting. Grow the seedlings under very bright light. When starting seeds in summer for a fall crop, I germinate them indoors, where temperatures are constantly cool, and then grow them in containers on the deck, under the partial shade of a patio umbrella. In any season, disturb the roots as little as possible when setting parsley plants out in the garden.

Parsley keeps some of its color and flavor when dried, and dried parsley flakes are hugely convenient to have in the kitchen. To keep them from blowing around, I place parsley in the dehydrator with the stems attached and strip off the leaves when they are almost dry.

Flat-leafed or Italian parsley also can be frozen. Place clean, dry leaves on a cookie sheet in the freezer until frozen, and then quickly transfer to airtight containers such as small freezer bags.

All types of parsley can be preserved as a frozen pesto base, and parsley is often combined with other herbs in mixed pestos, where it adds color, flavor, and a surprising amount of vitamins and minerals, too.

Finally, though I have yet to make it myself, I hear that parsley wine is pretty darn good.

Dry parsley when the plants are at their peak, which is usually early summer.

ROSEMARY
(*Rosmarinus officinalis*)

Fresh rosemary leaves are loaded with aromatic compounds that may stimulate the brain when inhaled, so crushing and sniffing a few sprigs may make you smarter. Rosemary's complex flavor tastes like a chord of mint, licorice, and pepper, which makes it invaluable for enriching stocks and sauces, or adding to homemade breads.

Rosemary grows into big woody bushes where it is winter hardy, from Zone 7 southward, but in colder climates it can be grown as an annual or as a potted plant brought into a cool room for the winter. You won't need much — a single potted rosemary plant will produce many more sprigs than you need in the course of the summer. If you plan to keep your rosemary through a cold winter, grow it in a pot sunk into the ground through summer so it will be easy to lift in the fall.

Rosemary is easy to dry, and because the leaves are narrow and hold little moisture, rosemary is one of the few culinary herbs that gives good results when air-dried in small bunches. Use small amounts in herbal pestos to add an interesting flavor, and chop fresh rosemary into summer squash, green beans, or other summer vegetables being prepared for the freezer.

SAGE
(Salvia officinalis)

Sage is a valuable plant in the edible landscape because of the soft texture of its gray-green leaves, and its gorgeous blue flowers produced on spikes just as hummingbirds arrive in late spring. Established plants usually survive winter from Zone 6 southward, but they may be so badly damaged that they are not worth keeping. In colder climates, start out spring with new purchased plants. Two should be enough.

The sister herb for poultry or potatoes, dried sage is welcome in herb blends. Stem tips can be dried in small bundles and hung so the leaves will dry straight, or you can use a dehydrator. One year I dried a beautiful batch by placing large sage leaves between paper towels and pressing them in an old phone book. Sautéed in a little oil, they made wonderful accents for winter meals. Sage wine may sound odd, and like other herb wines it is basically strong sweet tea that has been fermented and aged, but it is one of the better herb wines I have ever made.

THYME
(*Thymus* species)

Thyme comes in many confusing forms, so as with oregano, it is best to sample a leaf before choosing plants. Those identified as a cultivar of *Thymus vulgaris* are best for fresh eating and drying, and this species grows into an upright plant. Low-growing lemon thyme (*T. × citriodorus*) is tasty, too, but the leaves are so small that they are tedious to dry. All types of thyme like tough, gritty spots better than beds, so plants grown high and dry in a rock garden may do better than those grown in a moist, raised bed.

Thyme is easy to grow in most climates, but diseases encouraged by wet conditions are common in areas with warm, muggy summers. For a sure crop, cut and dry thyme in early summer, while the foliage is healthy. Under good conditions, you should get a second cutting later in the summer.

Fresh yet savory, thyme brings depth of flavor to a wide range of dishes, and it is indispensable in French and Creole cuisines. Dry thyme in the dehydrator so mildew never gets a chance at the somewhat furry little leaves.

> **Dry thyme in the dehydrator so mildew never gets a chance at the somewhat furry little leaves.**

TEA HERBS

ANY LANDSCAPE can be tweaked to include low-maintenance plants chosen for their value for making tea. I suppose any broth made by steeping plant parts in hot water can be called a tea, but a truly satisfying tea begins with an enticing aroma and then delivers complex flavors in every sip. All of the plants discussed on pages 304–309 — and dozens more — are imbued with flavor compounds that readily dissolve in hot water to produce tasty, aromatic teas. Many of these teas have healing properties, too.

The key to happiness in growing herbs for tea is to find plants that suit your climate so well that they cannot be held back, producing an abundance of easy-to-dry foliage with little investment of time and energy. Once you get to know the tea herbs your site and soil want to grow, the rest is easy — harvest and dry each tea herb in its season, and store the dried herbs in airtight jars in a cool, dark place. Once you have a store of dried tea herbs, you can mix up blends that feature the different flavors of your favorite tea plants. I make tea in quart canning jars, using about a half cup of dried herbs per quart of tea. It is easier to strain loose tea through a strainer after steeping than to try to contain dry herbs in a tea ball.

The queen of tea herbs is mint, which comes in forms to suit every taste. See Managing Your Mints on page 297 to review the best choices. Once you have chosen a mint or two, consider the six plants on pages 304–309, which always give satisfying results when grown for tea. Twenty more good tea plants are listed on pages 310–311.

CATNIP
(*Nepeta cataria*)

Catnip looks like a big, furry mint, and it is. In addition to hosting compounds that please cats, catnip leaves brew into a mild lemon-mint tea that complements the fruity flavor of chamomile. The two herbs are often combined to make a tea that helps settle the mind in preparation for sleep. Small amounts of catnip tea are an old remedy for colic in babies, too.

In the garden, catnip grows as a short-lived perennial or reseeding annual. Plants regrow quickly after stems are harvested, so each plant has a high yield potential. As long as you let one plant hold a few flower spikes until they turn brown, sufficient seeds will be shed to give rise to volunteer seedlings in spring, which you can dig and move to where you want them to grow. When allowed to bloom freely during the second half of summer, catnip blossoms attract a huge variety of bees and beneficial insects to the garden.

CHAMOMILE
(*Matricaria recutita*)

Chamomile is a cold-hardy annual that covers itself with small yellow-and-white flowers that smell of green apples, and these flowers are dried and made into tea. Chamomile's fruity, floral flavors are mild, so it is often paired with mints to create a satisfying tea widely believed to promote relaxation and sleep.

To get started with chamomile, start seeds for about six plants indoors in late winter, grow them under lights, and set them out under cloches about 6 weeks before your last frost date. Allow the ferny plants to grow freely until they bloom in late spring or early summer. Use scissors to snip off perfect blossoms, and dry them on a screen in a warm, dry place or in a dehydrator. Harvest flowers from each plant at least twice, but then allow some blossoms to stay on the plants until they shatter. Each mature chamomile blossom contains hundreds of tiny seeds, and chamomile easily sheds enough seeds to return as self-sown seedlings for a second year. You can further help chamomile reseed by piling the pulled plants (which are probably holding thousands of ripe seeds) where you would like to see chamomile seedlings appear the following season. This can be a temporary nursery bed, because chamomile seedlings are easy to dig and move to another location.

LEMON BALM
(*Melissa officinalis*)

Lemon balm tea has been used to manage anxiety since the Middle Ages, and lemon balm may have antiviral properties as well. Lemon balm's flavor can't carry a tea on its own, but add a few crushed blackberries and a stevia leaf to a quart batch, and you have the start of something good.

Lemon balm is easy to love in the garden because it looks rather handsome through the first half of summer, growing into a luminous mound of slightly hairy green leaves. Two plants are plenty to grow for tea. Start cutting 6- to 8-inch-long branches for drying when the plants are a foot tall; you should get a second cutting before the plants insist on blooming, furnishing nectar to honeybees and other insects for 2 months or more. Established plants persist for a couple of years, then disappear, but not without leaving behind a few self-sown offspring. If you'd rather not take a chance of losing your lemon balm, take a division from your mother clump in early summer and plant it in a new site.

> **Add a few crushed blackberries and a stevia leaf to a quart batch of lemon balm tea, and you have the start of something good.**

MONARDA
(*Monarda didyma*)

Monarda, also known as bee balm, is a native American woodland mint, more popular as a perennial flower than as a tea herb. It can be grown as both, and it is possible that harvesting one-half to one-third of the stem tips in late spring, as a tea herb, enhances the plant's performance as a flower by prolonging bloom time and improving air circulation around the remaining stems. Improved air circulation discourages powdery mildew, which is a persistent fungal disease for all but a few resistant varieties of monarda.

Monarda leaves breathe menthol notes into herb teas, and fully mature leaves in particular yield a bold, full-bodied beverage. If you grow the plants primarily for tea, grow at least three plants, which mature into clumps 3 feet across. You can harvest and dry bee balm flowers, too, but I find it impossible to take them from the many bees, butterflies, and hummingbirds that visit the blossoms from dawn to dusk. Instead, find places for monarda along woodland edges or in partial shade cast by buildings. I grow red, pink, and lavender strains, and I love them all, but hummingbirds and butterflies seem to like the lavender blossoms best.

> **Monarda leaves breathe menthol notes into herb teas, and older leaves in particular yield a bold, full-bodied beverage.**

RASPBERRIES
(*Rubus* species)

Raspberries grown for their delicious fruit deserve space in the landscape, but even in poor fruit years you can harvest raspberry leaves as tea herbs. In late spring, just as the plants bloom, pick individual leaflets that have darkened to medium green. Harvest leaves again in late summer, this time from new canes that grew in the current season. Again, favor mature, fully green leaves over tender new growth, which has fewer flavor compounds.

Dried raspberry leaves mix well with mints and other herbs like fennel seed and nettles. By itself, raspberry leaf tea is a popular supplement among women in pursuit of more regular periods and those trying to get pregnant.

STEVIA
(*Stevia rebaudiana*)

Stevia, also called sweet leaf plant, is indispensable to the tea gardener. Two fresh leaves will sweeten a quart of herb tea without adding calories, and the leaves are easy to dry, too. Fresh stevia brewed into tea lacks the chemical taste often found in commercial products. The key to using stevia is to use less, not more. In the garden, two to four plants will provide plenty of leaves for sweetening teas and other beverages.

A tender perennial, stevia is killed by temperatures cold enough to freeze the soil, so it is reliably winter hardy only to Zone 8 or warmer locations in Zone 7. Elsewhere, you can bring plants indoors for the winter, or simply buy a couple of new plants from a local greenhouse grower each spring. Do not waste your time trying to sprout and grow stevia seeds, which have low germination rates and grow very slowly. When you buy a plant, you can start picking stevia leaves immediately.

The Real Tea Plant

Commercial black tea is grown from a semi-tropical evergreen shrub, *Camellia sinensis*. Young leaves become green tea, while older ones are processed into darker teas. This species is hardy only to Zone 8, but a cultivar from Russia called 'Sochi' is worth trying in a protected site as far north as Zone 6.

TWENTY MORE PLANTS TO USE IN TEAS

Once you have a few essential tea plants in place, start experimenting with the plants listed below, which can be grown as tea herbs for blending or used therapeutically for a variety of conditions.

PLANT	PARTS USED	USES AND MEDICINAL PROPERTIES
Alfalfa (*Medicago sativa*)	Leaves, flowers	Nutritious green tea, good for blending with other herbs.
Burdock (*Arctium lappa*)	Roots	Dried roots provide a bitter note in teas; used in some detoxification therapies.
Calendula (*Calendula officinalis*)	Flower petals	Orange or yellow petals add a colorful touch and nutritional boost to pale teas.
Chicory (*Cichorium intybus*)	Roots	When chopped and roasted, bitter chicory roots can be used as a coffee substitute.
Clovers (*Trifolium* species)	Leaves, flowers	Leaves impart a slight acidic tang; tea from leaves and flowers is used to moderate menopausal symptoms.
Dandelion (*Taraxacum officinale*)	Leaves, roots	Dried leaves can be blended with other herbs; slow-roasted roots are used as coffee or chai tea substitute.
Echinacea (*Echinacea* species)	Leaves, roots, flowers	Boosts immune system functioning and may shorten the duration of colds and flu.
Fennel (*Foeniculum vulgare*)	Leaves, seeds	Imparts anise flavor to teas, good for digestion and sore throats.
Hibiscus (*Hibiscus sabdariffa*)	Flowers	Collect bracts just after petals fall and dry them; the tropical annual strain known as roselle provides the best zesty flavor.
Hops (*Humulus lupulus*)	Flowers	Slightly bitter tea is used to promote sleep; also used to flavor beer.
Hyssop (*Hyssopus officinalis*)	Leaves, flowers	Very flavorful bitter mint with showy blooms; easy to grow in large containers.
Lavender (*Lavandula angustifolia*)	Flowers	A few lavender flowers in tea enhance the aroma and promote relaxation.
Lemongrass (*Cymbopogon citratus*)	Leaves	Fast-growing tropical grass can be grown in containers; leaves keep their pungent lemon flavor when dried.
Marshmallow (*Althaea officinalis*)	Leaves, roots	Persistent perennial in moist shade; teas soothe the digestive and urinary tracts, used as therapy for chronic bladder infections.
Nettles (*Urtica dioica*)	Leaves	First herb of spring, loaded with antioxidants; nettle tea is used as therapy for enlarged prostate gland.
Passionflower vine (*Passiflora incarnata*)	Leaves	Often combined with lemon balm and chamomile to reduce anxiety and restore calm.
Rhubarb (*Rheum × hybridum*)	Stems	Small pieces of dried rhubarb add a lemony zing to any herb tea.
Rose (*Rosa rugosa*)	Leaves, flowers, berries	Ripe berries, or rose hips, contain an abundance of vitamins and impart a citrusy flavor to teas; teas made from dried flower buds are used in Chinese medicine.
Sweet cicely (*Myrrhis odorata*)	Leaves, seedpods	A lovely soft-textured perennial for partial shade, sweet cicely leaves and green seedpods have a sweet, aniselike flavor.
Valerian (*Valeriana officinalis*)	Roots	One of the most potent herbs you can take to promote sleep, but its musky flavor must be masked by other herbs; also used to reduce anxiety in dogs.

rosebuds

echinacea
blossoms

nettles

hyssop

calendula petals

lemongrass

Index

Page numbers in *italic* indicate illustrations and photographs.
Page numbers in **bold** indicate charts and tables.

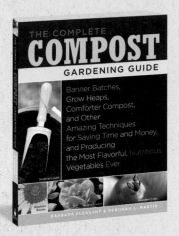

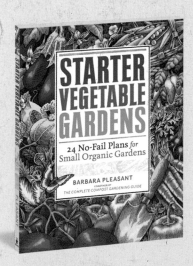